LEARNING TO PROGRAM WITH MATLAB

Building GUI Tools

Craig S. Lent
Department of Electrical Engineering
University of Notre Dame

WILEY

VP & PUBLISHER:	Don Fowley
ASSOCIATE PUBLISHER:	Dan Sayre
EDITORIAL ASSISTANT:	Jessica Knecht
MARKETING MANAGER:	Christopher Ruel
DESIGNER:	Kenji Ngieng
SENIOR PRODUCTION MANAGER:	Janis Soo
ASSOCIATE PRODUCTION MANAGER:	Joyce Poh

This book was set by MPS Limited, Chennai. Cover and text printed and bound by Courier Westford.

This book is printed on acid free paper. ∞

Founded in 1807, John Wiley & Sons, Inc. has been a valued source of knowledge and understanding for more than 200 years, helping people around the world meet their needs and fulfill their aspirations. Our company is built on a foundation of principles that include responsibility to the communities we serve and where we live and work. In 2008, we launched a Corporate Citizenship Initiative, a global effort to address the environmental, social, economic, and ethical challenges we face in our business. Among the issues we are addressing are carbon impact, paper specifications and procurement, ethical conduct within our business and among our vendors, and community and charitable support. For more information, please visit our website: www.wiley.com/go/citizenship.

Evaluation copies are provided to qualified academics and professionals for review purposes only, for use in their courses during the next academic year. These copies are licensed and may not be sold or transferred to a third party. Upon completion of the review period, please return the evaluation copy to Wiley. Return instructions and a free of charge return mailing label are available at www.wiley.com/go/returnlabel. If you have chosen to adopt this textbook for use in your course, please accept this book as your complimentary desk copy. Outside of the United States, please contact your local sales representative.

Library of Congress Cataloging-in-Publication Data

Lent, Craig S., 1956–
    Learning to program with MATLAB : building GUI tools / Craig S. Lent,
  Department of Electrical Engineering, University of Notre Dame.
        pages cm
    Includes index.
    ISBN 978-0-470-93644-3 (pbk. : acid-free paper)   1. Computer programming.
        2. Visual programming (Computer science)   3. MATLAB.   4. Graphical user interfaces
        (Computer systems)   I. Title.
  QA76.6.L45   2013
  005.4'37—dc23

                                                                                    2012041638

Printed in the United States of America

10 9 8 7 6 5 4 3 2 1

To Tom Finke, Pat Malone, the late Katy McShane, and all the other amazing teachers at the Trinity School campuses in South Bend, IN, Eagan, MN, and Falls Church, VA.

Contents

Preface

To learn how to program a computer in a modern language with serious graphical capabilities, is to take hold of a tool of remarkable flexibility that has the power to provide profound insight. This text is primarily aimed at being a first course in programming, and is oriented toward integration with science, mathematics, and engineering. It is also useful for more advanced students and researchers who want to rapidly acquire the ability to easily build useful graphical tools for exploring computational models. The MATLAB programming language provides an excellent introductory language, with built-in graphical, mathematical, and user-interface capabilities. The goal is that the student learns to build computational models with graphical user interfaces (GUIs) that enable exploration of model behavior. This GUI tool-building approach has been used at multiple educational levels: graduate courses, intermediate undergraduate courses, an introductory engineering course for first-year college students, and high school junior and senior-level courses.

The MATLAB programming language, descended from FORTRAN, has evolved to include many powerful and convenient graphical and analysis tools. It has become an important platform for engineering and science education, as well as research. MATLAB is a very valuable first programming language, and for many will be the preferred language for most, if not all, of the computational work they do. Of course, C++, Java, Python, and many other languages play crucial roles in other domains. Several language features make the MATLAB language easier for beginners than many alternatives: it is interpreted rather than compiled; variable types and array sizes need not be declared in advance; it is not strongly typed; vector, matrix, multidimensional array, and complex numbers are basic data types; there is a sophisticated integrated development and debugging environment; and a rich set of mathematical and graphics functions is provided.

While computer programs can be used in many ways, the emphasis here is on building computational models, primarily of physical phenomena (though the techniques can be easily extended to other systems). A physical system is modeled first conceptually, using ideas such as momentum, force, energy, reactions, fields, etc. These concepts are expressed mathematically and applied to a particular class of problem. Such a class might be, for example, projectile motion, fluid flow, quantum evolution, electromagnetic fields, circuit equations, or Newton's laws. Typically, the model involves a set of parameters that describe the physical system and a set of mathematical relations (systems of equations, integrals, differential equations, eigensystems, etc.). The mathematical solution process must be realized through a computational algorithm—a step-by-step procedure for calculating the desired quantities from the input parameters. The behavior of the model is then usually visualized graphically, e.g., one or more plots, bar graphs, or animations.

A GUI tool consists of a computational model and a graphical user interface that lets the user easily and naturally adjust the parameters of the model, rerun the computation, and see the new results.

The experience that led to this text was the observation that student learning is enhanced if the students themselves build the GUI tool: construct the computational model, implement the visualization of results, and design the GUI.

The GUI is valuable for several reasons. The most important is that exploring model behavior, by manipulating sliders, buttons, checkboxes, and the like, encourages a focus on developing an intuitive insight into the model behavior. Insight is the primary goal. Running the model many times with differing inputs, the user can start to see the characteristic behavior of physical system represented by the model. Additionally, it must be recognized that graphically driven tools are what students are accustomed to when dealing with computers. A command line interface seems crude and retrograde. Moreover, particularly for engineering students, the discipline of wrapping the model in a form that someone *else* could use encourages a design-oriented mentality. Finally, building and delivering a sophisticated mathematical model that is operated through a GUI interface is simply more rewarding and fun.

The GUI tool orientation guides the structure of the text. Part I (Chapters 1 through 8) covers the fundamentals of MATLAB programming and basic graphics. It is designed to be what one needs to know prior to actual GUI building. The goal is to get the student ready for GUI building as quickly as possible (but not quicker).

In this context, Chapter 4 (matrices) and Chapter 6 (animation) warrant comment. Because arrays are a basic MATLAB data class and solving linear systems a frequent application, this material is included in Part I. An instructor could choose to cover it later without disrupting the flow of the course. Similarly, the animation techniques covered in Chapter 6 could be deferred. The animation process does, however, provide very helpful and enjoyable practice at programming FOR loops. Many GUI tools are enhanced by having an animation component; among other advantages, animation provides a first check of model behavior against experience. The end of Chapter 6 also includes a detailed discussion of the velocity Verlet algorithm as an improvement on the Euler method for solving systems governed by Newton's second law. While this could be considered a more advanced topic, without it, models as simple as harmonic motion or bouncing balls fail badly because of nonconservation of energy.

Part II covers GUI tool creation with the GUIDE (graphical user interface development environment) program, which is part of MATLAB. Chapters 9 and 10 are the heart of the text and take a very tutorial approach to GUI building. Chapter 10 details a simple, but widely useful, technique for transforming a functioning MATLAB program into a GUI tool. Readers already familiar with MATLAB, but unfamiliar with using GUIDE, can likely work through these two chapter in a couple hours and be in short order making GUI tools.

Part III covers more advanced techniques in GUI building, graphics, and mathematics. It is not meant to be comprehensive; the online MATLAB help documentation is excellent and will be the main source for many details. The text covers what, in many cases, is the simplest way to invoke a particular function; more complicated uses are left for the student to explore using the documentation.

This approach—having students write GUI tools for specific problem domains—grew out of the author's experience teaching undergraduate electromagnetics courses and graduate quantum mechanics courses in electrical engineering at the University of Notre Dame. These areas are characterized by a high level of mathematical abstraction, so having students transform the esoteric mathematics first into code, and then into visualizable answers, proved invaluable.

The text began as a set of lecture notes for high school students at Trinity School at Greenlawn, in South Bend, Indiana. Since 2005, all Trinity juniors have learned MATLAB using this approach and have used it extensively in the physics and calculus courses that span the junior and senior year. The two other Trinity School campuses, one in Falls Church, Virginia, and the other in Eagan, Minnesota, adopted the curriculum soon after the Greenlawn campus. The last chapter on mathematics is largely shaped by the material covered in the Trinity senior year. The author is profoundly grateful to the faculty and students of Trinity Schools, for their feedback, love of learning, and courage. Special thanks to Tom Finke, the remarkable head of Math and Science for Trinity Schools, and to Dr. John Vogel of Trinity School at Meadow View, for very helpful reviews of the manuscript. All author's royalties from this text will go to support Trinity Schools. I'm very grateful to Tom Noe and Linda DeCelles for their help in preparing the manuscipt.

Since 2010, this approach to learning MATLAB, and the earlier preprints of the text, has been used in the Introduction to Engineering course for first-year students in the College of Engineering at Notre Dame. In addition to learning to make MATLAB GUI tools, students employ them as part of a semester project completed in small teams. Each project normally has a substantial physical apparatus (involving significant construction), as well as an associated computational model. Some of the more specialized graphics topics included in Part III have been selected because they tend to arise in these projects. The course includes several other modules in addition to MATLAB and is the creation of Prof. Jay Brockman, a masterful teacher with profound pedagogical insights.

It is worth noting that in both the first-year college engineering and high school contexts, students benefit from a brief experience with a simpler programming language. At Notre Dame, this simpler language is the Lego robotics ROBOLAB® language for programming Lego Mindstorms® robots. The high school curriculum at Trinity introduces students to programming with a four-week course on the Alice language, developed by Carnegie Mellon University. These "ramp languages" allow students to become accustomed to programming as creating a sequence of instructions in a way that is insulated from syntax errors.

A note on formatting: Numerous examples, programs, and code fragments are included in highlighted text. When the example is meant to illustrate the behavior of MATLAB commands typed in the Command window, the MATLAB command prompt ">>" is included, as in

```
>> disp('Hello, world!')
Hello, world!
```

Program listings, by contrast, contain the code as it would be seen in the Editor window.

```
%% greetings.m
%  Greet user in cheery way
%     Author: Calvin Manthorn
greeting='Hello, world!';
disp(greeting);
```

After many decades of nearly daily use, the author still finds a durable and surprising joy in writing MATLAB programs for research, teaching, and recreation. It is hoped that, through all the details of the text, this comes through. May you, too, enjoy.

MATLAB Programming

Getting Started

This chapter will introduce the basics of using MATLAB, first as a powerful calculator, and then as a platform for writing simple programs that automate what a calculator would do in many steps. The emphasis here will be on performing basic mathematical operations on numbers.

The MATLAB integrated development environment is the program that runs when you launch MATLAB. You will use it to operate MATLAB interactively, and to develop and run MATLAB programs.

The concept of a MATLAB variable is important to grasp. It is not identical with the familiar mathematical notion of a variable, though the two are related. MATLAB variables should be thought of as labeled boxes that hold a number, or other type of information.

MATLAB has many built-in functions for evaluating common mathematical functions. More complicated MATLAB functions, including those of your own making, will be explored further in Chapter 7.

After completing this chapter you should be able to:

- Use the MATLAB integrated development environment to operate MATLAB interactively from within the Command window.
- Create and name MATLAB variables, and assign them numerical values.
- Invoke several built-in MATLAB mathematical functions (like sine, cosine, and exponential functions).
- Get more information on MATLAB statements and functions using the `help` and `doc` commands.
- Write a simple program that sets the values of variables, calculates some quantities, and then displays the results in the Command window.
- Run through a program line by line using the MATLAB debugger in the Editor window.

3

1.1 Running the MATLAB IDE

MATLAB is normally operated from within the MATLAB integrated development environment (IDE). You can launch MATLAB in the Windows environment by double-clicking on the shortcut on your desktop, or by selecting it from the Start | Programs menu.

The IDE is organized into a header menu bar and several different windows. Which windows are displayed can be determined by checking or unchecking items under the Layout menu on the HOME tab. Some important windows for working with MATLAB are:

Command window. This is the main interactive interface to MATLAB. To issue a MATLAB command, type the command at the >> prompt and press Enter on the keyboard.

Workspace browser. Each variable defined in the current workspace is represented here. The name, class (type), value, and other properties of the variable can be shown. Choose which properties to show using the View—Choose Columns menu from the header menu bar. A recommended set to display is: Name, Value, and Class. Double-clicking on a variable brings up the Variable Editor window. The icon representing numbers is meant to symbolize an array, i.e., a vector or matrix. MATLAB's basic data type is the array—a number is treated as a 1×1 array.

Current Folder browser. In Windows parlance, the current folder is the same as the current directory. Without further instruction, MATLAB will save files in the current folder and look for files in the current directory. The browser displays files and other directories (folders) that reside in the current directory. Icons at the top of the browser allow the user to move up a directory (folder) level or to create a new folder. Double-clicking on a displayed folder makes it the current folder.

Editor window. The MATLAB editor is where programs are written. Launch the Editor window by typing "edit" in the Command window and pressing Enter. It doubles as part of the debugger interface, which is covered in detail later. The editor "knows" the MATLAB language and color codes language elements. There are many other convenient features to aid code-writing.

Figures window. Graphics is one of the main tools for visualizing numerical quantities. The results of executing graphics-related commands, such as those for plotting lines and surfaces, are displayed in the Figures window.

Variable Editor. The value or values held in a particular variable are displayed in a spreadsheet-like tool. This is particularly useful for arrays (matrices and vectors).

Manipulating windows

As usual in Windows, the currently active window is indicated by the darkening of its blue frame. Each window can be undocked using the small pull-down menu near the upper right-hand corner of the window. Undocked windows can be arranged on the screen using the usual Windows mouse manipulations. An undocked window can be docked again using the small arrow button (this time the arrow points downward) in the upper right-hand corner of the window.

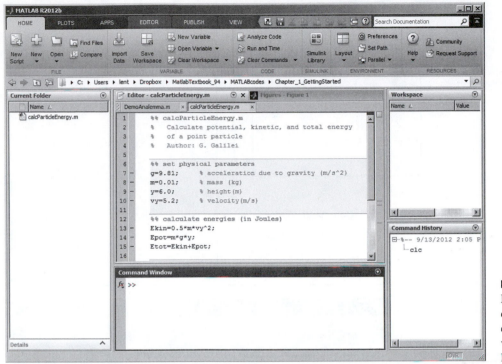

FIGURE 1.1 The MATLAB integrated development environment (IDE) with the default layout.

Windows can be manipulated within the IDE by clicking and dragging the top frame of the window. Outlines of the drop position of the window appear and disappear as the mouse is moved around. This takes some practice.

More than one IDE window can share the same screen pane. Choose between active windows in a single pane by using the tabs at the top, side, or bottom of the of the pane.

The default window layout in the IDE is shown in Figure 1.1. A (strongly) recommended setup for the desktop includes three panel areas, as shown in Figure 1.2. In the upper left quadrant of the IDE position the Workspace browser, Current Folder browser, and (optionally) the Figures window. One of these three is visible at any time, with the others being accessible by clicking the labeled tab. In the lower left, have the Command window open. The right portion is then devoted to the Editor window, where most of your programming work will take place. It really helps the development process to adopt this setup, or something very like it.

1.2 MATLAB variables

A MATLAB variable is simply a place in the computer's memory that can hold information. Each variable has a specific address in the computer's memory. The address is not manipulated directly by a MATLAB program. Rather, each variable is associated with a name that is used to refer to its contents. Each variable has a *name*, such as x, initialVelocity, or studentName. It also has a *class* (or *type*) that specifies what kind of information is stored in the variable. And, of course, each variable usually has a *value*, which is the information

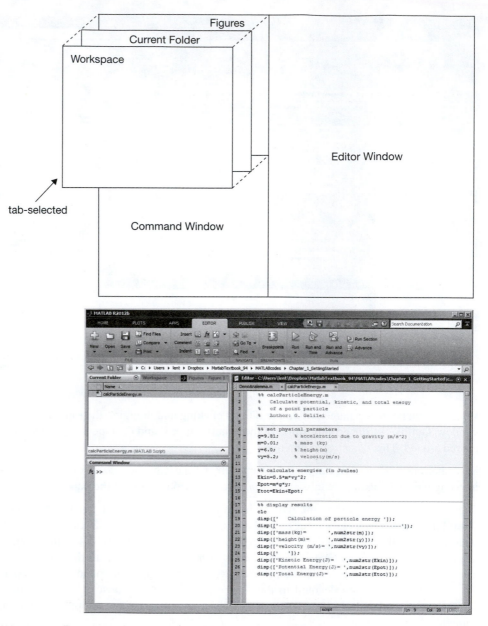

FIGURE 1.2 Recommended layout of the MATLAB IDE windows.

actually stored in the variable. The value may be a structured set of information, such as a matrix or a string of characters.

Numbers are stored by default in a variable class called *double*. The term originates in the FORTRAN variable type known as "double precision." Numbers in the double class take 64 bits in the computer's memory and contain 16 digits of precision. Alphanumeric strings, such as names, are stored in variables of the *char* class. Boolean variables, which can take

FIGURE 1.3   A schematic representation of MATLAB variables a, vinit, and fName. Each has a name, class (type), and a current value.

the value *true* or *false*, are stored in variables of the *logical* class. Logical true and false are represented by a 1 and a 0. Other variable classes will be discussed later.

Variable assignment statements

The equals sign is the MATLAB assignment statement. The command a=5 stores the value 5 in the variable named a. If the variable a has not already been created, this command will create it, then store the value. The class of the variable (its type) is determined by the value that is to be stored. Assignment statements can be typed into the Command window at the command prompt, a double greater-than symbol, ">>".

```
>> a=4;                     % class double
>> fname='Robert';         % class char
>> temperature=101.2;      % class double
>> isDone=true;            % class logical
```

In these examples, everything after the percent sign is a comment, information useful to the reader but ignored by MATLAB.

The assignment statement will cause MATLAB to echo the assignment to the Command window unless it is terminated by a semicolon.

```
>> a=4.2
a =
     4.2000
>> a=5.5;
>>
```

Multiple commands can be put on one line if they are separated by semicolons, though this is generally to be avoided because it degrades readability. We will occasionally do this in the text for brevity.

The right-hand side of the assignment statement can be an *expression*, i.e., a combination of numbers, arithmetic operators, and functions.

```
>> a=4*7+2.2;
>> r=a+b;
>> b=sin(3.28);
>> x2=x1+4*sin(theta);
>> zInit=1+yInit/cos(a*xInit);
>> k=k+1;
```

The general form of the assignment statement is

```
            <variable name>=<expression>;
```

The expression is first evaluated, then the value is stored in the variable named on the left-hand side of the equals sign. If variables appear in the expression on the right-hand side of the equals sign, the expression is evaluated by replacing the variable names in the expression with the values of the variables *at the time the statement is executed.* Note that this does not establish an ongoing relationship between those variables.

```
>> a=5;
>> b=7;
>> c=a+b     % uses current values of a and b
c =
      12
>> a=0;
>> b=-2;
>> c
c =
      12       % kept same value despite a and b changing
```

The equals sign is used to store a result in a particular variable. The only thing permitted to the left of the equals sign is the variable name for which the assignment is to be made. Though the statement a=4 looks like a mathematical equality, it is in fact *not* a mathematical equation. None of the following expressions are valid:

```
>> r=a=4;                    % not a valid MATLAB statement
>> a+1=press-2;              % not a valid MATLAB statement
>> 4=a;                      % not a valid MATLAB statement
>> 'only the lonely'='how I feel'; % not a valid MATLAB
                                          statement
```

By contrast this, which makes no sense as mathematics, is quite valid:

```
>> nr=nr+1;                  % increment nr
```

Variable names

Variable names are case-sensitive and must begin with a letter. The name must be composed of letters, numbers, and underscores; do not use other punctuation symbols. Long names are permitted but very long names should be used judiciously because they increase the chances for misspellings, which might go undetected. Only the first 31 characters of the variable name are significant.

`xinit`	okay
`VRightInitial`	okay
`4You2do`	not okay
`Start-up`	not okay
`vector%1`	not okay
`TargetOne`	okay
`ThisIsAVeryVeryLongVariableName`	okay
`ThisIsAVeryVeryLongVariablename`	okay, but different from previous
`x_temp`	okay

Variable workspace

The currently defined variables exist in the MATLAB workspace. [We will see later that it's possible for different parts of a program (separate functions) to have their own separate workspaces; for now there's just one workspace.] The workspace is part of the dynamic memory of the computer. Items in the workspace will vanish when the current MATLAB session is ended (i.e., when we quit MATLAB). The workspace can be saved to a file and reloaded later, although use of this feature will be rare. The workspace can be managed further using the following commands:

`clear a v g`	clears the variables a v g from the workspace
`clear`	clears all variables from the workspace
`who`	lists the currently defined variables
`whos`	displays a detailed list of defined variables
`save`	saves the current workspace to the file called matlab.mat
`save foobar`	saves the current workspace to the file called foobar.mat
`load`	loads variables saved in matlab.mat into the current workspace
`load foobar`	loads variables saved in foobar.mat into the current workspace

1.3   Numbers and functions

While real numbers (class double) are precise to about 16 digits, the display defaults to showing fewer digits. The command `format long` makes the display show more digits. The command `format short`, or just `format`, resets the display.

Large numbers and small numbers can be entered using scientific notation. The number 6.0221415×10^{23} can be entered as `6.0221415e23`. The number -1.602×10^{-19} can be entered as `-1.602e-19`.

Complex numbers can be entered using the special notation `5.2+2.1i`. The square root of -1 is represented in MATLAB by the predefined values of `i` and `j`, although these can be overwritten by defining a variable of that name (not recommended). MATLAB also recognizes the name `pi` as the value 3.141592653589793. This can also be overwritten by defining a variable named `pi`, an extraordinarily bad idea.

Internally MATLAB represents real numbers in normalized exponential base-2 notation. The range of numbers is roughly from as small as 10^{-308} to as large as 10^{308}.

Standard numerical operations are denoted by the usual symbols, and a very large number of functions are available. Some examples follow.

+	addition
–	subtraction
*	multiplication
/	division
^	exponentiation, e.g., 1.3^3.2 is $1.3^{3.2}$
`sin(x)`	returns the sine of x
`sind(x)`	returns the sine of x degrees
`cos(x)`	returns the cosine of x
`cosd(x)`	returns the cosine of x degrees
`tan(x)`	returns the tangent of x
`tand(x)`	returns the tangent of x degrees
`atan(x)`	returns the inverse tangent of x
`atand(x)`	returns the inverse tangent of x in degrees
`acos(x)`	returns the inverse cosine of x
`acosd(x)`	returns the inverse cosine of x in degrees
`asin(x)`	returns the inverse sine of x
`asind(x)`	returns the inverse sind of x in degrees
`exp(x)`	returns e^x
`log(x)`	returns the natural logarithm of x
`log10(x)`	returns the $\log_{10}(x)$
`sqrt(x)`	returns the square root of x
`abs(x)`	returns the absolute value of x
`round(x)`	returns the integer closest to x
`ceil(x)`	returns the smallest integer greater than or equal to x
`floor(x)`	returns the largest integer less than or equal to x
`isprime(n)`	returns true if n is prime
`factor(k)`	returns prime factors of k
`sign(x)`	returns the sign (1 or −1) of x; `sign(0)` is 0
`rand`	returns a pseudorandom number between 0 and 1
`rand(m)`	returns an $m \times m$ array of random numbers
`rand(m,n)`	returns an $m \times n$ array of random numbers

See more in the interactive help on the HOME tab: Help | Documentation | MATLAB | MATLAB functions (near the bottom).

1.4   Documentation

There are many MATLAB commands and functions. To get more information on a particular command, including syntax and examples, the online facilities are accessed from the
Command window using the `help` and `doc` commands.

>   `help <subject>`   returns brief documentation on MATLAB feature <subject>
>   `doc <subject>`   returns full documentation on MATLAB feature <subject>
>   can also be accessed by searching MATLAB Help for <subject>

For example, `help rand` gives brief information about the `rand` command, whereas `doc`
`rand` produces a fuller explanation in the Help browser.

1.5   Writing simple MATLAB scripts

With this brief introduction, you can start to write programs. The most basic form of a
program is a simple MATLAB script. This is just a list of MATLAB commands that are
executed in order. This amounts to a set of simple calculations that likely could be executed
on a calculator. Writing them as a program may save effort if the calculations are to be
performed repeatedly with different sets of inputs. (Even so, the real power of a computer
program rests in the more elaborate ways of controlling the calculation that we will get to
later.)

Let's consider an example from physics and compute the potential energy, kinetic energy,
and total energy of a point particle near the Earth's surface. (It's not necessary that you know
this physics.) You will need to specify the acceleration due to gravity g, the particle's mass
m, position y, and velocity v_y. From these things you can compute the relevant energies
using the formulas:

$$E_{kinetic} = \frac{1}{2}mv_y^2$$

$$E_{potential} = mgy$$

$$E_{total} = E_{kinetic} + E_{potential}$$

The following program performs this calculation. Type it into the Editor. The double percent
signs mark the beginning of sections; the lines will display automatically before each section.

```
%% calcParticleEnergy.m
%    Calculate potential, kinetic, and total energy
%    of a point particle
%    Author: G. Galilei

%% set physical parameters
g=9.81;      % acceleration due to gravity (m/s^2)
m=0.01;      % mass (kg)
y=6.0;       % height(m)
vy=5.2;      % velocity(m/s)
```

```
%% calculate energies (in Joules)
Ekin=0.5*m*vy^2;
Epot=m*g*y;
Etot=Ekin+Epot;

%% display results

disp(['   Calculation of particle energy ']);
disp(['------------------------------------------']);
disp(['mass(kg)=        ',num2str(m)]);
disp(['height(m)=       ',num2str(y)]);
disp(['velocity (m/s)= ',num2str(vy)]);
disp([' ']);
disp(['Kinetic Energy(J)   = ',num2str(Ekin)]);
disp(['Potential Energy(J) = ',num2str(Epot)]);
disp(['Total Energy(J)     = ',num2str(Etot)]);
```

Save the program by selecting "EDITOR | Save | Save As ..." and enter calcParticle Energy in the File Save dialog box. The dialog box will automatically add the ".m" extension to the filename; this indicates the file is a MATLAB program. You can save any changes and run the program by pressing the green "Run" button at the top of the Editor tab.

Let's look at some important features of this simple program.

Block structure

Virtually all programs should have at least this sort of block structure:

- A header block that starts with the name of the file and includes a description of what the program is supposed to do. This block is all comments. Though ignored by MATLAB itself, this is crucial communication to the reader of the program. Include the name of the program's author.

- A block that sets the input parameters. These could be further broken down into different sorts of input.

- A block or set of blocks that does the main calculation of the program.

- If appropriate, a block that displays, plots, or communicates the results of the program.

Use the double percent signs to separate different blocks of the program and label each block appropriately.

Appropriate variable names

Choose variable names that make clear the nature of the quantity being represented by that variable. The program would run fine if you have used variable names like j2mjl and xjwxss, but it's hugely valuable to use a name like Ekin and Epot for the kinetic and potential energies. Putting some thought into making the code clear pays big dividends as programs become more complex.

Useful comments

Similarly, adding helpful comments that document the program is very important. Comments can be overdone—one doesn't need to put a comment on every line. But the usual temptation is to undercomment.

Units

For physical problems that involve quantities whose values depend on the units employed, the code needs to specify which units are being used.

Formatting for clarity

Blank lines are ignored by the MATLAB interpreter and so can be used to make the program visually clearer. The important role of indenting text will be described later.

Basic display command

The last three lines print out the results to the Command Window. The `disp` command will be explained further in the next chapter. For the moment, let's just take this pattern to be a useful one in printing out a number and some explanatory text on the same line. To print out the number stored in the variable `vinit` with the explanatory text "Initial velocity (m/s):", use the MATLAB statement

```
disp(['Initial velocity (m/s):',num2str(vinit)]);
```

All the punctuation here is important, including the difference between round and square brackets. This is in fact a very common MATLAB idiom, with the form

```
disp(['<text>',num2str(<variablename>)]);
```

Change the inputs several times and rerun the program. Test the program by trying some special cases. For example, when the velocity is zero, you expect the kinetic energy to be zero. When running the program several times, you may notice that the output, which appears in the Command window, becomes hard to read. One can't easily distinguish the recent results from those from previous runs, and the values for the energies don't appear in a nice column making comparison easy. You can improve this by altering the last section of the program:

```
...
%% display results
disp('----------------------------------------------------');
disp(['Kinetic Energy (J)   = ',num2str(Ekin)]);
disp(['Potential Energy (J) = ',num2str(Epot)]);
disp(['Total Energy (J)     = ',num2str(Etot)]);
disp(' ');
```

Type in the change and note the improved clarity of the output. This is a very simple example of formatting the program and the output for clarity. A computer program should communicate to both the computer and to human readers.

1.6   A few words about errors and debugging

Programming languages demand a degree of logic, precision, and perfection that is rarely produced by human beings on their first (or second, or third) attempts. Programming errors—bugs—are inevitable. Indeed, programmers accept that developing functioning programs *always* involves an iterative process of writing and debugging. So don't be surprised if you are not an exception to this. Expect to make errors. It doesn't mean you're not good at this; it just means you're programming.

Error messages are your friends

Some programming errors are insidious—they produce results that are wrong but look plausible and never generate an error message. Or they don't produce wrong results until a special series of circumstances conspires to activate them. These errors are usually the result of the programmer not thinking through the logic of the program quite carefully enough, or perhaps not considering all the possibilities that might arise. To have an error detected for you by MATLAB when you try to run the program is, by contrast, a wonderful moment. MATLAB has noticed something is wrong and can give you some clues as to what the problem is so you can fix it right now. An appropriate response is "Wow, great! An error message! Thanks!" It is sometimes just a case of misspelling, or not being sufficiently careful with the syntax of a command. Or it may take more careful debugging detective work. But at least it has been brought to your attention so you can fix it.

Often one error produces a cascade of other errors and subsequent error messages. Focus on the *first* error message that occurs when you try to run the program. The error message will frequently report the line number in your program where it noticed things going awry. Read the error message (the first one) and look at that line in your program and see if you can tell what the problem is. It may have its origin before that line—perhaps a variable has a value that is unexpected (and wrong) because of a previous assignment statement. In any case, try to fix that problem and then rerun the program.

Sketch a plan on paper first

Before starting to write the program, write out a plan. This can be written in a combination of English and simplified programming notation (sometimes called pseudocode). Think through the variables you need and the logic of your solution plan. Time spent planning is not wasted; it will shorten the time to a working program.

Start small and add slowly

This is the key to writing a program. Don't write the whole program at once. Start with a small piece and get it debugged and working. Then add in another element and get it working. And so on. It's often wise to rerun and test the code after adding each brief section. The Fundamental Principle of Program Development is: "Start small and add gradually."

1.7   Using the debugger

The debugger is useful to see what is going on (or going wrong) when the program executes. Here you will mostly want to employ it simply to visualize program execution. The debugger lets you execute the program one line at a time.

It's often helpful in debugging a script to make the first command in the script the `clear` command, which removes all variables from memory. This prevents any history (i.e., previously set variables) from influencing the program. It may also reveal an uninitialized variable. A step-by-step method for examining the program in the debugger is as follows:

1. Save the program to a file.

2. Make sure the Workspace browser is visible.

3. Place a breakpoint (stop sign) in the program. On the left side of the Editor, next to the line numbers, are horizontal tick marks next to each executable line. Mouse-clicking on a tick mark will set a breakpoint, which will be indicated by a red stop sign appearing. Put the breakpoint at the first executable line, or at a place just before where you think the trouble is occurring.

   If the stop sign is gray instead of red, it means you haven't saved the file. Save the file and continue.

4. Run the program by pressing the green "Run" button on the EDITOR tab or by invoking the program name in the Command window.

5. Press the "Step" button on the EDITOR tab to step through the program line by line, executing one statement at a time. Look in the Workspace browser to see the current values of all variables. In the Command window the ">>" prompt becomes "K>>" to indicate that any command can also be typed (from the keyboard) as well.

6. Exit the debugger by pressing the Quit Debugging button on the EDITOR tab.

7. Clear all breakpoints by pressing "Breakpoints | Clear All" on the EDITOR tab, or by toggling off the stop signs with the mouse.

Looking ahead

The variables employed thus far have each contained a single number. The next chapter will describe variables that hold arrays of numbers or arrays of characters. The ability to manipulate numerical arrays will immediately make MATLAB command much more powerful—able to process large amounts of data at a time. Handling character-based data will produce more flexibility in interacting with the user, as well as adding an entirely different kind of information that can be processed by a program.

PROGRAMMING PROBLEMS

For the problems below write well-formatted MATLAB programs.

- Each program should include a title comment line, a brief description of what the program does, your name as the program author, and separate sections labeled "set parameters," "calculate <whatever>," and "display results." Begin each section with a comment line that starts with "%%".

- Create informative and readable variable names.

- Use comments appropriately so that a reader sees clearly what the program is doing. Specify the units of physical quantities.

- Use display statements (`disp`) to show both the problem input parameters and solution results. Pay attention to spaces and blank lines in formatting the output statements clearly.

Forming good programming habits pays off. Clear well-written code is easier to understand and change.

1. **Quadratic roots.** Write a program, `quadroots.m`, for finding the roots of the second-order polynomial $ax^2 + bx + c$. Use the quadratic equation. The inputs are the coefficients a, b, and c and the outputs are z_1 and z_2. The program should produce (exactly) the following output in the Command window when run with $(a, b, c) = (1, 2, -3)$:

```
====================
Quadratic Solver

coefficients
  a = 1
  b = 2
  c = -3
roots
  z1 = 1
  z2 = -3
```

2. **Rolling dice.** Write a program, `ThrowDice.m`, which generates the sum from randomly throwing a pair of fair dice. Use the `randi` function.

3. **Right triangle.** Write a program, `triangle.m`, that finds the length of the hypotenuse and the acute angles in a right triangle, given the length of the two legs of the right triangle.

4. **Running to the Sun.** Write a program, `sunrun.m`, to calculate how many hours it would take to run to the Sun if averaging a five-minute mile. Display the answer in seconds, hours, and years. (The distance from the Earth to the Sun is 93 million miles.)

5. **Gravitational force.** Write a program, `gforce.m`, to find the gravitational force (in Newtons) between any two people using $F = Gm_1m_2/r^2$ with gravitational constant $G = 6.67300 \times 10^{-11} N \cdot m^2/kg^2$. Run the program to find the gravitational force exerted on one person whose mass is 80 kg by another person of mass 60 kg who is 2 m away and report this value in the Command window.

6. **Shoes on the Moon.** Write a program, `moonshoes.m`, to estimate the number of shoes that it would take to cover the surface of the moon (which has a radius of 1740 km). Choose a shoe length and width.

7. **Kite string.** Write a program, `kitestring.m`, to calculate the amount of string needed to fly a kite at a height `kiteHeight` and at an angle `theta` to the horizon. Assume the person holds the kite a distance `holdHeight` above the ground and wants to have a minimum length of `stringWound` wound around the string holder. Run the program for a height of 8.2 m, an angle of $2\pi/7$, with 0.25 m of string around the holder, which is held 0.8 m above the ground.

8. **Calculating an average.** Write a program, randavg.m, that calculates the average of five random numbers between 0 and 10, which are generated using rand. Reset the random number generator using the rng('shuffle') command before finding the random numbers.

9. **Stellar parallax.** In the 16th century, Tycho Brahe argued against the Copernican heliocentric model of the universe (actually the solar system), because he reasoned that if the Earth moved around the Sun, you would see the apparent angular positions of stars shifting back and forth. This phenomenon is known as the stellar parallax, and it wasn't measured until the 19th century because it's so small. The stars are much farther away than anyone in the 16th century imagined. The star closest to the Sun is Proxima Centauri, which has an annual parallax $\delta\theta = 0.7$ arcseconds. That means that over six months the apparent position in the sky shifts by a maximum angle of seven-tenths of one 3600th of a degree. Write a program, parallax.m, to calculate how far away a one-inch diameter disk would need to be to subtend the same angle. Express the answer in feet and miles.

10. **Elastic collisions in one dimension.** When two objects collide in such a way that the sum of their kinetic energies before the collision is the same as the sum of their kinetic energies after the collision, they are said to collide elastically. The final velocities of the two objects can be obtained by using the following equations.

$$v_{1f} = \left(\frac{m_1 - m_2}{m_1 + m_2}\right) v_{1i} + \left(\frac{2m_2}{m_1 + m_2}\right) v_{2i}$$

$$v_{2f} = \left(\frac{2m_1}{m_1 + m_2}\right) v_{1i} + \left(\frac{m_2 - m_1}{m_1 + m_2}\right) v_{2i}$$

Write a program, Collide.m, that calculates the final velocities of two objects in an elastic collision, given their masses and initial velocities. Use $m_1 = 5$ kg, $m_2 = 3$ kg, $v_{1i} = 2$ m/s, and $v_{2i} = -4$ m/s as a test case.

11. **Kinetic friction.** The magnitude of the kinetic friction, F_{fric}, on a moving object is calculated using the equation:

$$F_{fric} = \mu_k N$$

where μ_k is the coefficient of kinetic friction, and N is the normal force on the moving object. If the object is on a surface parallel to the ground, the normal force is simply the weight of the object, $N = mg$, where $g = 9.8 \, m/s^2$, the acceleration due to gravity, and mass is measured in kg. Write a program, Friction.m, which calculates the force of kinetic friction on a horizontally moving object, given its mass and the coefficient of kinetic friction. Run the program with each of the following sets of parameters:

    a. $m = 0.8$ kg $\mu_k = 0.68$ (copper and glass)

    b. $m = 50$ g $\mu_k = 0.80$ (steel and steel)

    c. $m = 324$ g $\mu_k = 0.04$ (Teflon and steel)

12. **Light travel time.** Write a program, LightTime.m, to calculate the time it takes light to travel (a) from New York to San Francisco, (b) from the Sun to the Earth, (c) from Earth to Mars (minimum and maximum), (d) from the Sun to Pluto.

13. **Finite difference.** Consider the function $f(x) = cos(x)$. Write a program, FiniteDiff.m, to calculate the finite-difference approximation to the derivative of $f(x)$ at the point $x = x_0$ from the expression:

$$\left.\frac{df(x)}{dx}\right]_{x=x_0} \approx \frac{f(x_0 + \Delta x) - f(x_0)}{\Delta x}$$

Run the program with smaller and smaller numbers for Δx to see that the approximation converges to a limit. Find the limit for various values of x_0, including $x_0 = 0, \frac{\pi}{4}, \frac{\pi}{2}, \pi, \frac{5\pi}{4}$, and 2π. Could you have predicted the results you get?

14. **Total payment.** The monthly payment, P, computed for a loan amount, L, that is borrowed for a number of months, n, at a monthly interest rate of c is given by the equation:

$$P = \frac{L * c(1+c)^n}{(1+c)^n - 1}$$

Write a program, TotalPayment.m, to calculate the total amount of money a person will pay in principal and interest on a $10,000 loan that is borrowed at an annual interest rate of 5.6% for 10 years.

15. **Logistic population growth.** A food-limited animal population can be described by the function:

$$P(t) = P_0 + (P_f - P_0)\left[\frac{2}{1 + e^{-t/\tau}} - 1\right]$$

Where τ represents a characteristic growth time, P_0 is the initial population, and P_f is the final population. Write a program, LogisticGrowth.m, to calculate the population at a specific time t. Pick sensible values for the parameters.

16. **Triangulating height.** A surveyor who wants to measure the height of a tall tree positions his inclinometer at a distance d from the base of the tree and measures the angle θ between the horizon and the tree's top. The inclinometer rests on a tripod that is 5 feet tall. Write a program, Triangulate.m, to calculate the height of the tree. Use reasonable values for d and θ.

17. **Resistors in parallel.** The total resistance R of two resistors, R_1 and R_2, connected in parallel, is given by:

$$\frac{1}{R} = \frac{1}{R_1} + \frac{1}{R_2}$$

Write a program, Rparallel.m, to calculate the total resistance R for resistors connected in parallel for each of the following pairs of resistors.

    a. $R_1 = 100 \ k\Omega$ $R_2 = 100 \ k\Omega$

    b. $R_1 = 100 \ k\Omega$ $R_2 = 1 \ \Omega$

    c. $R_1 = 100 \ k\Omega$ $R_2 = 10 \ M\Omega$

18. **Compound interest.** The value V of an interest-bearing investment of principal, P, after N_y years is given by:

$$V = P\left(1 + \frac{r}{k}\right)^{kN_y}$$

where k is the number of times per year the investment is compounded, and r is the interest rate (5% interest means $r = 0.05$). Write a program, CompInterest.m, to calculate the value of such an investment for realistic parameters. Then consider the limiting case of a $1 investment at 100% interest compounded (nearly) continuously with $k = 1 \times 10^9$ for one year. What is the value of the investment after one year in the limiting case? (Do you recognize this number?)

19. **Paint coverage.** A typical latex paint will cover about 400 square feet per gallon of paint. Write a program, CalcPaint.m, that determines the number of gallons a consumer should purchase to have at least a minimum amount of paint to apply two coats of paint to a room with a given length, width, and wall height, a given number of windows with specified dimensions and doorways of specified dimensions. Run the program for a $16' \times 20'$ room with ceiling height $8'$ with four $30'' \times 4'$ windows and two $3' \times 7'$ door openings.

Strings and Vectors

Most people are familiar with manipulating numbers from experience with calculators. Computers, however, can deal with many types of data besides individual numbers.

Groups of character symbols, which can form words, names, etc., are stored in MATLAB variables called "strings." It turns out to be surprisingly important to manipulate strings as well as numbers. What sort of operations do you want to perform on strings? Strings can be combined together by concatenation ('chaining together'). Substrings can be extracted by using indexing to refer to just part of a string. Sometimes you may want the string (e.g., '1.34') that corresponds to a number (1.34), and sometimes you may want the number that corresponds to a string. A common motif is to concatenate strings representing words (e.g., `'The answer is '`) and numbers (e.g., `'3.44'`), and display the result in the Command window with the `disp` command.

The `input` command enables the program to get information, either strings or numbers, from the user. Following a prompt, the user types the information into the Command window. This will enable construction of programs that interact with the user. Part II will describe how to use a graphical user interface to let the user input information in a way that's even more convenient and flexible.

MATLAB also has a class of variables that hold, not just single numbers, but arrays of numbers, for example [134.2, 45, 12.4, 1.77]. One-dimensional arrays like this are called vectors, and can be of any length. Two-dimensional arrays, called matrices, are described in Chapter 4.

Vectors can be manipulated mathematically in many ways, including the basic operations of addition, subtraction, multiplication, and division. Most MATLAB mathematical functions will work on vectors as well as individual numbers. Several special vector functions make it easy to manipulate large quantities of information in a very compact form. Vectors of pseudorandom numbers, created with functions `rand` and `randi`, will prove very useful in creating simulations using techniques developed later in the text.

After mastering the material in this chapter you should be able to write programs that:

- Create and manipulate string variables.
- Output well-formatted information to the user in the Command window.
- Get either string or numerical information from the user through the Command window.
- Create and manipulate variables that hold numerical vectors.
- Perform mathematical operations on entire arrays of numbers.
- Generate vectors of pseudorandom numbers for use in simulation programs.

2.1   String basics

MATLAB stores alphanumeric strings of characters in the variable class *char*. Strings can be entered directly by using single quotes.

```
firstname='Alfonso';
lastname='Bedoya';
ideal='Buy low, sell high';
```

The value of the string can be displayed using the `disp` command.

```
>> disp(firstname)
Alfonso
>> disp(lastname)
Bedoya
```

Strings can be concatenated (merged together) using square brackets. The general syntax is

```
<newstring>=[<str1>,<str2>,<str3>,...];
```

```
>> fname=[firstname,lastname];
>> disp(fname)
AlfonsoBedoya
>> fullname=[firstname,' ',lastname];
>> disp(fullname)
Alfonso Bedoya
>> disp([ideal, ', young ', firstname, '!' ] );
Buy low, sell high, young Alfonso!
```

It's worth examining this last example carefully. The square brackets are being used to concatenate four strings: (1) the value stored in `ideal`, (2) the string `', young '`, (3) the string stored in `firstname`, and (4) the string `'!'`. Notice the role that spaces play in producing the desired result.

It is important to keep in mind the distinction between a number and a character string representing that number. The number 4.23 may be stored in a variable named `vel`, of type double. A string named `velstring` can store the string `'4.23'`. That is to say `velstring` contains the character `'4'` followed by the character `'.'`, the character `'2'`, and the character `'4'`. Converting from a number to a string can be done by the function `num2str`. Converting from a string to a number is accomplished by using either `str2num` or `str2double` (preferred).

Some very useful string-related functions are described below.

`num2str(x)`	returns a string corresponding to the number stored in x
`str2num(s)`	returns a number corresponding to the string s
`str2double(s)`	returns a number corresponding to the string s (also works with cell arrays of strings, defined later)
`length(s)`	returns the number of characters in the string sName
`lower(s)`	returns the string s in all lowercase
`upper(s)`	returns the string s in all uppercase
`sName(4)`	returns the 4th character in the string sName
`sName(4:6)`	returns the 4th through the 6th characters in the string sName

2.2 Using the `disp` command to print a variable's value

A common MATLAB idiom is to print to the Command window an informational string including the current value of a variable. This is done by (a) the `num2str` command, (b) string concatenation with square brackets, and (c) the `disp` command.

```
>> vinit=412.43;
>> disp(vinit)  % minimal
   412.4300
>> disp(['Initial velocity = ',num2str(vinit),' cm/s'])
Initial velocity = 412.43 cm/s
```

2.3 Getting information from the user

When the program runs, it can ask the user to enter information using the `input` command. The command is written differently, depending on whether the user's input is to be interpreted as a string or a number. For example, to prompt the user to provide the value of `nYears`, use

```
      nYears=input('Enter the number of years: ');
```

The program will display the string 'Enter the number of years:' in the Command window and then wait for the user to enter a number and press Enter or Return on the keyboard. The value the user enters will be interpreted as a number that is to be stored in the variable named nYears. If the user enters something that is not a number, an error normally results.

> *NOTE: MATLAB will actually evaluate what the user types as a MATLAB expression. For example, if the user types in sqrt(2)/2, MATLAB will first evaluate it, then assign the variable the value that results. If the user happens to type in an expression involving currently defined variables, MATLAB will evaluate that as well. This is a powerful and potentially extremely confusing feature that should be avoided by beginners.*

To prompt the user to enter a name, use

```
firstName=input('Please enter your first name: ','s');
```

The second argument 's' tells the function to interpret the user's input as a character string.

2.4   Vectors

We've seen how to store numbers in variables. It's often convenient to store not just one number, but a set of numbers. This can be done using arrays. An array stores an indexed set of numbers. Here we will consider one-dimensional arrays, also known as vectors; two-dimensional arrays, known as matrices, are treated later. Higher-dimensional arrays are possible, though you won't use them much. Note that MATLAB vectors can be much longer than the usual spatial vectors composed of the x, y, and z coordinates of a point. Vectors in MATLAB can be a single element, or may contain hundreds or thousands of elements.

Vectors can be entered using square brackets (the commas between elements are optional but help readability).

```
>> vp=[1, 4, 5, 9];
>> disp(vp)
     1     4     5     9
```

In this example, vp is the name of the entire vector. You can access individual elements of the vector using an integer index.

```
>> disp(vp(2))
     4

>> disp(vp(4))
     9
```

Think of this vector as an indexed set of boxes holding the elements of vp. Individual vector elements are accessed as vp(1), vp(2), vp(3), and so on. Elements of the vector can be individually changed.

```
>> vp(1)=47;
>> vp(3)=1.2;
>> disp(vp)
   47.0000     4.0000     1.2000     9.0000
```

The vector index always starts with 1. The vector vp, in the previous example, is a row vector. The other type of vector is a column vector, which is entered with semicolons separating the elements.

```
>> vc=[5; 3; 1; 2];
>> disp(vc)
     5
     3
     1
     2
```

A row vector contains several columns; a column vector contains several rows.

Transpose operator

The vector transpose operator is the single quote mark. It exchanges rows with columns, thus turning a row vector into a column vector and vice versa.

```
>> disp(vp)
   47.0000     4.0000     1.2000     9.0000

>> disp(vp')
   47.0000
    4.0000
    1.2000
    9.0000
```

The single quote mark can be hard to read clearly and might be mistaken for dust on the screen—consider putting a comment in the code to alert the reader to the transposition. (The single quote transpose operation also takes the complex conjugate, but this makes no difference for real numbers.)

2.5 Operations on vectors

Multiplication by a scalar

Multiplying a vector by a number results in each element of the vector being multiplied by the number. This is an example of a so-called "element-by-element operation."

```
>> disp(vp)
    47.0000     4.0000     1.2000     9.0000

>> a=0.5*vp
a =
    23.5000     2.0000     0.6000     4.5000
```

Addition with a scalar

Adding a number and a vector results in adding the number to each element of the vector. As always, subtracting is simply adding a negative.

```
>> disp(vp)
    47.0000     4.0000     1.2000     9.0000

>> a=vp+2
a =
    49.0000     6.0000     3.2000    11.0000

>> a=vp-5
a =
    42.0000    -1.0000    -3.8000     4.0000
```

Element-by-element operation with two vectors

If two vectors are the same size (an important requirement), then the sum (or difference) of the vectors is defined element by element.

```
>> a=[1, 4, 18];
>> b=[9, 1, 2];
>> a+b
ans =
    10      5     20
>> a-b
ans =
    -8      3     16
```

Element-by-element multiplication or division must be indicated with the compound symbols .* and ./, respectively.

```
>> a=[1, 4, 18];
>> b=[9, 1, 2];
>> a./b
ans =
    0.1111     4.0000     9.0000
```

```
>> a.*b
ans =
     9     4    36
```

The compound symbol `.^` is used to indicate element-by-element exponentiation.

```
>> a=[1, 2, 4, 5]; b=a.^2;
>> disp(b)
     1     4    16    25
```

Functions of vectors

Many MATLAB functions operate on vectors element by element. For example:

```
>> thetaDeg=[0, 30, 45, 60, 90];
>> r=1;
>> x=r*cosd(thetaDeg);
>> y=r*sind(thetaDeg);
>> disp(x)
    1.0000    0.8660    0.7071    0.5000         0

>> disp(y)
         0    0.5000    0.7071    0.8660    1.0000

>> disp(x.*x+y.*y)
     1     1     1     1     1
% illustrating trig identity sin^2(t)+cos^2(t)=1
```

Length of vectors

The `length` function returns the number of elements in the vector.

```
>> v=[3, 5, 7, 9, 13, 55];
>> nv=length(v)
nv =
     6
```

Subarrays

The colon operator can be used to index a subset of the vector.

```
>> v=[3, 5, 7, 9, 13, 55];
>> a=v(2:5)
a =
     5     7     9    13
```

Individual elements can also be picked out to form a new vector.

```
>> b=v([1, 3, 6])
b =

    3     7    55
```

(Note that the square brackets are important here.)

The symbol end is interpreted as meaning the index of the last element in the vector.

```
>> a=[1, 3, 4, 5];
>> disp(a(2:end))
    3     4     5
```

Concatenating vector

Vectors can be put together to form other arrays. This is exactly analogous to string concatenation and is also accomplished with square brackets.

```
>> a=[1, 2, 3];b=[4, 5, 6];
>> c=[a,b];
>> disp(c)
    1     2     3     4     5     6
>> c2=[b, a]; c3=[20, a, 21];
>> disp(c2)
    4     5     6     1     2     3

>> disp(c3)
   20     1     2     3    21
```

2.6   Special vector functions

A vector of N ones is returned by ones(1,N). A vector of N zeros is returned by zeros(1,N). A vector of N random numbers between 0 and 1 is returned by rand(1,N).

```
>> g0=ones(1,5);disp(g0)
    1     1     1     1     1
>> p0=zeros(1,5);disp(p0)
    0     0     0     0     0
>> rv=rand(1,5);disp(rv)
    0.6154    0.7919    0.9218    0.7382    0.1763
```

Among the most useful functions is `linspace`, which generates a vector with a set of equally spaced points. The syntax is:

$$var = \texttt{linspace}(initial\ value,\ final\ value,\ number\ of\ points)$$

```
>> t=linspace(0, 90, 7);
>> disp(t)
     0    15    30    45    60    75    90
```

This is often used for generating a grid of equally spaced coordinates in space or time.

The colon operator (:) also creates an equally spaced vector of numbers. The expression `1:10` generates a vector of integers from 1 to 10. The default spacing between numbers is 1. The spacing between numbers in the array, called the *stride*, can also be set as the middle number between two colons.

```
>> 1:2:10
ans =
     1     3     5     7     9

>> 0:0.2:1.3
ans =
          0    0.2000    0.4000    0.6000    0.8000    1.0000    1.2000
>> 5:-0.5:3

ans =

     5.0000    4.5000    4.0000    3.5000    3.0000
```

Statistical functions

Some useful statistical vector functions include:

`max(v)`	value of the smallest element of array v
`min(v)`	value of the largest element of array v
`sum(v)`	sum of the elements of array v
`mean(v)`	average value of the elements of array v
`median(v)`	median of the elements of array v
`mode(v)`	mode of the elements of array v
`std(v)`	standard deviation the elements of array v
`sort(v)`	returns vector sorted in ascending order

The median x_{med} of a set of numbers $\{x_i\}$ is a number such that half of the x_i are larger than x_{med} and half are smaller. The median of $[1, 2, 3, 4]$ is 2.5. The mode of the set $\{x_i\}$ is the value that occurs most often. If several numbers occur with the same frequency, the smallest of those is returned by the function. The sample standard deviation of a set of numbers x_i is given by:

$$s = \sqrt{\frac{1}{n-1}\sum_{i=1}^{n}(x_i - \bar{x})^2} \tag{2.1}$$

where $\bar{x}$ is the mean of the set.

For example:

```
>> x=[2, 1, 2, 5, 6, 10, 11, 10];
>> median(x)
ans =
      5.5000
>> mean(x)
ans =
      5.8750
>> mode(x)
ans =
      2
>> std(x)
ans =
      4.0510
```

2.7 Using rand and randi

The command r=rand generates a random number in the interval $[0, 1]$. The command rv=rand(1,1000) generates a vector of 1000 random numbers. The command randi(30,1,200) generates a vector of 200 random numbers from 1 to 30.

The functions rand and randi actually use a pseudorandom number generator. True random numbers cannot be produced by a computer program but rather require a random physical process. While the numbers generated will be very evenly distributed, the same numbers will be produced for every MATLAB session. A nice way around this is to change the seed of the generator, using a number derived from the clock of your computer. That way, each MATLAB session will produce a different set of pseudorandom numbers. To initialize rand or randi with a clock-generated seed, put the command:

```
rng('shuffle')
```

near the beginning of the program. This initialization command should not be inside a simulation loop (see Chapter 5). It only really needs to be executed once per MATLAB session.

In earlier versions of MATLAB initialize the random number generator using:

```
RandStream.setDefaultStream ...
      (RandStream('mt19937ar','seed',sum(100*clock)));
```

or

```
rand('seed',sum(100*clock));
```

Looking ahead

A very common computational task is to represent a mathematical function, or a set of measured data, by enumerating ordered pairs such as $\{(x_1, y_1), (x_2, y_2), (x_3, y_3) \ldots\}$. To visualize this set, you may often want to plot these points, perhaps connected by line segments. The vectors developed in this chapter make it natural to represent a set of ordered pairs like this by a pair of MATLAB vectors x and y, which have the same length and store the components of the pairs: $x_3 = $ x(3) and $y_3 = $ y(3), etc. The next chapter describes how to make plots from pairs of MATLAB vectors. Visualizing the relationship between tabulated sets of data (vectors) is a real strength of MATLAB.

PROGRAMMING PROBLEMS

1. **Greeting.** Write a MATLAB program, greeting.m, that asks for the first name of the user and then greets the user. Something like this:

   ```
   What is your first name? Alfonso
   Good morning, Alfonso! Glad to be computing with you today.
   ```

2. **Quadratic roots2.** Write a program, quadroots2.m, to prompt the user to enter in turn a, b, and c, and then calculate the roots of the quadratic equation. Something like this:

   ```
   ************************************

   Quadratic Solver for ax^2+bx+c=0
   Please enter a: xx
   Please enter b: xx
   Please enter c: xx
   The roots are:
           Z1=xxxxx
           Z2=xxxxx
   ************************************
   ```

3. **Pig Latin.** Write a program, piglatin.m, prompting the user to enter a string that starts with a consonant to be translated into pig Latin. The rule for pig Latin is the following: move the first letter of the word to the end with an added "ay." For example, the word "hello" translates into "ellohay." Translate the user's word and then display to the user the word and the pig Latin translation. (This program need not handle digraphs like "th" correctly.)

4. **Sum next 10.** Write a program, sum10.m, which asks the user for an integer and then finds the sum of that number and the next nine integers following that number. Report the result to the user, which should look something like: The sum of the integers from 4 through 13 is 85.

5. **Unit vector.** A unit vector is a vector of length one. It is often desirable to find a unit vector in the same direction as a given vector. Such a vector can be determined by computing $v/|v|$ where $|v| = \sqrt{v_1^2 + v_2^2 + v_3^2 + \cdots + v_n^2}$. Write a program, `unitvector.m`, that finds a unit vector for any four-dimensional vector.

6. **Trig identity.** Write a program, `trigid.m`, that takes an array of five angles and computes two new arrays, the sines of the elements in the first array, and the cosines. Then use array operations to show that $\cos^2(x) + \sin^2(x) = 1$ for each angle in the original array.

7. **Test statistics.** Write a program, `teststats.m`, that prompts the user to enter 5 test scores. Then compute the mean, median, mode, and variance for the scores entered using the appropriate MATLAB functions. (Use `help <function>` or `doc <function>` if you need information on these functions.) Report the results for these test scores to the user.

8. **Box features.** Write a program, `box.m`, that asks the user to input the dimensions of a box and then calculates the surface area and volume of the box. Report the results to the user in the command window.

9. **Poor Encryption.** After registering with a particular website, a student is assigned a 9-character password that contains no numbers. The student needs to email the password to a parent so that the parent has access to the site as well, but is concerned that someone may hack the email and obtain the password. Write a program, `encrypt.m`, that asks the student for the password and a 10-digit telephone number (without dashes). Then use the telephone number to separate characters in the password to create a new 19-character password that the student can email to a parent. The parent can then eliminate the phone numbers in the 19-character password to obtain the correct password.

10. **Better encryption.** The previous problem is clearly rather poor encryption. Can you do better? Write two programs, `myEncrypt.m` and `myDecrypt.m`, that use a different scheme to encrypt a string and decrypt it.

11. **Password.** Write a program, `password.m`, that asks for a user's first name, middle initial, last name, and 10-digit cell phone number. Create a six-character password for the user, using the first letter of the first name, the middle initial, the first two letters of the last name and the last two digits of the telephone number. Report the password to the user. All letters in the password should be lowercase.

12. **Take order.** Write a MATLAB program, `Take Order.m`, which greets the customer, takes the customer's name, and the number of different types of thurgins they want to order. Running the program should look something like this (be careful with spaces):

```
>> TakeOrder
Please enter your name: Buford
Good morning, Buford. We have a variety of thurgins to choose
from today.
How many nurvels would you like? 7
How many tombits? 12
How many weenives? 3
That will be 22 thurgins total.
Thanks for your order, Buford.
```

13. **Take order 2.** Make an expanded version, TakeOrder2.m, of the previous program, which also computes the total cost of the order. Say nurvels are $0.55 each, tombits are $0.45, and weenives have gone up to $1.23 each. Print out a full summary of the transaction.

14. **Vector products.** Write a program, dotcross.m, that finds the dot product and cross product of two three-dimensional row vectors. Recall that the dot product of two three-dimensional vectors is defined to be $v \cdot w = v_1w_1 + v_2w_2 + v_3w_3$ and the cross product of two vectors is defined to be the vector $v \times w = (v_2w_3 - v_3w_2, v_3w_1 - v_1w_3, v_1w_2 - v_2w_1)$. Display the results in the Command window.

15. **Terminal velocity.** Objects dropped from a great height fall with increasing speed until the drag force from the air balances the force due to gravity. The terminal velocity in air (for sufficiently massive bodies like pennies or people) is given by:

$$v_t = \sqrt{\frac{2mg}{\rho A C_d}}$$

Where m is the mass of the object, g is the acceleration due to gravity ($9.81 \, m/s^2$), ρ is the density of air ($1.18 \, kg/m^3$), A is the cross vertical sectional area of the object (m^2), and C_d is the dimensionless drag coefficient, which depends on the details of the shape and is about 0.3. Write a program, TerminalVel.m, that prompts the user for the m and A, and computes the terminal velocity in m/s and in mi/hr, displaying both in a well-formatted style. Use your program to estimate the difference in speed between a skydiver falling feet-first and lying horizontally.

16. **Squares of numbers.** Write a program, squares.m, that uses linspace to create and array of integers from 10 to 20 inclusive and then computes and reports the square of each integer.

17. **Squares with user input.** Modify the squares.m program to allow a user to enter a range of integer values (e.g., from 15 to 30) and then compute and report the square of each integer. Call the program squares2.m.

18. **User paint.** Write a program, userpaint.m, which asks the user for the dimensions on the room to be painted, the dimensions of the windows in the room, the number of windows, the dimensions of door openings in the room, and the number of door openings. Compute the number of gallons of paint needed to paint the room, assuming a gallon of paint covers 400 square feet, and report the result to the user. Personalize the program by asking the user for a first name, and report the results with a greeting using the first name.

19. **Take order 3.** Write a new program, TakeOrder3.m, which stores the user input of each type of thurgin in an array. Represent the price of each thurgin (as given in the problem above) in a second array and compute the total cost of the thurgins ordered using array operation(s). Finally, report to the user the total cost of the thurgins ordered.

20. **Furniture sales.** A discount furniture store sells four types of bedroom sets. The cost (in dollars) of each set can be represented by the array Cs = [199, 268, 500, 670]. The price at which the store sells each set can be represented by the array Ps = [398, 598, 798, 998]. In a particular quarter the number of sets sold of each type can be

represented by the array $Ns = [35, 25, 20, 10]$. Write a program, `furniture.m`, that calculates and reports:

a. The total number of bedroom sets sold.

b. The total revenue received by the store from the number of sets sold.

c. The profit realized by the store from the sale of bedroom sets.

21. **Rental receipts.** Cheap Rentals offers four types of vehicles: compacts; full-sized; vans; SUV's. The daily rental fees for each type of vehicle are $25, $38, $53, and $72, respectively. The following represents their July business, where the number stated is the days rented from each of its three locations: Airport; Campus; Elkhart.

Airport: compacts 250; full-sized 150; vans 180; SUV's 86.

Campus: compacts 160; full-sized 44; vans 60; SUV's 20.

Elkhart: compacts 210; full-sized 112; vans 120; SUV's 78.

Represent the fees and days rented at each location in four appropriate arrays. Then write a program, `rentals.m`, which uses array operations to compute and report:

a. The total number of rental days for July at each location.

b. The total number of rental days for July for the company.

c. The total revenue received at each location in July.

d. The total revenue received by the company in July.

Plotting

MATLAB is exceptional among programming languages for the power of its built-in graphics capabilities. This chapter will introduce the fundamentals of making two-dimensional linear plots.

In MATLAB, a basic x-y plot is constructed from two MATLAB vectors that define a set of points in the plane. The points are often connected by line segments so that, if the density of points is high, a smooth curve results. Separate MATLAB commands control the axis scaling, color of the lines, labeling of the axes, appearance of grid lines, and other aspects of the plot.

One of the most common graphics tasks is tabulating and plotting a mathematical function. One can use the `linspace` command to create a regularly spaced array of points representing the independent variable, and then use MATLAB vector math to create a tabulation of the values of a specific function, the dependent variable, at those points. The `plot` command, and associated formatting commands, can then be used to make a graph of the function. For some kinds of data, bar plots or histogram plots are a more natural way to represent the information graphically.

After mastering the material in this chapter you should be able to write programs that:

- Create x-y plots of tabulated information.
- Adjust the scaling of the plot axes, add labels to the axes, and put a title on the plot.
- Tabulate (x, y) pairs representing a function $y = f(x)$, and create a plot that graphically displays the function.
- Plot several functions on one graph.
- Produce bar charts and histograms.
- Add annotations to a plot using lines and text.

3.1   The plot command

The plot command produces a two-dimensional plot and is the workhorse of MATLAB graphics. It creates a plot that represents graphically the relationship between two vectors (either 1-by-N or N-by-1 arrays). Consider two vectors, v1 and v2 (see Figure 3.1).

```
v1=[1, 3, 4, 6, 5, 2];
v2=[1, 2, 2, 3, 4, 2];
plot(v1,v2,'-o');
axis([0 7 0 5]);
```

The plot command has the general form:

```
plot(<vector of x-values>,<vector of y-values>,<style-option
string>)
```

The vectors must be of the same length and are interpreted as forming a series of (x, y) pairs to be plotted. By this we simply mean that the values in the first vector will be plotted on the horizontal axis and the values in the second vector will be plotted on the vertical axis. This is very important in understanding how the plot command works. The plot

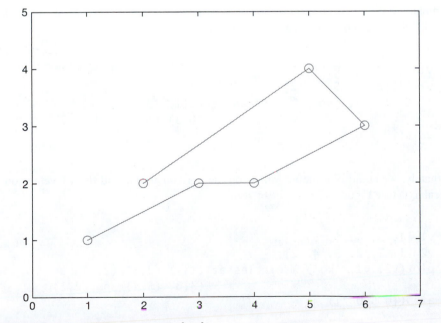

FIGURE 3.1   The result of plot(v1,v2,'-o').

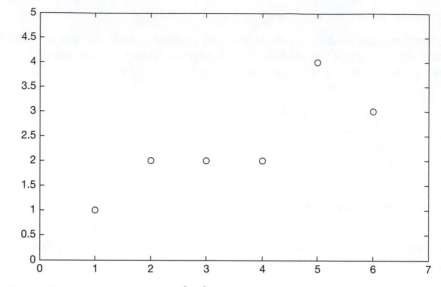

FIGURE 3.2 The result of plot(v1,v2,'ko').

command simply draws markers at (x, y) points and/or connects the points with straight line segments. The command itself is in no way concerned with functional relationships; it is just connecting points.

To emphasize this, let's just plot the points themselves. If the style-option string is 'ko', then a black circle is plotted at each of the points.

```
>> v1=[1, 3, 4, 6, 5, 2];
>> v2=[1, 2, 2, 3, 4, 2];
>> plot(v1, v2, 'ko') % circles at (1,1) (3,2) (4,2)
                   %                 (6,3) (5,4) and (2,2)
>> axis([0 7 0 5])
```

Alternately, we could plot the v2 values on the horizontal axis and the v1 values on the vertical axis (see Figure 3.3).

```
>> v1=[1, 3, 4, 6, 5, 2];
>> v2=[1, 2, 2, 3, 4, 2];
>> plot(v2, v1, 'ko') % circles at (1,1) (2,3) (2,4)
                   %                 (3,6) (5,4) and (2,2)
>> axis([0 5 0 7])
```

A style-option string of '-o' produces lines connecting circles, as in Figure 3.1. If the style-option is omitted, the default is '-', which produces a solid line connecting points

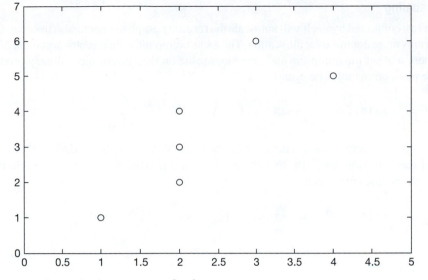

FIGURE 3.3   The result of `plot(v2,v1,'ko')`.

with no markers at the points. Other options for the style string control the color, the marker, and the line type.

Color		Marker		Line type	
b	blue	.	point	-	solid
g	green	o	circle	:	dotted
r	red	x	x-mark	-.	dashdot
c	cyan	+	plus	- -	dashed
m	magenta	*	star	(none)	no line
y	yellow	s	square		
k	black	d	diamond		
w	white	v	triangle (down)		
		^	triangle (up)		
		<	triangle (left)		
		>	triangle (right)		
		p	pentagram		
		h	hexagram		
		(none)	no marker		

The elements of the style-option string can be specified in any order. Some examples follow:

```
plot(x, y, 'r-d');  % red line and diamonds
plot(x, y, 'k:');   % black dotted line
plot(x, y, 'pg-.'); % pentagrams and green lines
```

Axis scaling

The `plot` command by itself will autoscale the resulting graph to encompass the data. Often one wants more control over the scaling. The `axis` command with a vector argument of four numbers will set the minimum and maximum value on the current plot (already produced by the plot command). The syntax is:

```
axis([xmin, xmax, ymin, ymax])
```

The commas separating the scaling limits are optional. If you want to let MATLAB autoscale one of these dimensions, set it to `inf` (infinity) for a maximum or `-inf` for a minimum. For example, the command:

```
axis([ -1, 1, -inf, inf])
```

sets the horizontal range to $[-1, 1]$, but lets MATLAB choose the vertical limits based on the data that is plotted.

Some other commonly used commands to control the axis behavior are follow:

axis manual	freezes the scaling at the current limits
axis auto	returns the axis scaling to its default, automatic mode
axis tight	sets the axis limits to the range of the data
axis equal	sets the aspect ratio so that tick mark increments on the x, y, and z axes are equal in size
axis square	makes the current axis box square in size
axis normal	undoes the effects of axis square and axis equal
axis off	turns off all axis labeling, tick marks, and background
axis on	turns axis labeling, tick marks, and background back on
grid on	draws grid lines on the graph

Plot labeling

In almost every instance, plots should be labeled. The key commands are `xlabel`, `ylabel`, and `title`, each of which takes a string argument. It is often convenient to construct a string for the title with information about the plot.

Note that the `plot` command creates a plot. *Commands that modify how the plot looks come **after** the `plot` command.* This is a very common source of errors and frustration for beginners. A typical sequence of commands to produce a plot follows this pattern:

1. Create a vector containing the independent variable. This will be plotted along the horizontal axis.

2. Create a vector containing the dependent variable. This will be plotted on the vertical axis.

3. Make the plot using the `plot` command.

4. Set the scaling, add axis labels, add a grid, add a title, etc.

The plot command clears the plotting area of whatever was previously plotted and overwrites it with the new plot.

3.2   Tabulating and plotting a simple function

A mathematical function $f(x)$ is usually defined on an infinite set of points in some domain, for example, $f(x) = 3x^2$ on the closed interval $x = [0, 3]$. Of course, one can only compute and plot the value of the function at a finite set of points. We can use MATLAB vector arithmetic to construct a graphical representation of the function $f(x)$. For example, the following program will create two MATLAB vectors, x and f, and construct a plot representing this function.

```
%% simpleplot.m
%    make a very simple plot of the function f(x)=3x^2.
%    Author: P.J. Pennypacker

%% set parameters
xmin=0;
xmax=3;
Nx=200;

%% set independent variable
x=linspace(xmin, xmax, Nx);

%% calculate function values
f=3*x.^2;

%% plot results
plot(x, f)
xlabel('x')
ylabel('f(x)=3x^2');
title('A simple plot')
grid on
```

By using many points (in this example, 200 points in the range $[0, 3]$), we visually approximate the continuum.

The basic steps in making a plot like this are:

1. Create a vector containing values of the independent variable, for example x, throughout the domain of the function. This is usually done using the linspace command. These values will be plotted along the horizontal axis.

2. Create a vector containing the function values computed element by element from the values stored in the x vector (or whatever the name of the vector holding the independent variable values happens to be).

3. Make the plot using the plot command.

4. Set the scaling, add axis labels, add a grid, add a title, etc.

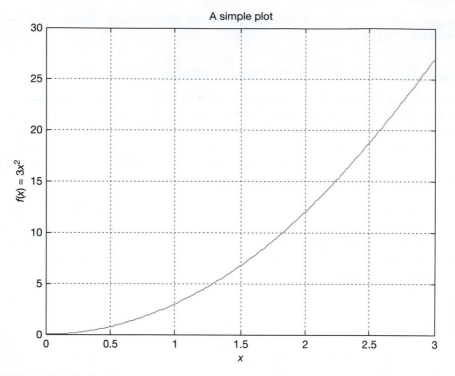

FIGURE 3.4 Result of running `simpleplot.m`.

Here's an example with a more complicated function—a polynomial multiplied by a damped exponential $x(t) = (at^2 + bt + c)e^{-t/\beta}$. One might imagine this represents the horizontal motion $x(t)$ of a damped spring. Note that we're deliberately using variables that are not called f and x to emphasize that what matters is not the names of the variable but their roles as dependent or independent variables. Here the independent variable (which will be plotted on the horizontal axis) is t. To tabulate values of x, you first must specify the parameters a, b, c, and β.

```
%% plotdampedpolynomial.m
%    make a plot of the function
%        x(t)=(at^2+bt+c)*exp{-t/beta}.
%    Author: Milo Farnsworth

%% set parameters
tmin=0;
tmax=3;
Nt=200;
a=1;
b=-7;
c=1;
beta=0.4;
```

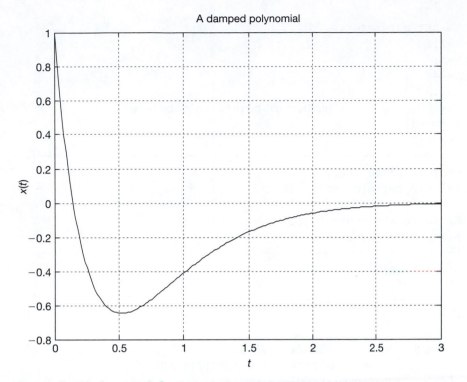

FIGURE 3.5 Graphical output of `plotdampedpolynomial.m`.

```
%% set independent variable
t=linspace(tmin, tmax, Nt);

%% calculate function values
x=(a*t.^2+b*t+c).*exp(-t/beta);

%% plot results
plot(t, x, 'k-')
xlabel('t')
ylabel('x(t)');
title('A damped polynomial')
grid on
```

Here is another example that computes a general cubic curve and plots the results.

```
% plotcubic.m
%    plot cubic ax^3+bx^2+cx+d on interval [-3,3]
%    Author: Harold Potter
```

```
%% set parameters
a=1;
b=1;
c=-4;
d=1;
Nx=200;              % number of points to tabulate
xmin=-3;
xmax=+3;

%% initialize array
x=linspace(xmin, xmax, Nx);

%% calculate cubic function
f=a*x.^3+ b*x.^2 +c*x +d;

%% plot results
plot(x, f, 'r');
axis([xmin, xmax, -inf, inf]);
xlabel('x')
ylabel('f(x)')
title(['Cubic ax^3+bx^2+cx+d',...
      ',   a=',num2str(a),' b=',num2str(b),...
      ', c=',num2str(c),...
      ', d=',num2str(d)]);
grid on
```

The ellipses (. . .) continue one line of MATLAB onto the next for readability. This program also illustrates the important practice of defining parameters at the top of the program (using MATLAB variables) rather than using numbers in the body of the program. It's much better to define and set values for variables xmin, xmax, and Nx and use them in the linspace command. Thus, rather than

```
% ... other commands here ...

x=linspace(-3, 3, 100);      % bad programming practice
```

it is much better to write:

```
% ... near top of program
xmin=-3;
xmax=3;
Nx=100;

% ... other commands here ...

x=linspace(xmin, xmax, Nx);            % good programming practice
```

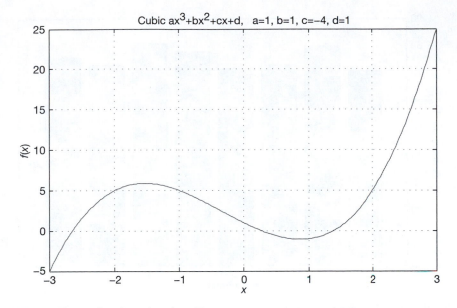

FIGURE 3.6   The results of running plotcubic.m.

The advantages of defining parameters near the top of the program are: (1) it's clear where to change things that alter the behavior of the program, and (2) subsequent calculations in the program can use these parameters and be kept consistent with the changes.

3.3   Bar graphs and histograms

One can display the values stored in a vector by creating a bar chart. The command `bar(v)` with a single vector argument creates a bar plot of the values of each element of v.

```
%% makebar1.m
%     demonstrate the use of a bar plot

%% set data
temperatures=[71, 80, 73, 72, 78, 81, 73, 76];

%% plot data as bar chart
bar(temperatures);
xlabel('Measurement');
ylabel('Temperature(F)');
grid on;
```

The same data can be plotted differently by (a) first sorting the data, and (b) scaling the vertical axis to reveal the differences between the data values more. This is accomplished by the following program.

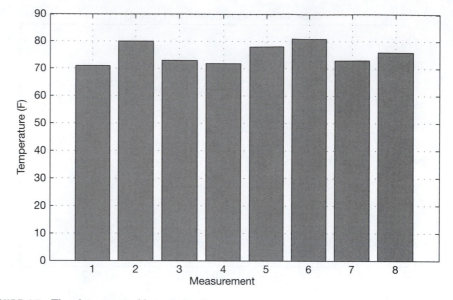

FIGURE 3.7 The plot generated by makebar1.m.

```
%% makebar2.m
%    demonstrate the use of a bar plot
%       sort the data and display with a zero
%       offset on the vertical axis
%       Author: S. Snape

%% set data
temperatures=[71, 80, 73, 72, 78, 81, 73, 76];
sortedTemps=sort(temperatures);
Tmin=65;
Tmax=85;

%% plot data as bar chart
bar(sortedTemps);
xlabel('Measurement')
ylabel('Temperature (F)');
grid on
axis([0, length(temperatures)+1, Tmin,  Tmax]);
```

Note that the zero of the vertical axis is now not seen. This presentation of the same data emphasizes the differences between the plotted values and de-emphasizes the information about their absolute values by hiding the zero of the vertical axis. Formatting a plot frequently involves choices about what one thinks is important in the function or data being presented.

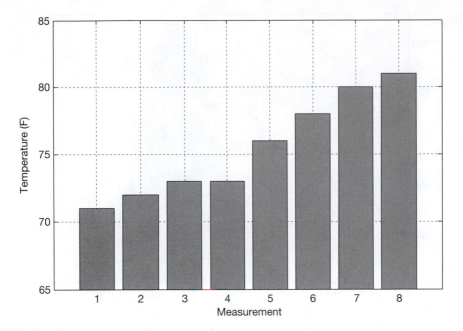

FIGURE 3.8   The plot generated by `makebar2.m`.

Histograms

Sometimes one is not interested in the details of a data set as much as in the distribution of the data. A histogram is a bar chart that plots the number of data points falling within various ranges of values. This is rarely useful unless there is a fair amount of data, so we'll make some using the MATLAB function `randn(1,N)`, which returns a normally distributed set of N pseudorandom numbers with a standard deviation of 1 and a mean value of 0. By shifting and stretching this distribution, the following program generates a distribution around `q0` with a standard deviation of `sigmaq`. The `hist` command produces a histogram plot of the data divided into `nbins` bins.

```
%% normHist1.m
%    make a histogram of normally distributed random numbers
%    Author: Norm Conquist

%% set parameters for data
Ndata=10000;
q0=1.5;         % mean of  q data
sigmaq=0.25;    % standard deviation of q data
qmin=0.0;       % min and max for plotting
qmax=2.5;
nbins=25;       % number of bins for histogram

%% generate simulation data
qdata=q0+sigmaq*randn(1,Ndata);
```

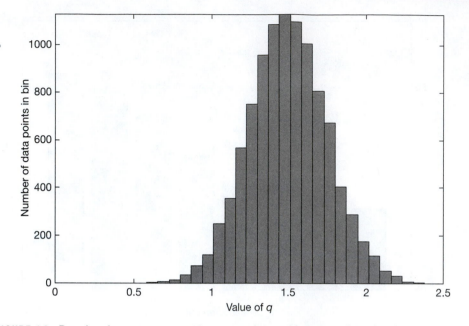

FIGURE 3.9 Running the program normHist1.m produces a histogram plot using the hist command.

```
%% plot histogram of data
hist(qdata, nbins);
xlabel('Value of q')
ylabel('Number of data points in bin')
axis([qmin, qmax, 0, inf]);
```

3.4   Drawing several plots on one graph

Normally, each time the plot command is invoked the graphics area is cleared and a new plot is drawn. If you want to combine more than one plot on the graph, there are two basic strategies. Several plots can be displayed on one set of axes using a plot command with multiple argument sets. Alternatively, one can use use the hold command to stop the graphics area from being cleared. The hold command is necessary to combine different kinds of plots, e.g., a bar plot and a line plot.

Multiple plots with a single plot command

The plot command can graph more than one set of x-data and y-data pairs. For example, to plot a sine wave and a cosine wave on the same graph, additional x-y pairs are included as arguments to the plot command.

```
%% plotSineCosine.m
%     make a plot with sine and cosine on the
```

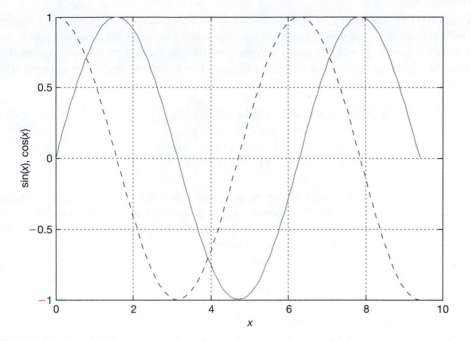

FIGURE 3.10 Running the program `plotSineCosine.m` produces multiple curves on one graph.

```
%       same graph
%       Author: Morton B. Thistlewaite

%% set parameters
Nx=300;
xmax=3*pi;

%% calculate functions
x=linspace(0, xmax, Nx);
y1=sin(x);
y2=cos(x);

%% plot results
plot(x, y1, x, y2);  % plots y1 vs x and y2 vs x
grid on
xlabel('x')
ylabel('sin(x), cos(x)')
```

To clarify which lines correspond to which functions, one can add a `legend` command of the form

```
legend('sin(x)', 'cos(x)');
```

where the order of the label strings corresponds to the order in the `plot` statement.

A single `plot` statement can be used to plot an arbitrary number of curves on the same axis. Each curve is comprised of straight line segments connecting the tabulated points, but if there are enough points, the result becomes indistinguishable from a smooth curve. The color, line-type, and data point indicators for each curve are specified by an optional style string. The general form is:

```
plot(x1vec, y1vec, stylestring1 ,...
        x2vec, y2vec, stylestring2 ,...
            <as many as you like>
        xNvec, yNvec, stylestringN)
```

Continuing the `plot` statement across several lines using the ellipses (. . .) is optional, but recommended for clarity. This construction can be used to draw lines on the graph by specifying explicitly the coordinates of each point. For example, we can modify the previous plot to draw a vertical red line at $x = \pi$.

```
%% plotSineCosine2.m
%      make a plot with sine and cosine on the
%      same graph
%      Author: Foghorn Leghorn

%% set parameters
Nx=100;
xmax=3*pi;

%% calculate functions
x=linspace(0, xmax, Nx);
y1=sin(x);
y2=cos(x);

%% plot results
plot(x, y1,...
       x, y2, '--',...
       [pi, pi],[-10, 10],'r');
axis([0, xmax, -1, 1]);

xlabel('x')
ylabel('sin(x), cos(x)')
legend('sin(x)', 'cos(x)');
```

Although the added red line goes from the point $(\pi, -10)$ to $(\pi, +10)$, the `axis` scaling statement limits the graph to showing just the range $y = [-1, 1]$. With this construction, many curves (and lines) can be plotted on one graph. The result is shown in Figure 13.11.

Combining multiple plots with a hold command

As already mentioned, the `plot` command normally first clears the plotting area of whatever has been previously plotted and creates a new plot. The `hold on` command keeps

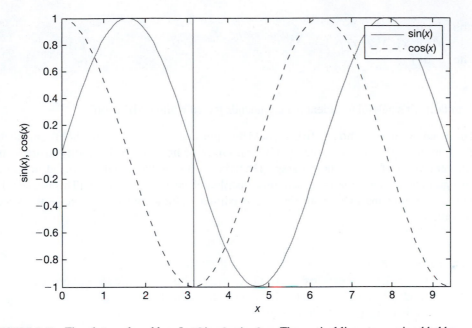

FIGURE 3.11   The plot produced by `plotSineCosine2.m`. The vertical line at $x = \pi$ is added by using multiple arguments in the `plot` command.

whatever has been plotted on the axes in place, and allows new plotting commands (e.g., `plot` or `bar`) to add to what has already been plotted. The command `hold off` returns the graphics to normal mode.

```
%% holdPlot.m
%    make a plot with sine and 1.2*cosine on the
%    same graph to demonstrate hold command
%    Author: Polly Gnomiel

%% set parameters
Nx=300;
xmax=3*pi;

%% calculate functions
x=linspace(0, xmax, Nx);
y1=sin(x);
y2=cos(x);

%% plot results
plot(x, y1)
axis([0, xmax, -1, 1]);
xlabel('x')
ylabel('sin(x), 1.2*cos(x)')
grid on
```

```
hold on
   plot(x, 1.2*y2, '--')
hold off
```

For clarity, it's helpful to indent the commands issued while `hold` is on.

The behavior shown in `holdPlot.m` could be replicated without using the hold commands by using a single `plot` command. The real utility of `hold` is in the ability to stack up different kinds of plots. The program `plotHist2.m` uses the `hold` command to plot a histogram bar plot and then adds a normal distribution curve to the graph. (This is a simple way to compare the two—matching the maximum values—but more precise ways are possible.)

```
%% normHist2.m
%    make a histogram of normally distributed random numbers
%       add plot of normal distribution function
%       Author: N. Schwartzkopf

%% set parameters for data
Ndata=10000;
q0=1.5;         % mean of  q data
sigmaq=0.25;    % standard deviation of q data
qmin=0.0;       % min and max for plotting
qmax=2.5;
nbins=25;       % number of bins for histogram

%% generate simulation data
qdata=q0+sigmaq*randn(1,Ndata);

%% plot histogram of data
[nq, qs]=hist(qdata, nbins);    % returns histogram
                                %    data without plotting
bar(qs, nq);                    % makes histogram plot
xlabel('Value of q')
ylabel('Number of data points in bin')
axis([qmin, qmax, 0, inf]);

%% overlay plot of normal distribution function
Nq=200;
qa=linspace(qmin, qmax, Nq);

Pq=max(nq)*exp( -(qa-q0).^2/(2*sigmaq^2));
hold on
  plot(qa, Pq, 'k', 'LineWidth', 2)
hold off
```

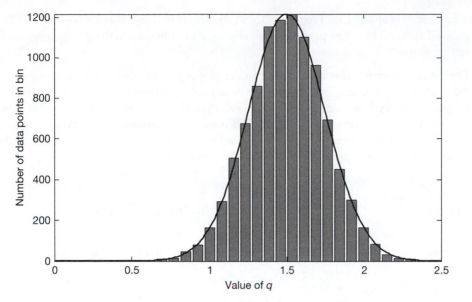

FIGURE 3.12 Result of `normHist2.m`, which uses `hold` to stack a bar chart and a plotted curve.

Thickening plotted curves

In Figure 3.12, it is helpful to make the plotted curve thicker than usual so it is visible against the bar plot. This is accomplished in `normHist2` by adding another modifier to the `plot` command, which specifies the value of the LineWidth property of the line, measured in points (see the next section).

3.5 Adding lines and text

A plot statement always clears the figure before drawing the plot. By contrast, the `line` and `text` commands add graphical elements to an existing plot without redrawing the figure.

The `line` command takes as arguments a vector of x values and a vector of y values. The points need not actually fall on a line; the command simply connects the points defined by the (x, y) pairs in the same way as the `plot` command. An extended version adds a pair of strings that determine the appearance of the line.

```
line(x, y);
line(t, v, 'Color', 'blue');
```

This is an instance of setting what is called a property-value pair. One of the properties of a line is named Color (capitalization is relevant). The value of the Color property can be a string such as 'blue', 'green', 'red', etc. Abbreviations 'b', 'g', and 'r' also work. Another property for a line is named LineWidth, which takes on values of 0.5 (the default), 1, 2, etc., representing the width of the line measured in points. A point is 1/72 of an inch. The permissible values for LineWidth are positive real numbers. See the MATLAB documentation under 'Line Properties' for a complete (very long) list of properties and their allowed values. These line properties can also be altered in calls to the `plot` command by setting property–value pairs.

The `text` command adds a text string to the plot at starting position x, y, (now scalars rather than vectors). Text objects can also be altered by setting property–value pairs. One property is named FontSize, which takes on values of 12, 16, 18, etc. The permissible values for FontSize are integers. See the MATLAB documentation under 'Text Properties' for a complete list of properties and their allowed values. See Appendix B for a brief description of formatting mathematical expressions in a text command.

```
text(4, 0.5, 'This is a label')
text(4, 0.5, 'This is a green label', 'Color', 'g')
```

Try entering the following commands interactively at the command line prompt.

```
>> axis([0, 20, 0, 20])
>> text(4, 1, 'This is a label')
>> text(4, 3, 'This is a big red label', 'Color', 'r',
    'FontSize', 14)
>> line([0, 5, 10, 15],[10, 7, 6, 1])
>> line([0, 5, 10, 15],[0, 15, 6, 0],'Color','r')
```

The program `PlotGaussWithLines.m` illustrates the use of both of these commands.

```
%% PlotGaussWithLines.m
%    plot a gaussian curve and annotate one standard deviation
%    Author: Vic Vector

%% set parameters
q0=1.5;         % mean of distribution
sigmaq=0.25;    % standard deviation
qmin=0.0;       % min and max for plotting
qmax=2.5;

Nq=200;
qa=linspace(qmin, qmax, Nq);
% (relative) height of marks at one-sigma points

TicHeight=0.3;

%% calculate normalized gaussian function
prefactor=1/sqrt(2*pi*sigmaq^2);
Gauss=prefactor*exp( -(qa-q0).^2/(2*sigmaq^2) );
fmax=max(Gauss);
```

```
%% plot function
plot(qa, Gauss)
xlabel('q')
ylabel('Normal distribution')
axis([qmin, qmax, 0, 1.2*fmax]);
grid on

%% add annotations at standard deviation marks
qupper=q0+sigmaq;
qlower=q0-sigmaq;
% find exact value of function at one-sigma points
fupper=prefactor*exp( -(qupper-q0).^2/(2*sigmaq^2) );
flower=prefactor*exp( -(qlower-q0).^2/(2*sigmaq^2) );

% length of vertical lines are determined by TicHeight and fmax
MarkLength=TicHeight*fmax;
line([qupper, qupper],[fupper-MarkLength/2,
      fupper+MarkLength/2],... 'Color','r');
line([qlower, qlower],[flower-MarkLength/2,
      flower+MarkLength/2],... 'Color','r');

text(q0+1.2*sigmaq,fupper, '+\sigma', 'Color', 'r');
text(q0-1.6*sigmaq,flower, '-\sigma', 'Color', 'r');
```

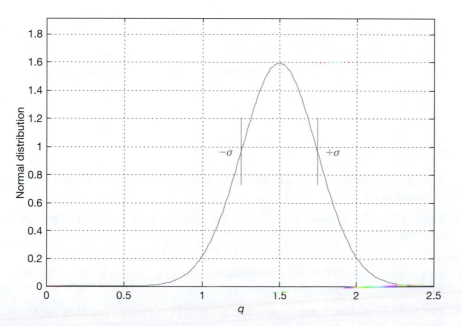

FIGURE 3.13 The graph produced by the program PlotGaussWithLines.m. A Gaussian is plotted with labeled vertical lines at plus and minus one standard deviation σ.

Looking ahead

The plotting commands covered in this chapter are the bread and butter of MATLAB graphics. Subsequent chapters detail more capabilities that can enhance graphical visualization of information. Visualization techniques are always best employed with an eye toward increasing insight, rather than just show. Chapter 6 describes methods for making graphics that move—animations. Well-conceived animations can make computational tools far more effective at communicating model behavior to the user. Creating animations requires the programming constructs of Chapter 5. The graphical user interfaces (GUI) capability of Part II (Chapters 9–11) enables the user to interact with the program and displayed graphics. More advanced graphics commands, including three-dimensional plotting, are explored in Chapter 13.

PROGRAMMING PROBLEMS

1. **Plotting points.** Write a program, `ConnectPoints.m`, that plots the points defined by the two arrays $x = [0, 1, 2, -2, -1, 0]$ and $y = [0, 0, 1, 1, 0, 0]$. Each point should be plotted as a star, and the points should be connected with line segments.

2. **Plot parabola.** Write a program, `plotparabola.m`, that plots the function $f(x) = ax^2 + bx + c$ for x on the interval $[-3, 3]$. Use `linspace` to define a vector of x values and calculate $f(x(k))$ at each point $x(k)$. Try various values of a, b, and c.

3. **Plot sine curve.** Write a program, `sinewave.m`, that plots the function

$$f(x) = \sin\left(\frac{x}{\lambda}\right)$$

for x in the interval $[-3p, 3p]$. Use `linspace` to define a vector of x values and calculate $f(x(k))$ at each point $x(k)$. Try various values of $\lambda > 0$.

4. **Plot Series.** Write a program, `AvSequence.m`, that plots the sequence defined by:

$$f_1 = 0$$
$$f_2 = 1$$
$$f_k = \frac{(f_{k-1} + f_{k-2})}{2} \quad \text{for } k > 2$$

for k up to 20. Since this f is actually only defined on the integers, you should plot using, for example: `plot(f, 'o-')`.

5. **Plotting damped motion.** Write a program, `plotdamped.m`, that plots the following function:

$$f(x) = e^{\frac{-x}{a}} \cos\left(2\pi \frac{x}{\lambda}\right)$$

Choose an appropriate domain for the function and vary the parameters a and λ (by changing the values set in the program and rerunning).

6. **Plot ballistic motion.** Write a program, `plotballistic.m`, that plots the following function:

$$h(t) = h_0 + v_0 t - \frac{1}{2} g t^2$$

Let $g = 9.8$ and $h_0 \geq 0$. Choose an appropriate domain for the function and vary the parameters h_0 and v_0 (by changing the values set in the program).

7. **Plot derivative.** A numerical approximation of the derivative at every point in an interval, except the endpoints, can be determined by the expression:

$$\left. \frac{df(x)}{dx} \right]_{x=x_0} \approx \frac{f_{n+1} - f_{n-1}}{2\Delta x}$$

The derivatives at the endpoints can be approximated by:

$$\left. \frac{df(x)}{dx} \right]_{x=x_1} \approx \frac{f_2 - f_1}{\Delta x}$$

$$\left. \frac{df(x)}{dx} \right]_{x=x_n} \approx \frac{f_n - f_{n-1}}{\Delta x}$$

Write a program, Plotdfdx.m, that plots the function $y = (\sin(\pi x))^{10}$ and this numerical approximation of the derivative of the function on the interval $[0, 1]$.

8. **Plot the logistic function.** Write a program, plotlogistic.m, that plots the following function:

$$p(y) = \frac{1}{1 + e^{-\left(\frac{y - y_0}{a}\right)}}$$

Choose an appropriate domain for the function and vary the parameters y_0 and a (by changing the values in the program).

9. **Harmonic motion plot.** Write a program, plotharmonic.m, that plots harmonic motion of x in time, as described by the following equation:

$$x(t) = A \cos(\omega t + \varphi)$$

In this equation, A is the amplitude of the motion, ω is the angular frequency, and φ is the phase shift, all of which are constants in the equation. Run the program with the values

$$A = 2, \text{ and } \varphi = \frac{\pi}{2}.$$

Pick a value for the period T that is related to ω by the relation $\omega = \frac{2\pi}{T}$. Also pick a good value for the final time T_f that sets the range of $t = [0, \ldots, T_f]$.

10. **Creative plot.** Draw a figure of your own choosing on a piece of graph paper and write a MATLAB program, plotoriginal.m, to draw the figure. Drawing the figure should require at least four different sections of code and use the MATLAB hold function to keep adding new elements to the same set of axes. The title of your plot and the figure itself should clearly communicate the image to a viewer.

11. **Probabilities for three dice.** Write a program ThreeDiceProb to calculate and display the probability $P(N)$ of rolling three dice and getting a total (sum of the face values) of N. Use the Monte Carlo technique, simulating many repeated rolls of the dice and estimating the probability by the fraction of rolls with each result. Display the probabilities as a bar graph. You may find the hist(x,bins) function useful.

12. **Probabilities for multiple dice.** Extend the previous problem to calculate $P(N)$ for any number $N_d > 1$ of dice.

Matrices

The name MATLAB is derived from "Matrix Laboratory," so it's no surprise that this programming language is particularly strong at handling matrices. Matrices and vectors have many applications in science and engineering. Mathematically a matrix is simply a two-dimensional array of numbers. Given a matrix **A**, one specifies a particular element with two integer indices. For example, the element in the 2nd row and 3rd column is written $A_{2,3}$. In MATLAB, this would be denoted A(2,3).

Many of the techniques for manipulating matrices are straightforward extensions of those for manipulating vectors described in Chapter 2. Array indexing and element-by-element mathematical operations behave just as in the case of vectors. Several operations on matrices are new, however: the matrix-vector product, matrix-matrix multiplication, the inverse of a matrix, and the determinant of a matrix.

A very common use for matrix operations is to characterize a system of linear equations that you want to solve simultaneously. Section 4.3 describes how to use matrix operations to solve such a linear system, and includes as and extended example an electric circuit problem.

After mastering the material in this chapter you should be able to write programs that:

- Create matrices explicitly from numbers or vectors.

- Multiply matrices by vectors or other matrices.

- Extract individual elements or subarrays from a matrix.

- Find the inverse or determinant of a matrix.

- Solve a matrix equation of the form $\mathbf{Ax} = \mathbf{b}$.

- Solve a system of simultaneous linear equations by casting them in the form of a matrix equation and then solving the matrix equation.

4.1   Entering and manipulating matrices

In MATLAB you can enter a matrix by writing the elements inside square brackets with the rows separated by semicolons.

```
>> P=[1, 4, 6; 2, 7, -3]
P =

     1     4     6
     2     7    -3
```

A matrix with the same number of rows as columns is called a square matrix.

```
>> A=[ 1, 2, 3; 9, 8, 3; 0, 5, 8]
A =

     1     2     3
     9     8     3
     0     5     8
```

Here A is the name of a MATLAB variable that represents the entire matrix. Individual matrix elements are specified by their row index and column index, integers, which represent the position of the element in the array. A specific element is indicated using round brackets (i.e., parentheses). The element of A that appears in the 3rd row, 2nd column is referenced as A(3,2)—the first index refers to the row and the second refers to the column.

```
>> A(3,2)
     ans = 5
>> A(2,2)
     ans = 8
>> A(1,3)
     ans = 3
```

Individual elements can appear on the left-hand side of the equals sign in an assignment statement, and so they can be individually assigned values (overwriting the previously stored values).

```
>> A(1,2)=10;
>> A(2,2)=12;
>> disp(A)
     1    10     3
     9    12     3
     0     5     8
```

If used in the place of an array index, a colon by itself indicates *all* the elements of the corresponding row or column.

```
>> disp(A)
       1      10       3
       9      12       3
       0       5       8

>> disp(A(1,:))        %  the first row, all columns
       1      10       3

>> disp(A(:,2))        %  all  rows, second column
      10
      12
       5
```

The colon can also be used to specify a range of values for the row and/or column index.

```
>> disp(A)
       1      10       3
       9      12       3
       0       5       8

>> disp(A(1:2,1:2))
       1      10
       9      12

>> disp(A(2:3,:))
       9      12       3
       0       5       8
```

A vector of individual index values can be used to reference noncontiguous elements of a matrix.

```
>> disp(A)
       1      10       3
       9      12       3
       0       5       8

>> disp(A([1,3],[1,3]))
       1       3
       0       8

>> disp(A([1,3],:))
       1      10       3
       0       5       8
```

Size of a matrix

A matrix is said to have size $n \times m$, where n is the number of rows and m is the number of columns. The MATLAB function `size` returns these values in two variables.

```
>> disp(A)
      1    10     3
      9    12     3
      0     5     8

>> size(A)
ans =
      3     3

>> B=[1, 4, 17, 3; 2, 5, 12, 7];
>> [nrowB,ncolB]=size(B)
nrowB =
      2
ncolB =
      4
```

Matrix transpose

Taking the transpose of a matrix exchanges rows with columns. In MATLAB the transpose operator is the single quote symbol.

```
>> disp(B)
      1     4    17     3
      2     5    12     7

>> disp(B')
      1     2
      4     5
     17    12
      3     7

>> disp(A)
      1    10     3
      9    12     3
      0     5     8

>> disp(A')
      1     9     0
     10    12     5
      3     3     8
```

[Note: The single quote transpose operator actually takes the transpose and also takes the complex conjugate of each element. This distinction does not matter for real matrices, only those with complex elements (i.e., numbers with both a real and imaginary part). If you want to take just the transpose of a complex matrix, without conjugation, use a period followed by a single quote, e.g., `Btrans = B.';`.]

4.2 Operations on matrices

Arithmetic operations with a scalar

Multiplying a matrix by a scalar (i.e., just a single number, not an array) simply multiplies each element of the matrix by the number. The same holds for division, addition, and subtraction.

```
>> disp(A)
     1    10     3
     9    12     3
     0     5     8

>> s=2;
>> disp(A*s)
     2    20     6
    18    24     6
     0    10    16

>> disp(A/s)
    0.5000    5.0000    1.5000
    4.5000    6.0000    1.5000
         0    2.5000    4.0000

>> disp(A+s)
     3    12     5
    11    14     5
     2     7    10

>> disp(A-s)
    -1     8     1
     7    10     1
    -2     3     6
```

Addition and subtraction of two matrices with the same size

If two matrices are the same size (they must have both the same number of rows and the same number of columns), then addition and subtraction are defined to be element-by-element.

```
>> disp(A)
     5     5     3
     2     4     3
     0     0     1
```

```
>> disp(B)
     2     1     2
     4     3     0
     4     1     2

>> disp(A+B)
     7     6     5
     6     7     3
     4     1     3

>> disp(A-B)
     3     4     1
    -2     1     3
    -4    -1    -1
```

Functions of matrices

Most MATLAB mathematical functions will take a matrix argument and return a matrix whose values are computed element-by-element. For example, if the i,jth element of A is $a_{i,j}$ and $B = sin(A)$, then the i,jth element of B is $sin(a_{i,j})$. Here is an example using the function sind to calculate the sine for a matrix of angles that are measured in degrees:

```
>> Atheta=[0, 30, 45, 60, 90; 90, 120, 135, 150, 180];
>> disp(Atheta)
     0    30    45    60    90
    90   120   135   150   180

>> disp(sind(Atheta))
          0    0.5000    0.7071    0.8660    1.0000
     1.0000    0.8660    0.7071    0.5000         0
```

Matrix multiplication

Two matrices can be multiplied together if their dimensions are appropriately matched. We can multiply two matrices A and B together if the number of columns of A is the same as the number of rows of B. Consider the product $C = AB$. If A is an $n \times p$ matrix and B is a $p \times m$ matrix, then the product C is an $n \times m$ matrix. The standard mathematical notation for the element of a matrix A in the ith row and jth column is $A_{i,j}$. The elements of the product C are then given by

$$C_{i,j} = \sum_{k=1}^{p} A_{i,k} B_{k,j}$$

where the sum goes over all the columns of A and the rows of B. This means simply

$$C_{i,j} = A_{i,1} B_{1,j} + A_{i,2} B_{2,j} + A_{i,3} B_{3,j} + \cdots + A_{i,p} B_{p,j}.$$

For example:

$$AB = \begin{pmatrix} 2 & 3 & 0 & 3 \\ 3 & 0 & 0 & 1 \\ 1 & 1 & 3 & 4 \end{pmatrix} \begin{pmatrix} 0 & 3 \\ 2 & 1 \\ 2 & 2 \\ 3 & 2 \end{pmatrix} = \begin{pmatrix} 15 & 15 \\ 3 & 11 \\ 20 & 18 \end{pmatrix} = C$$

The $(1, 1)$ element of the product is computed by taking the inner product of the first row of A with the first column of B, thus $C_{1,1} = 2 \cdot 0 + 3 \cdot 2 + 0 \cdot 2 + 3 \cdot 3 = 15$ and $C_{3,2} = 1 \cdot 3 + 1 \cdot 1 + 3 \cdot 2 + 4 \cdot 2 = 18$.

An important special case is when A and B are both $N \times N$. Then both AB and BA are well defined but in general $AB \neq BA$—matrix multiplication is not commutative.

By default in MATLAB, the multiplication symbol * is interpreted as matrix multiplication. The expression A*B, where A and B are matrices, will result in the computation of the product according to the rules of matrix multiplication, providing the dimensions of the two matrices are appropriate. (If the dimensions are not right, an error message results and execution is terminated.) For example, doing the matrix multiplication above is as simple as:

```
>> A =[ 2      3      0      3;...
        3      0      0      1;...
        1      1      3      4];
>> B =[ 0      3;...
        2      1;...
        2      2;...
        3      2];
>> C=A*B;
>> disp(C)
     15      15
      3      11
     20      18
```

The identity matrix

For square $N \times N$ matrices, there is a unique $N \times N$ identity matrix I that has ones on the diagonal and zeros everywhere else.

$$I = \begin{pmatrix} 1 & 0 & 0 & \cdots & 0 \\ 0 & 1 & 0 & \cdots & 0 \\ 0 & 0 & 1 & \cdots & 0 \\ \vdots & \vdots & \vdots & \ddots & \vdots \\ 0 & 0 & 0 & \cdots & 1 \end{pmatrix} \tag{4.1}$$

The identity matrix has the property that, for any square matrix A, $AI = IA = A$. The matrix I plays the role for matrix multiplication that the number 1 plays in multiplication of real numbers. The MATLAB function eye(N) returns the $N \times N$ identity matrix.

```
>> I=eye(4);
>> disp(I)
     1     0     0     0
     0     1     0     0
     0     0     1     0
     0     0     0     1
```

The inverse of a matrix

Many, but not all, square matrices have a multiplicative inverse. If the inverse of A exists, it is usually written A^{-1} and is a matrix of the same size as A that satisfies

$$A^{-1}A = AA^{-1} = I. \tag{4.2}$$

As one might expect, the inverse of the inverse is the original matrix.

$$(A^{-1})^{-1} = A \tag{4.3}$$

In MATLAB the inverse of a matrix can be calculated using the function inv.

```
>> disp(A)
     3     3     2     1
     3     3     4     3
     3     1     1     1
     1     0     2     2

>> B=inv(A);
>> disp(B)
    1.0000   -1.0000    0.0000    1.0000
   -2.5000    2.5000    1.0000   -3.0000
    6.0000   -5.0000   -3.0000    6.0000
   -6.5000    5.5000    3.0000   -6.0000
```

We can check the inverse property directly:

```
>> disp(B*A)
    1.0000    0.0000         0    0.0000
    0.0000    1.0000    0.0000         0
   -0.0000   -0.0000    1.0000         0
   -0.0000   -0.0000    0.0000    1.0000
```

[Note: Several elements are not exactly zero here, though inspection reveals that they are less than 10^{-14}. This is because some of the careful cancellation of terms that makes the product zero off the diagonal aren't exact on a computer (any computer) that has to treat numbers with finite precision.]

The determinant of a matrix

The determinant of a square matrix is a real number that can be useful in characterizing certain properties of the matrix. The determinant of a matrix can be calculated in MATLAB using the `det` function.

```
>> disp(A)
     3      3      2      1
     3      3      4      3
     3      1      1      1
     1      0      2      2

>> disp(det(A))
    -2
```

For our present purposes, perhaps the determinant is most useful as a check on the existence of the matrix inverse. If the determinant is zero, then the matrix has no inverse and is termed "singular." If two rows or two columns are identical, or a multiple of one another, then the matrix is singular.

```
>> A(1,:)=2*A(2,:);
>> disp(A)
     6      6      8      6  % 1st row is 2x second row
     3      3      4      3
     3      1      1      1
     1      0      2      2
>> disp(det(A))
     0
>> disp(inv(A))
Warning: Matrix is singular to working precision.
   Inf    Inf    Inf    Inf
   Inf    Inf    Inf    Inf
   Inf    Inf    Inf    Inf
   Inf    Inf    Inf    Inf
```

Matrix-vector multiplication

Vectors are just matrices with a length of 1 in one dimension or the other; column vectors are $N \times 1$ matrices and row vectors are $1 \times N$ matrices. So the rules of matrix multiplication still apply.

Consider one case that will be of particular interest: A square $N \times N$ matrix multiplies a column vector u of length N. The result is another column vector of length N.

$$Au = b \tag{4.4}$$

Each element of the vector b is computed by taking the inner product of a row of A and the column vector u. This is equivalent to the set of equations

$$A_{1,1}u_1 + A_{1,2}u_2 + A_{1,3}u_3 + \cdots + A_{1,1}u_N = b_1$$
$$A_{2,1}u_1 + A_{2,2}u_2 + A_{2,3}u_3 + \cdots + A_{2,N}u_N = b_2$$
$$A_{3,1}u_1 + A_{3,2}u_2 + A_{3,3}u_3 + \cdots + A_{3,N}u_N = b_3 \qquad (4.5)$$
$$\vdots \qquad\qquad \vdots \quad \vdots$$
$$A_{N,1}u_1 + A_{N,2}u_2 + A_{N,3}u_3 + \cdots + A_{N,N}u_N = b_N$$

Each element of the vector b is a linear combination of the elements of u, with the weighting coefficients being given by the appropriate row of the matrix A.

4.3 Solving linear systems: The backslash operator

A problem that arises frequently in many fields is that physical or mathematical analysis yields a set of coupled equations precisely of the form shown in equation (4.5). In many situations, the numbers on the right-hand side are known but the u's are unknown quantities we'd like to determine. Once we put the problem in this form, we recognize that finding the simultaneous solution to this set of linear equations is equivalent to finding a vector u that satisfies

$$Au = b \qquad (4.6)$$

where we know all the elements of A and b.

One way to solve this problem would be to calculate the inverse of A and multiply both sides of (4.5) by it.

$$Au = b \qquad (4.7)$$
$$A^{-1}Au = A^{-1}b \qquad (4.8)$$
$$u = A^{-1}b \qquad (4.9)$$

This can be calculated in MATLAB with the command u=inv(A)*b;. As it turns out, this approach is almost always unwise. Calculating the full matrix inverse of a matrix is costly in terms of computation time and, more importantly, the precise cancellations of many terms that occur make it less accurate and stable than other methods. Simpler and more stable numerical solutions are obtained in MATLAB using the "backslash" operator. The solution of $Au = b$ is obtained by writing

```
u=A\b;  % solve linear system A*u=b
```

This notation invokes clever linear solvers that are far more efficient and stable than taking the inverse. The notation is meant to suggest b being "divided" by A from the left, as in $u = A^{-1}b$.

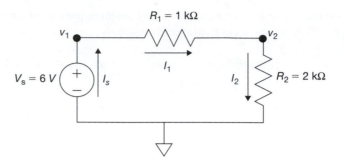

FIGURE 4.1 Schematic of a simple circuit consisting of a voltage source connected to two resistors in series.

Extended example: Solving circuit problems

An electrical circuit is characterized by voltages and currents. Electrical current is the flow of charge through circuit elements. A useful analogy is the flow of water through pipes. Electrical voltage is a measure of the potential energy of electric charge. The voltage corresponds to the height of a pipe in the water analogy: i.e., the gravitational potential energy of water in the pipe is like the electrical potential energy of the charge in the circuit. Water flows downhill, from higher areas to lower areas; charge flows from higher voltage to lower voltage.

A circuit, like the one shown schematically in Figure 4.1, is composed of different circuit elements: wires, voltage sources, and resistors. (There are other possible circuit elements we won't discuss here.) Each circuit element can be characterized by the way current and voltage are related for that element.

Wire segments

Each wire segment is characterized by the current flowing through the wire, I, and the electrical voltage (electrical potential) of the wire, V. Except at very high frequencies, a wire is an isopotential surface, which means that the voltage everywhere along the wire is the same. We label with circles particular points in the circuit called *nodes*, which help in analyzing the circuit. Every point connected to the node by only a wire has the same voltage. The voltage at the node is called the "nodal voltage."

Wire junctions

When wires come together and form a junction, the current must satisfy Kirchoff's current law (KCL) which expresses the conservation of charge. If we let I_k be the current flowing *into* the junction from the kth node, we must have:

$$I_1 + I_2 + I_3 + \cdots + I_N = 0$$

Using this notation, we see that some currents coming into the junction must be negative, meaning that they represent a flow of current out from the junction. The flows in and out must all balance, or charge would build up at the junction.

Voltage sources

A voltage source keeps the voltage difference between its two terminals at a constant value, here V_s. It will provide whatever current is necessary so that this voltage difference is maintained. The plus and minus signs indicate on which side the value of the voltage is greater.

$$v_+ - v_- = V_s$$

Resistors

A resistor is characterized by Ohm's law, which relates the current *through* the resistor to the voltage *across* the resistor.

$$V = IR$$

By "voltage across the resistor" we simply mean the difference between the voltage on the two terminals of the resistor. The sign of the difference is determined by the convention that we take the voltage on the *upstream* side of the resistor (the side from which the current flows) minus the voltage on the *downstream* side. (If we are wrong about assigning the direction of current flow, the math will take care of things—currents and voltages will come out with a negative sign.)

Ground

The arrow-like symbol at the bottom of Figure 4.1 symbolizes a connection to the electrical ground. Ground is simply a reference potential taken to be 0. The voltage on any part of the circuit that is grounded is always 0.

Relationships between current and voltage for various circuit elements are summarized in Figure 4.2.

Let's analyze the circuit shown in Figure 4.1. We label node 1 with voltage v_1 and node 2 with voltage v_2. The current through each element is labeled I_s, I_1, and I_2, respectively. We will use the individual current and voltage relationships for each element.

1. The voltage source on the left maintains the voltage difference between v_1 and ground at V_s, so we know:

$$v_1 - 0 = V_s \tag{4.10}$$

2. We can use KCL at node 1 and insist that the sum of the currents entering the node be zero:

$$I_s - I_1 = 0 \tag{4.11}$$

3. Similarly for the current flowing into node 2:

$$I_1 - I_2 = 0 \tag{4.12}$$

4. For resistor R_1 we can use Ohm's law to write:

$$v_1 - v_2 = I_1 R_1 \tag{4.13}$$

5. And for resistor R_2:

$$v_2 - 0 = I_2 R_2 \tag{4.14}$$

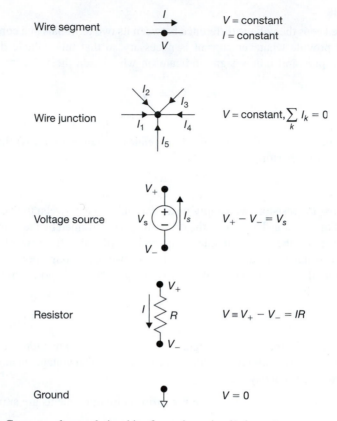

FIGURE 4.2 Current–voltage relationships for various circuit elements.

We need to solve equations (4.10) through (4.14) simultaneously. These are five equations for the five unknowns v_1, v_2, I_1, I_2, and I_s. The source voltage V_s we treat as a known quantity, since it must be specified in order to solve the problem. The resistances R_1 and R_2 are known parameters. Even though in this case, we could easily solve this system of equations by algebraic manipulation, we want to take a systematic approach so we learn a method that works for solving more complicated problems in the future.

We begin by rewriting equations (4.10) through (4.14) so that the unknown variables are on the left side of each equation and known values are on the right. We will also choose a specific order in which to write the unknowns: v_1, v_2, I_1, I_2, I_s.

$$v_1 - 0 = V_s$$
$$-I_1 + I_s = 0$$
$$I_1 - I_2 = 0 \qquad (4.15)$$
$$v_1 - v_2 - R_1 I_1 = 0$$
$$v_2 - R_2 I_2 = 0$$

Now let's write these equations out explicitly, showing the dependence on each of the five unknowns. Again, we keep all unknown quantities on the left, and known quantities on the right of the equals sign.

$$1v_1 + 0v_2 + 0I_1 + 0I_2 + 0I_s = V_s$$
$$0v_1 + 0v_2 - 1I_1 + 0I_2 + 1I_s = 0$$
$$0v_1 + 0v_2 + 1I_1 - 1I_2 + 0I_s = 0 \qquad (4.16)$$
$$1v_1 - 1v_2 - R_1I_1 + 0I_2 + 0I_s = 0$$
$$0v_1 + 1v_2 + 0I_1 - R_2I_2 + 0I_s = 0$$

Writing the equations out in this way makes it easier to recognize that these five equations can be written as one matrix equation of the form $\mathbf{Au} = \mathbf{b}$, where $\mathbf{u}$ is the column vector of the unknowns.

$$\underbrace{\begin{bmatrix} 1 & 0 & 0 & 0 & 0 \\ 0 & 0 & -1 & 0 & 1 \\ 0 & 0 & 1 & -1 & 0 \\ 1 & -1 & -R_1 & 0 & 0 \\ 0 & 1 & 0 & -R_2 & 0 \end{bmatrix}}_{\mathbf{A}} \underbrace{\begin{bmatrix} v_1 \\ v_2 \\ I_1 \\ I_2 \\ I_s \end{bmatrix}}_{\mathbf{u}} = \underbrace{\begin{bmatrix} V_s \\ 0 \\ 0 \\ 0 \\ 0 \end{bmatrix}}_{\mathbf{b}} \qquad (4.17)$$

$u = A \backslash B$

Each individual equation in (4.16) corresponds to the equation for the corresponding row of (4.17). Writing the MATLAB program to solve this problem is now straightforward. We construct the matrix A and column vector b as defined by (4.17), and then solve the matrix equation $\mathbf{Au} = \mathbf{b}$ by using the MATLAB linear solver command u=A\b. The elements of $\mathbf{u}$ can then be interpreted as the values of v_1, v_2, I_1, I_2, and I_s. An example of a solution is shown in the following example.

```
% simpleCircuit1.m
%    use linear solver for two resistors in
%    series example circuit
%          Author: Tansy Wagwheel

%% set parameters
Vs=6;    % volts
R1=1e3;  % ohms
R2=2e3;

%% form matrix and solve
%   unknowns vector u= [v1; v2; I1; I2; I3];
%    form linear system Au=b
A=[ 1   0   0   0  0 ;...
    0   0  -1   0  1 ;...
    0   0   1  -1  0 ;...
    1  -1  -R1  0  0 ;...
    0   1   0  -R2 0];
```

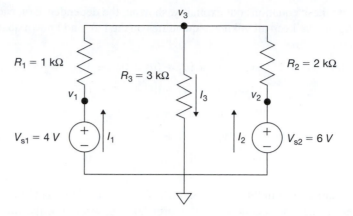

FIGURE 4.3 Schematic of a circuit with two voltage sources.

```
% right hand side column vector
b=[Vs; 0; 0; 0; 0];
% solve linear system
u=A\b;

%% print out results
v1=u(1);
v2=u(2);
I1=u(3);
I2=u(4);
I3=u(5);

clc
disp(['=====================']);
disp(['Vs=  ',num2str(Vs), ' volts']);
disp(['R1=  ',num2str(R1), ' ohms']);
disp(['R2=  ',num2str(R2), ' ohms']);
disp('    Solution:')
disp(['    v1=  ',num2str(v1), ' volts']);
disp(['    v2=  ',num2str(v2), ' volts']);
disp(['    I1=  ',num2str(I1), ' amps']);
disp(['    I2=  ',num2str(I2), ' amps']);
disp(['    I3=  ',num2str(I3), ' amps']);
```

Now let's apply this method to the slightly more complex circuit shown in Figure 4.3.

We can simplify the analysis a little by recognizing that the nodal voltages at v_1 and v_2 will be exactly the voltage set by the voltage sources. The unknowns therefore are $v_3, I_1, I_2,$ and I_3. Ohm's law for each resistor gives us:

$$-v_3 - R_1 I_1 = -v_1$$
$$-v_3 - R_2 I_2 = -v_2 \qquad (4.18)$$
$$v_3 - R_3 I_3 = 0$$

KCL at node 3 requires:

$$I_1 + I_2 - I_3 = 0 \qquad (4.19)$$

We see that equations (4.18) and (4.19) together give us four simultaneous linear equations for the four unknowns. We can then write them in matrix form as

$$\begin{bmatrix} -1 & -R_1 & 0 & 0 \\ -1 & 0 & -R_2 & 0 \\ 1 & 0 & 0 & -R_3 \\ 0 & 1 & 1 & -1 \end{bmatrix} \begin{bmatrix} v_3 \\ I_1 \\ I_2 \\ I_3 \end{bmatrix} = \begin{bmatrix} -v_1 \\ -v_2 \\ 0 \\ 0 \end{bmatrix} \qquad (4.20)$$

A MATLAB program to solve this linear system is shown in simpleCircuit2.m.

```
% simpleCircuit2.m
%   use linear solver for two-branch circuit
%     Author: Tansy Wagwheel II


%% set parameters
v1=1; % volts
v2=1;
R1=2e3; % ohms
R2=2e3;
R3=2e3;


%% form matrix and solve
%   unknowns vector u= [v3; I1; I2; I3];
%     form linear system Au=b
A=[ -1  -R1  0    0;...
    -1   0  -R2   0;...
     1   0   0   -R3;...
     0   1   1   -1];
% right hand side column vector
b=[-v1; -v2; 0; 0];
% solve linear system
u=A\b;


%% print out results
v3=u(1);
I1=u(2);
I2=u(3);
I3=u(4);


clc
disp(['====================']);
disp(['v1=  ',num2str(v1), ' volts']);
disp(['v2=  ',num2str(v2), ' volts']);
disp(['R1=  ',num2str(R1), '  ohms']);
disp(['R2=  ',num2str(R3), '  ohms']);
```

```
disp(['R3=   ',num2str(R3),   ' ohms']);
disp('    Solution:')
disp(['       V3=  ',num2str(v3), ' volts']);
disp(['       I1=  ',num2str(I1), ' amps']);
disp(['       I2=  ',num2str(I2), ' amps']);
disp(['       I3=  ',num2str(I3), ' amps']);
```

4.4 Special matrix functions

The functions ones(n,m) and zeros(n,m) return an $n \times m$ matrix of ones or zeroes. When invoked with one argument, they return a square matrix of that size.

```
>> A=ones(4,3);
>> disp(A)
     1     1     1
     1     1     1
     1     1     1
     1     1     1

>> B=zeros(3,4);
>> disp(B)
     0     0     0     0
     0     0     0     0
     0     0     0     0

>> C=ones(5)
>> disp(C)
     1     1     1     1     1
     1     1     1     1     1
     1     1     1     1     1
     1     1     1     1     1
     1     1     1     1     1
```

The function rand(n,m) similarly returns an $n \times m$ matrix of pseudorandom numbers between 0 and 1. A single argument yields a square matrix of random numbers. For random integers, use randi(p,n,m), which returns an $n \times m$ array of pseudorandom integers in the interval $[1,p]$, or randi([r,p],n,m), which returns integers in the interval $[r,p]$.

```
>> A=rand(3,4);
>> disp(A)
    0.3500    0.6160    0.8308    0.9172
    0.1966    0.4733    0.5853    0.2858
    0.2511    0.3517    0.5497    0.7572
```

```
>> B=rand(3);
>> disp(B)
    0.7537    0.0759    0.7792
    0.3804    0.0540    0.9340
    0.5678    0.5308    0.1299

>> C=randi(5,3,4);
>> disp(C)
    2    5    4    3
    1    4    4    5
    3    2    1    4
```

Looking ahead

In MATLAB, matrices and vectors are simply particular examples of *arrays*. An array is an aggregation of numbers that are referenced by a set of indices—a single index for a vector, two indices for a matrix. The array name refers to the whole; individual array elements are referenced using indices. The array notion can be extended in several ways. First, *multidimensional arrays* extend the concept to any number of indices. For example, one might have a four-dimensional array V(ix,iy,iz,it). These are handled just like the matrices in this chapter. Arrays can also hold other data classes besides real numbers. These other data classes—complex numbers, handles, function handles, and structures—are described in Chapter 8. Cell arrays, also described in Chapter 8, are very much like regular arrays, but a single cell array can contain contain elements from several different classes.

PROGRAMMING PROBLEMS

1. **Programming magic.** Look up the MATLAB magic function in the online documentation. Write a MATLAB program, MagicSquare.m, that does the following:
   - generates and displays a magic square named M of size 7×7.
   - displays the element in the third row, fourth column of M.
   - displays the block of values in rows 2 through 4 and columns 5 through 7 of M.
   - displays the sum of the elements in row 3.
   - displays the sum of the elements in columns 1 through 3.

2. **Simultaneous linear equations.** Write a MATLAB program, Solve5.m, that solves the following system of equations and displays the results.

$$a + 2b - d + 7e = 36$$

$$-4a + 78b + 53c - 28d - 47e = -36$$

$$92a + 29b + 63c + 38d + 42e = 701$$

$$74a + 63b - 9c - 7d + 49e = 390$$

$$-49a - 99b + 84c + 12d + 7e = 88 \qquad (4.21)$$

3. **Concession stand.**   Write a program, ConcessionStand.m, that uses vector-matrix multiplication to tabulate and display the cost of each of the following orders. Assume that a hot dog costs $3.00, a brat costs $3.50, and a Coke costs $2.50.

	hot dogs	brats	cokes
order 1	2	1	3
order 2	1	0	2
order 3	2	2	2
order 4	0	5	1

4. **Intersection of two lines.**   Consider two lines given by the following two equations.

$$2x - y = 10$$
$$3x + 2y = 1$$

Solve for the intersection of the two lines by constructing a matrix equation and solving the linear system with MATLAB. Plot the two lines on the domain $x \in [0, 5]$ and plot the calculated interception point as a red circle.

5. **Linear system of equations.**   Solve the system

$$x + 2y + z = -1$$
$$x - 3y + 2z = 1$$
$$2x - 3y + z = 5$$

for $x, y,$ and z.

6. **Airspeed.**   An airplane flying with the prevailing wind from Los Angeles to New York takes 4.5 hours. Flying against the wind on the return trip takes 5.3 hours. If the distance between these cities is 2500 miles, find the airspeed of the airplane and the wind speed.

7. **Pauli matrices.**   The Pauli matrices are defined as follows:

$$\sigma_x = \begin{pmatrix} 0 & 1 \\ 1 & 0 \end{pmatrix} \quad \sigma_y = \begin{pmatrix} 0 & -i \\ i & 0 \end{pmatrix} \quad \sigma_z = \begin{pmatrix} 1 & 0 \\ 0 & -1 \end{pmatrix}$$

The commutator (square brackets) and anticommutator (curly brackets) of two matrices are defined by:

$$[A, B] \equiv AB - BA \qquad \{A, B\} \equiv AB + BA$$

Show the following relations by direct calculation using MATLAB.

a. $[\sigma_x, \sigma_y] = 2i\sigma_z$

b. $[\sigma_x, \sigma_z] = -2i\sigma_y$

c. $[\sigma_y, \sigma_z] = 2i\sigma_x$

d. $\sigma_x\sigma_x = \sigma_x\sigma_x = \sigma_x\sigma_x = I$

e. $\{\sigma_x, \sigma_x\} = \{\sigma_y, \sigma_y\} = \{\sigma_z, \sigma_z\} = 2I$

f. $\{\sigma_x, \sigma_y\} = \{\sigma_x, \sigma_z\} = \{\sigma_y, \sigma_z\} = 0$

g. $-i\sigma_x\sigma_y\sigma_z = I$

Control Flow Commands

The simplest programs consist of a series of commands that are executed in order, one after the other. Because MATLAB has some very powerful commands, such a program can be quite useful. The real power of programming becomes apparent, though, when we can structure a program so that (a) which commands are executed depends on the values currently stored in variables, and (b) some commands can be executed repeatedly. Statements that don't directly execute an action, but rather control which other commands will be executed, are called "control flow commands." In MATLAB the if statement allows conditional execution, and repetitive execution, making "loops," is accomplished using the for or while statements.

After mastering the material in this chapter you should be able to write programs that:

- Use an if statement to conditionally execute a block of commands.

- Express complex logical conditions using a combination of logic operators.

- Create logical variables that function as program flags or switches.

- Repeatedly execute a command block a set number of times using a for loop.

- Repeatedly execute a command block until a logical condition is met using a while loop.

- Use a switch-case statement to conditionally execute one of several command blocks, depending on the value of a variable.

- Express an algorithmic solution to a problem by a combination of several control flow commands.

5.1 Conditional execution: The if statement

The if statement tells the computer to execute a block of commands if a specified condition is true. An example of an if statement in a program is:

```
% ifdemo.m
ageThreshold=50;

age=input('Please enter your age: ');
if age>ageThreshold
    disp('  Wow, getting up there.');
end

disp('Thanks!')
```

Let's consider this simple case carefully because it contains the core of what makes a computer program so potentially powerful. The variable age is created and given an initial value based on the user's input. When the if statement is executed, the computer checks to see if the expression following the if is true or false. If it is true, it executes the commands in the block (always indented) between the if and the corresponding end statement. If the statement following the if is false, then that block of statements is skipped and the next statement executed is the one that follows the end.

The key point in the previous example code is: whether or not the condition, age > ageThreshold, is true is determined by the *present value* of the relevant MATLAB variables—in this case, the values stored in age and ageThreshold. *That is the only basis on which the computer can make a decision—the values that are stored in variables when the decision needs to be made.* The program is not evaluating an abstract question, such as "Is the user old or not?" It's only capable of evaluating a very concrete and immediate question: "Is the value currently stored in age greater than the value stored in ageThreshold or not?" We could extend this little program to reuse the age variable at a later time.

```
% ifdemo2.m
ageThreshold=50;

age=input('Please enter your age: ');
if age>ageThreshold
    disp('  Wow, getting up there.');
end

age=input('How old is your brother Artemeus?: ');
if age<12
    disp('Oh, still a young sprout.');
end

disp('Thanks!')
```

The second if statement evaluates whether the value now stored in age (at the time this if statement is executed) is less than 12 or not. You may ask why we don't always know ahead of time what the values of variables will be—after all, we write the program that assigns values to variables. In these examples, we don't know exactly what will happen when the program is run because we don't know what the user will answer. In many programs, we don't know exactly what will happen because we can't anticipate precisely what the computation will have done up to that point. If we knew in advance, we wouldn't have to do the calculation. This is actually a clue to the immense usefulness of computer programs—they can respond to conditions that we need not have anticipated in detail. Despite being completely determined by the inputs, programs can generate surprising results.

There are several forms of the if statement. The most basic form can be written schematically as:

```
if <logical expression>
    <block of statements>
end
```

In this form, the block of statements is executed if <logical expression> is true. We discuss forming more complicated logical expressions in the next section. Every if statement must be terminated with an end statement.

For example:

```
if x<0
   ineg=45;
   x=alpha*abs(j);
end
```

Another form includes an else block that is executed if the condition expressed in the logical expression is *not* met:

```
if <logical expression>
    <block1>
else
    <block2>
end
```

In this case, <block 1> is executed if the logical expression is true, and <block 2> is executed if the logical expression is false.

It is useful to type in and run the following program. Run the program also with the debugger (page 14) to see execution shift from the top branch of the if statement to the bottom, depending on what the user inputs.

For example:

```
% PrimeCheck.m
%  prompt for number, check if it's prime or not
%     using isprime function
%     Author: B.J. Honeycutt
%
disp(' ');
disp('---- Prime number checker  ----');
n=input('Enter number to check: ');
if isprime(n)
    disp(['Yes! ',num2str(n),' is prime!']);
else
    disp(['No, ',num2str(n),' is not prime.']);
end
disp(' ');
```

Any conditional branch can itself contain conditional statements—i.e., if statements can be nested.

```
% EvenOrOdd.m
% pick a number between 3 and 100 inclusive
n=randi([3,100]);

% use the remainder function to classify as even or odd
% and further classify odds and prime or not using isprime
%  function
if rem(n,2)>0
    if isprime(n)
        disp([num2str(n),': odd and prime']);
    else
        disp([num2str(n),': odd and composite']);
    end
else
    disp([num2str(n),': even']);
end
```

Using appropriate indentation is crucial in making such nested statements readable. You can use the smart indenter by selecting a block of your program text in the Editor and then clicking the Indent icon on the EDITOR menu bar (or typing Ctrl-I) to automatically format the code.

The most general and flexible form uses if, elseif, and else statements, along with the mandatory end.

```
    if <logical expression 1>
        <block1>
```

```
        elseif <logical expression 2>
            <block2>
        elseif <logical expression 3>
            <block3>
        elseif <logical expression 4>
            <block4>
        else
            <block5>
        end
```

The `else` statement is optional. Each logical expression is checked in order, and the first one that is true results in the following block being executed. If none is true, the block following the `else` statement, if there is one, is executed.

Note that `elseif` is one word; this is not equivalent to nesting the if-else-end statements. Also note that MATLAB will execute only one of the blocks, the *first* one for which the logical expression is true, or the `else` block.

This example uses more complicated logical expressions that are explained in the next section ("&&" means "and"):

```
if (x >= -100)&&(x <= -5)
    f(ix)=0;
elseif (x > -5)&&(x <= 0)
    f(ix)=1;
elseif (x >  0)&&(x <= 5)
    f(ix)= -1;
elseif (x >  5)&&(x <= 100)
    f(ix)=0
else
    disp('Error—function out of range [-100,100]');
end
```

5.2   Logical expressions

The `if` statement—and the `while` statement explained in the Section 5.5—use a logical expression to decide which execution path to take. Logical expressions evaluate to a value of *true* or *false*. This is a different kind of information than a number, though MATLAB represents a false with 0 and a true with 1. In fact, any nonzero value is interpreted as a logical true.

Logical expressions are constructed from logical and relational operators:

&&   AND

|| OR

      &   element-by-element AND for arrays

      | element-by-element OR for arrays

      ~   not

    ==   is equal to

    ~=   is not equal to

    >   is greater than

    <   is less than

    >=   is greater than or equal to

    <=   is less than or equal to

For example:

```
% doubledice.m
%    simulate the roll of two dice
%    check if the result is snake eyes, craps, or sevens
%    Author: J.P. Morgan Chase

%% Roll dice
dice1=randi([1,6]);
dice2=randi([1,6]);

%% display outcome
disp(['dice 1: ', num2str(dice1), '  dice 2: ', num2str(dice2)]);
sum=dice1+dice2;

%% interpret result
if (dice1==1) && (dice2==1)
      disp('Snake eyes')
end

if sum==7
      disp('Sevens')
elseif (sum==2) || (sum==3) || (sum==12)
      disp('Craps')
end
```

Note that the test for equality is done with a *double* equals sign, which distinguishes it from the single equals sign used in the assignment statement. Use spaces and parentheses to make logical statements more readable. The logical expression:

```
(dice1==1) && (dice2==1)
```

which can be read "the value of dice1 is equal to 1 AND the value of dice2 is equal to 1," is clearer than:

```
dice1==1&&dice2==1
```

although to MATLAB they are equivalent. (Remember, you write a program to be understood by humans as well as computers. And one of the humans you are trying to be understood by is your future self.)

5.3   Logical variables

It is often useful to store a logical value, `true` or `false`, in a variable. For example, you may want to keep track of whether or not certain conditions have been met for a particular calculation to proceed. A variable named `isReady` could be set directly.

```
isReady=true;
```

It could also be set by evaluating a logical expression.

```
isReady=(numWorkingCylinders > 4) && (fuel > fuelMin)
```

The value of the logical variable is displayed encoded as either a 1 or a 0. Logical variables are sometimes used as so-called "flags" or "switches," which are set at one stage of program execution to control how a later stage behaves. In the following example, the nature of a calculated function, and also how it's plotted, are determined by the state of logical switches `isDamped` and `gridOn` set near the top of the program.

```
% PlotOscillations.m
%     plot oscillatory motion of mass on spring
%        Author: Cy Newsoyd

%% set parameters
Tperiod=2.3;   % period (seconds)
ymax=1.2;      % amplitude (meters)
phase=pi/3;    % phase (radians)
Tmax=5*Tperiod;
Nt=300;

gridOn=false;
isDamped=true;
tau=8.2;           % characteristic damping time

%% calculate function
t=linspace(0, Tmax, Nt);
y=ymax*cos(2*pi*(t/Tperiod)-phase);
if isDamped
    y=y.*exp(-t/tau);
end
```

```
%% plot result
plot(t, y);
xlabel('time(s)');
ylabel('position (m)');
if gridOn
    grid on
end
```

Choose logical variable names so they naturally sound like something that would be true or false. For example:

```
isDone
isFullNetwork
isTriangle
isIsoceles
gotName
```

You can also choose names that are a compressed verbal form—plotAll is understood to be true if it's true that the program should plot all the relevant variables. Similarly:

```
plotEigs    % true if eigenvalues should be plotted
showFull
ticksLarge  % true if the tick marks on the plot should be large
doVerbose   % print out lots of information
```

5.4   for loops

The for loop executes a block of instructions repeatedly. The for command creates a variable called the "loop variable," stores an initial value in it, and increments its value each time the instruction block is executed. The loop variable is most often an integer. For example, the following displays the numbers from 1 through 7:

```
% count to N
N=7;
for k=1:N
    disp(['k= ',num2str(k)]);
end
disp('Done!');
```

This for statement tells the computer to do the following:

1. Set the value of loop variable k to 1 (if k doesn't exist, it is created).

2. Check to see if the value of k is greater than the value of N (the loop index maximum). If it is, then exit the loop and continue execution with the statement following the end.

3. Execute the `disp` statement, using the current value of k.

4. Increment k, i.e., increases the value stored in k by 1.

5. Jump back to step 2.

For N=7, the previous `for` loop is equivalent to the following:

```
k=1;    % k is now 1
  disp(['k= ', num2str(k)]);
k=k+1;  % k is now 2
  disp(['k= ', num2str(k)]);
k=k+1;  % k is now 3
  disp(['k= ', num2str(k)]);
k=k+1;  % k is now 4
  disp(['k= ', num2str(k)]);
k=k+1;  % k is now 5
  disp(['k= ', num2str(k)]);
k=k+1;  % k is now 6
  disp(['k= ', num2str(k)]);
k=k+1;  % k is now 7
  disp(['k= ', num2str(k)]);
disp('Done!');
```

The syntax for the simplest form of the `for` statement is:

```
for <index>=<initial value>:<final value>
    <block>
end
```

The value of the loop variable is set to the initial value and then the block is executed. The value of the index is then incremented by one, and the block is executed again. This repeats until the index exceeds the final value.

The MATLAB Editor will indent the block within the loop automatically. Indentation is important for making the program readable, and should always be done (for the benefit of human readers—the computer doesn't care).

The value of the increment can also be specified.

```
for <index>=<initial value>:<increment>:<final value>
    <block>
end
```

For a positive increment, the block will be repeatedly executed as long as the index is less than or equal to the final value. For example, `for ix= 3:3:10 ...` end will execute three times, with `ix= 3, 6, 9`. For a negative increment, the block will be repeatedly executed as long as the index is greater than the final value.

For example:

```
% countByThrees.m
% count by 3s to  N
N=32;
for k=3:3:N
    disp(['k= ',num2str(k)]);
end
disp('Done!');

Output:
k= 3
k= 6
k= 9
k= 12
k= 15
k= 18
k= 21
k= 24
k= 27
k= 30
Done!
```

Another example (worth typing in and running):

```
% DrawStarBounce.m
%    draw bouncing star on command line
%    Author: Meadowlark Lemon

%% set parameters
Nb=32;          % number of blank spaces to move
dt=0.005;       % pause this long to make motion visible
Nbounce=4;      % number of bounces

%% loop to display
for kbounce=1:Nbounce
    for kb=1:Nb
        disp([blanks(kb), '*']);
        pause(dt)
    end
    for kb=Nb:-1:1
        disp([blanks(kb), '*']);
        pause(dt)
    end
end
```

The previous program uses the `blanks(n)` command, which returns a string with n blank spaces.

For loops can be nested within each other and with other control flow statements.

```
% diceRoll.m
%     find value for each possible roll of 2 dice
for iDice1=1:6
    for iDice2=1:6
        rollValue=iDice1+iDice2;
        disp([num2str(iDice1), ' & ',num2str(iDice2)]);
        disp(['      Role value: ',num2str(rollValue)]);
    end
end
```

Good programming practice

It's a useful convention to choose loop variable names that begin with "i," "j," "k," or "n." Use names that suggest the nature of the loop. For example, in the `DrawStarBounce` program, kb represents the current count of blanks and kbounce represents the current count of bounces.

Never change the value of the loop variable within the loop.

MATLAB will permit non-integer values for loop variables, but this should be avoided. It's almost always better to use an integer loop variable as an index into an array of real values, often constructed with `linspace`. So rather than this:

```
for s = [0:0.1:1]
    disp(s)
end
```

do this:

```
s = linspace(0, 1, 11);
for is=1:length(s)
    disp(s(is))
end
```

It will prove more flexible.

5.5 while loops

A `for` loop is a *count-controlled* loop—the number of times the loop executes is determined when the loop starts. There are situations where the number of times you want the loop repeated is not known at the beginning. For example, you might want to repeat a block of statements until a certain condition is met. This type of loop is called a "condition-controlled" loop and is implemented in MATLAB using the `while` command.

```
% continue to add up whole numbers until total
% exceeds, or is equal to, maxSum
maxSum=200;
tot=0;
k=0;
while tot < maxSum
    k=k+1;
    tot=tot+k;
end
disp(['Sum of first ',num2str(k),' integers = ',num2str(tot)]);
```

The general form is:

```
while <condition>
    <block>
end
```

This is a very general structure—any logical expression can be the <condition> and any set of executable statements can form the <block>. Any variables that are needed to evaluate the condition must be created and given values before the while is executed. If the <condition> is initially false, the <block> will not be executed at all. If it is true, the <block> is executed once, and then the <condition> is checked again. The <block> will be repeatedly executed until <condition> becomes false. A corollary is that if the block does nothing to change the <condition>, it will loop forever.

To stop a runaway program, type Ctrl-C in the Command window.

The following program illustrates the programming motif of repeating until a desired result is obtained.

```
% sayamen.m
% ask for an "Amen!" until you get one
%    Author: James Brown

%% set logical variable initially to indicate not done
gotAmen= false;

%% main logical loop
while ~gotAmen
   response=input(' Give me an Amen! ' ,'s');
   if strcmp(lower(response),'amen!')
      disp('Thank you!')
      gotAmen=true;
   else
      disp('I say it again:')
   end
end
```

Here the function `strcmp` is used to compare two strings; it returns the value "true" if the two strings are identical. This is important because strings cannot in general be tested for equality with the double equals sign.

```
name=input('Tell me my name: ','s');
if name=='Rumpelstiltskin' % FAILS —
                            % use: if strcmp(name, ...
                            % 'Rumpelstiltskin')
    disp('Oh no! You win!')
else
    disp('Wrong–o!');
end
```

5.6   Other control flow commands

Switch-case statement

A frequently encountered task is to execute different blocks of code depending on the value of an integer or a string. This can be done with the `if-elseif-else-end` construction, but is streamlined by using the switch-case command. An example using an integer switch follows:

```
% switchStooge1.m
disp(' ')
iStooge=input('Enter stooge number: ');

switch iStooge
    case 1
        disp('Moe Howard')
    case 2
        disp('Larry Fine')
    case 3
        disp('Curly Howard')
    otherwise
        disp('Error:  Just three stooges.')
end
disp(' ')
```

Here is an example using a string for the switch variable.

```
% switchStooge2.m
disp(' ')
nameStooge=input('Enter stooge name: ','s');

switch lower(nameStooge)
    case 'moe'
        disp('Moe Howard:')
```

```
            disp('   Why I oughta ...!')
        case 'larry'
            disp('Larry Fine:')
            disp('   Hey Moe, hey Moe!')
        case 'curly'
            disp('Curly Howard:')
            disp('   Nyuk, nyuk, nyuk!')
        case {'shemp','curly-joe'}
            disp('Rare stooges not processed.')
        otherwise
            disp('Error:  stooge unknown.')
    end
disp(' ')
```

Behind the scenes, the `switch` statement evaluates which case to use by comparing the string stored in `nameStooge` with each case name string, using `strcmp`. Notice the use of `lower` to remove sensitivity to the capitalization of the input.

A single code block can handle more than one match in a `switch` statement if one puts the alternatives in curly brackets.

```
switch monthStr
    case 'February'
        nDays=28;
    case {'September', 'April', 'June', 'November'}
        nDays=30;
    otherwise
        nDays=31;
end
```

Break statement (not recommended)

Normally, a `for` loop repeats until the loop index is greater than the loop index maximum. Similarly, a `while` loop repeats until the the logical expression is false. But these loops can also be exited using the `break` command. When the `break` command is encountered, the currently executing loop is terminated and control moves to the statement following the loop's terminating `end` statement. This is often used with a logical condition as in the following example:

```
for istep=1:N
   %<block of statements>
   if height(istep)<0    % if height becomes negative,
                              stop looping
       break
   end
end
```

Use of the break statement can lead to code that is difficult to debug, so its use should be avoided. This can always be accomplished by transforming the for loop into a while loop with the appropriate logic, or by altering the logical condition in the while statement.

PROGRAMMING PROBLEMS

1. **Age.**   Write a program, YourAge.m, that asks the user's name and age, then greets the user, and classifies the user as young, old, or young at heart. Add your own refinements to the categories by age. Use the if-elseif-else-end construction.

2. **Goodbye.**   Write a program, GoodBye.m, that prints "Good-bye!" repeatedly by shifting it over to the right (use the string function blanks):

```
Goodbye!
 Goodbye!
  Goodbye!
   Goodbye!
    Goodbye!
     Goodbye!
      Goodbye!  ...
```

3. **Tabulating roots and squares.**   Write a program, TabRoots.m, that uses a for loop to tabulate for each positive integer n, its square, square root, and e^n. The output should look like this:

```
n= 1
    sqrt(n)= 1
    n^2= 1
    exp(n)= 2.7183
n= 2
    sqrt(n)=1.4142
    n^2= 4
    exp(n)= 7.3891
n= 3
    sqrt(n)= 1.7321
    n^2= 9
    exp(n)= 20.0855
n= 4
    sqrt(n)= 2
    n^2= 16
    exp(n)= 54.5982
n= 5
    sqrt(n)= 2.2361
    n^2=25
    exp(n)- 148.4132
```

4. **Fibonacci numbers.** The Fibonacci numbers are the numbers in the sequence

$$0, 1, 1, 2, 3, 5, \ldots,$$

where the first two Fibonacci numbers are defined to be 0 and 1 and each subsequent number is obtained by finding the sum of the two previous Fibonacci numbers. These numbers are important in biology as well as in computing algorithms. Starting from `fib(1)=0` and `fib(2)=1`, write a program, `fibonacci.m`, that computes the first N Fibonacci numbers and finds their sum.

5. **Toss a coin.** Write a program, `CoinToss.m`, that asks the user to call a coin toss in the air (h or t). The program should then honestly (randomly) generate a head or tail using `randi`, and declare whether the user won or lost. Allow the user to continue to play until the user wants to stop.

6. **Partial sum of integers.** Write a program, `SumUpTo.m`, that uses a `for` loop to calculate the sum of the positive integers up to N. Set the value of N near the beginning of the program. ($N = 100$ was Gauss's famous trick.) That is, find and print:

$$P(n) = \sum_{k=1}^{n} k$$

7. **Finding prime numbers.** Write a program, `FindPrimes.m`, that examines each integer from 1 to N to see if the number is a prime. If it is prime (and only then), print out the number. Use the MATLAB function `isprime(k)`, which returns the value `true` if k is prime. The program should print out all the primes less than or equal to N. Use $N = 100$ as a test case.

```
>> FindPrimes
N= 100
Found Prime: 2
Found Prime: 3
Found Prime: 5
Found Prime: 7
Found Prime: 11 (etc.)
```

8. **Print laughing.** Write a program, `Laughing.m`, that types out a line with N Ha!s separated by spaces. Use a `for` loop to construct the string. It should work with any positive value of N.

```
>> Laugh
Ha! Ha! Ha! Ha! Ha! Ha! Ha! Ha!
```

9. **First π approximation.** Write a program, `PiSeries1.m`, that calculates an approximation to π by using the Euler solution to the Basel problem:

$$\frac{\pi^2}{6} \approx \sum_{k=1}^{N} \frac{1}{k^2}$$

Compute the sum for $N = 100$, 1000, 1×10^6, and 1×10^7.

10. **Second π approximation.** Write a program, `PiSeries2.m`, that calculates an approximation to π by using the Gregory-Leibniz series:

$$\frac{\pi}{4} \approx \sum_{k=0}^{N} \frac{(-1)^k}{2k+1}$$

Compute the sum for $N = 100$, 1000, 1×10^6, and 1×10^7.

11. **Calculate absolute value.** Write a program, `absvalue.m`, that gets a number from a user, then finds and displays its absolute value. Use an `if-then-else` construction rather than just the built-in `abs` function.

12. **Plot piecewise function.** Write a program, `plotPiecewise.m`, that plots the piecewise function $p(x)$ defined as follows, in the range $x = [-2, 2]$.

$$p(x) = \begin{cases} 2x + 3 & \text{if } x \in [-3/2, -1] \\ -sin(\pi x/2) & \text{if } x \in (-1, 1) \\ 2x - 3 & \text{if } x \in [1, 3/2] \\ 0 & \text{otherwise} \end{cases}$$

13. **Rolling dice (improved).** Write a program, `ThrowDice2.m`, that prints the results of rolling two fair dice (use `randi`). Also print out "boxcars" for double sixes and "snake eyes" for double ones.

14. **Drawing cards.** Write a program, `DrawCard.m`, that randomly selects a single card (from a full deck). Print the result as ace-spades, 5-hearts, king-diamonds, jack-clubs, etc.

15. **Number guessing game.** Write a program, `guessing.m`, that does the following: The computer generates a random integer between 1 and 20 (inclusive). The computer displays "I am thinking of a number between 1 and 20." It prompts the user to input a guess. While the guess is not equal to the computer's number, it tells the user whether the guess was too low or too high, and prompts for another guess. When the user guesses the right number, the computer congratulates the user and ends the game. (Hint: Use a `while` loop.) A run of the program (for which the user guessed 10 and 15 before correctly guessing 13) might look something like this:

```
>> guessing
I am thinking of a number
 between 1 and 20.
Enter your guess: 10
Too low
Enter your guess: 15
Too high
Enter your guess: 13
Right!
```

16. **Improved guessing game.** Write a program, `ImprovingGuessing.m`, in which the guessing game automatically repeats over and over until the user quits. Add the ability for the user to quit the program by inputting a `"q"` or a `"0."` At that point, print out the *average* number of guesses the user needed. In the previous example, the user only needed three guesses. If they have adopted a clever strategy, what is the maximum number of guesses the user should need on average?

17. **Counting by ones.** Write a program, `Countem.m`, that types out a line with N integers starting with n0, separated by commas and spaces. Use a `for` loop to construct the string.

```
>> Countem
NO= 5, N= 10
5, 6, 7, 8, 9, 10, 11, 12, 13, 14
```

18. **Rock-paper-scissors.** Write a program, `rps.m`, which plays the game rock-paper-scissors with the user. The user enters an `"r,"` `"p,"` `"s,"` or `"q"` to quit the game. The computer honestly (randomly) selects a choice, then tells the user who won, and prompts for another input. The computer keeps a running total of human wins and losses. Develop the program by writing some simpler versions first.

    a. **Version One.** Write a program, `rps1.m` that runs a single turn of the game. Generate the computer's choice using `rand`. Prompt the user for the choice `"r,"` `"p,"` or `"s."` Decide who won the turn (human or computer) and display the results.

    b. **Version Two.** Write a program, `rps2.m`, by adding to the user's options the choice `"q"` to quit. The program now plays the game over and over until the user enters a `q`.

    c. **Version Three.** Write a program, `rps3.m`, adding the feature that the program keeps a running total of wins and losses by human and computer and reports the cumulative results at the end of every turn.

19. **Hangman.** Write a program, `hangman.m`, that runs a game of hangman between two computer users. With the other player looking away, the first user should input a word, which is then cleared from the Command window. On each guess, the player should have the choice of guessing a word or a letter. Before each guess, the player should see a display of the word with asterisks in place of the letters the player has not guessed and the correct guesses so far filled in, and a list of all the letters the player has guessed up to that point.

20. **Monte Carlo integration.** One way to estimate the value of definite integrals in spaces with many dimensions is the Monte Carlo integration method. We illustrate the method here in two-dimensions. Consider the task of estimating the area of a circle of radius R. Inscribe the circle in a square with sides of length $2R$. To estimate the area, randomly pick N points in the square (use `rand`). Find how many points N_{in} are in the circle. The estimate for the area is then the fraction of all the points that are in the circle times the area of the square, $A \approx A_{MC} \equiv (N_{in}/N)4R^2$. Write a program, `MonteCarloCircle.m`, that implements this algorithm. Tabulate A_{MC} for $N = 10^k$ where $k = \{1, 2, \ldots, 7\}$. Make a graphical representation of the points "raining down" on the square with points inside the circle being a different color than points outside the circle.

21. **Pick a number.** Write a program `pickaNumber` that implements the following game. The program asks the user to mentally pick a small whole number n, but not report it. The program randomly picks 5 integers between 2 and 6: a, b, c, d, and e (don't disclose them to the user yet). The program then asks the user to do the following steps.

    1. Multiply the number n by a.

    2. Add b to the result.

    3. Multiply the result by c.

    4. Add d to the result.

5. Multiply the result by e and report the answer, n' (type it at the Command line).

The program then proudly announces the user's initial pick n.
Make your own version with a more complicated set of steps.

22. **Buffon's needle.** The question posed by the 18th-century French mathematician Georges-Louis Leclerc, the Count de Buffon, was this: Suppose a floor consists of parallel vertical strips of wood with equal width d, and a needle of length $L < d$ is dropped onto the floor. What is the probability P that the needle will lie across a line between two wood strips?

    a. Solve this problem by Monte Carlo simulation. The problem can be reduced to considering a single strip of width d on which the needle's center falls with uniform probability at a position $x \in [0, d]$. The angle θ that the needle makes with the horizontal is also uniformly distributed, $\theta \in [-\pi/2, +\pi/2]$. Write a program Buffon to estimate P by simulating the random dropping of N needles and determining the number N_c that cross the line on either end of the strip. An estimate of the probability of a needle falling across a line is then $P \approx N_c/N$. Use larger values of N until P is repeatable to at least 2 digits. Use a logical switch doGraphics that, when set to true, results in a graphical display of the needles appearing on the floor and the lines on either end of the strip. (The graphic will be overwhelmed if N is too large.)

    b. Buffon used double integration to obtain the result:

$$P = \frac{2L}{\pi d} \tag{5.1}$$

    This expression can be solved to give an expression for π in terms of the calculated (or measured) probability.

$$\pi = \frac{2L}{Pd} \tag{5.2}$$

    Use this expression to augment Buffon so that it also displays an approximation (very slowly converging) to π. Using this approach you can estimate π by physically dropping matches on a piece of paper with two lines on it and counting the crossings.

23. **Roulette.** Simulate a roulette game in which the player always bets on red (or equivalently, black, even, or odd). For the American roulette wheel there are 18 black spaces, 18 red spaces, and 2 green spaces (which are neither even nor odd). The probability of winning on a given spin is then $P_{win} = 18/38$. Assume the player starts with a stash of $100. On each spin the player bets the same amount, and must have at least that amount in the player's stash to continue the game. Play until the player cannot make another bet. After each spin of the wheel, plot the "trajectory" of the players stash up to that point, readjusting the scaling so the "present" is always near the right edge of the graph (remember to use drawnow). The program should be run the simulation continuously until play is over.

24. **Chuckaluck.** Simulate a game of chuckaluck, which proceeds as follows. The player picks a number [1, 6], places a bet, and three dice are rolled. If there are no dice that match the player's pick, he looses the bet. If there are one or more matches to the player's pick, the player wins and receives the number of matches times his bet as winnings. In your simulation, the player should start with an initial stash and bet the same amount each time. The player's pick should always be the same as well (it doesn't matter). Play until the player cannot make another bet. After each roll of the dice, plot the "trajectory" of the player's stash up to that point, readjusting the scaling so the "present" is always near the right edge of the graph (remember to use drawnow). The program should run the simulation continuously until play is over.

CHAPTER 6

Animation

Computational models are often enhanced by including an animation of model behavior. An animation can give the user an immediate sense of the system's dynamics. It also acts as a first intuitive check on the correctness of our model. For example, we all have some experience of how balls bounce, so an animation that shows a ball moving faster at the top of the bounce and slower near the bottom makes us immediately suspicious of the model. A correctly functioning model, including perhaps an animation and other analytical plots (e.g., showing the potential and kinetic energies of the bouncing ball), can enhance our understanding of the behavior.

Basic animation works the way a flip-book animation works—a series of still pictures with small differences between them are rapidly displayed to give the illusion of motion. This can be accomplished in MATLAB by repeatedly drawing with the `plot` command followed by the `drawnow` command, usually in a `for` loop. There are several tips and techniques offered here for making animations work well.

We try out these animation techniques by modeling the motion of particles being acted upon by specific forces. The motion is described by Newton's second law, $F = ma = m\, dv/dt$. We start with the simplest case, $F = 0$ and consider bounce conditions. The case when F is constant corresponds, for example, to motion under the gravitational force near the earth. For this case we develop an algorithm, called the improved Euler algorithm, for making many small steps from the initial condition into the future. Finally, we consider the most general case $F = F(x, v, t)$ and solve it using an algorithm called the Verlet method. This has the great advantage of conserving energy in most problems.

After mastering the material in this chapter you should be able to write programs that:

- Create animations by using the `plot`, `axis`, and `drawnow` commands in a `for` loop.

- Animate curves defined parametrically as functions of time.

- Combine several curves and lines in a single plot command so the animation can contain many graphical elements.

- Slow down an animation by inserting a `pause` command or speed it up by using an animation stride.

- Time march a solution to motion with zero acceleration, including bounce conditions.

- Time march a solution to motion with constant acceleration in one and two dimensions using the improved Euler method.

- Time march a solution to Newton's second law with changing forces using the Verlet method.

6.1 Basic animation

Let's start by animating the motion of a particle moving along a path. We'll represent the particle's position with a circle symbol, the kind used as a data marker in the plot command. This can be done conveniently by using an array to store the positions along the path we want the particle to take and using a for loop to redraw the plot at each time step. To start with, we'll simply move the particle along a line from $x = 0.1$ to $x = 0.9$ and keep its y-coordinate fixed at 0.3.

```
% SimpleAnimation.m
%    move a particle represented by
%    a circle symbol to illustrate
%    the basics of animation
%         Author: Fritz Freleng

%% set parameters
Nt=100;      % Number of time steps
xmin=0.1;
xmax=0.9;
yval=0.3;

%% create array
x=linspace(xmin,xmax,Nt);

%% animate position
for it=1:Nt
    plot(x(it), yval,'ro');
    axis([0, 1, 0, 1]);
    drawnow
end
```

Note that the first step involves setting up the array of values using linspace. Think of this array as containing the instantaneous values of the particle's x-coordinate at different times. (Notice how the parameters are segregated in the first section of the code, according to the canons of good programming practice.) The main action is in the for loop, which we can think of as stepping through these small time steps. Each time the body of the for loop is executed, the following things happen:

- The plot command clears the graphics frame and draws a new plot. The plot in this case draws a single point at the current position of the particle.

- The `axis` statement sets the scale for the image. This is important to include so that autoscaling is suppressed. Try running the program with the axis command commented out (by inserting a "%" at the beginning of the line) and see the result—very jerky.

- The `drawnow` command is necessary for a technical reason. It flushes the event queue to force graphical objects to be updated. Without it, you will see only the last plot. Try commenting out this line and see the result.

Because computers are fast, redrawing the plot each time isn't noticeable and the motion appears smooth.

In almost every case, animation requires that these three elements be in the animation `for` loop: (1) a command (or commands) that actually draws the picture as a snapshot in time, (2) the axis command, so autoscaling doesn't make the picture rescale from moment to moment, and (3) the `drawnow` command, to force the screen to redraw the updated plot each time.

Now let's modify the program to add two more features. We'll make the plotting a little more interesting by plotting a line from the particle's initial position to its current position. We can do that within the same `plot` command that creates the circle at the current position. Second, we can take control over the apparent speed of the motion by adding a `pause` command, which takes a time in seconds as its argument.

```
% SimpleAnimation2.m
%    move a particle represented by
%    a circle symbol to illustrate
%    the basics of animation
%      -added trailing line and speed control
%        Author: Fritz Freleng

%% set parameters
Nt=100;       % Number of time steps
xmin=0.1;
xmax=0.9;
yval=0.3;
dt=0.03;      % time step in seconds—change to vary speed

%% create array
x=linspace(xmin,xmax,Nt);

%% animate position
for it=1:Nt
    plot([x(1), x(it)],[yval, yval],'r',...    % plots line
         x(it), yval,'ro');                    % plots circle
    axis([0, 1, 0, 1]);
    pause(dt)
    drawnow
end
```

Examine the `plot` statement carefully. It plots a red line between the point $(x, y) = (\text{x(1)}, \text{yval})$ and the point $(x, y) = (\text{x(it)}, \text{yval})$. It then plots a red circle at the point $(x, y) = (\text{x(it)}, \text{yval})$. Animation of surprising complexity can be achieved by carefully thinking about what you want to draw at each timestep and making a single plot command with several parts that accomplishes just that.

Now let's step up the complexity of the plotting a bit more by making the particle move in a circle with radius R. Circular motion with period T can be described mathematically using a parametric representation as follows:

$$t = [0, 1]$$

$$x(t) = R \cos{(2\pi t/T)} \qquad (6.1)$$

$$y(t) = R \sin{(2\pi t/T)}$$

The strategy for implementing this in MATLAB is to construct a linear array of times from 0 to 1 using `linspace`, and then to calculate the corresponding values stored in the x and y arrays. This could be done using MATLAB vector notation, but for clarity we do it here in a `for` loop. The animation loop for `AnimateCircularMotion.m` plots a circle at the current position, but also plots a curve from the initial position, through all previously plotted positions, to the current position.

```
% AnimateCircularMotion.m
%    move a particle in a circle
%        Author: Delwyn Quight


%% set parameters
Nt=100;        % Number of time steps
R=1;           % radius of circle
T=1;           % period of motion (assume time goes from 0 to 1)
dt=0.03;       % time step in seconds—change to vary speed


%% initialize arrays
t=linspace(0,1,Nt)
x=zeros(1,Nt);
y=zeros(1,Nt);


%% calculate circular motion
for it=1:Nt
     x(it)=R*cos(2*pi*t(it)/T);
     y(it)=R*sin(2*pi*t(it)/T);
end


%% animate circular motion with trailing line
for it=1:Nt
     plot(x(1:it),y(1:it),'r',...   % plots curve
          x(it), y(it),'ro');       % plots point
     axis(1.2*[-1, 1, -1, 1]);
```

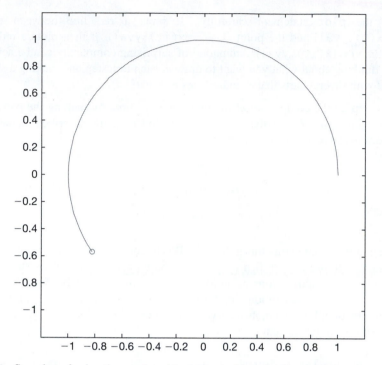

FIGURE 6.1 Snapshot of animation produced by AnimateCircularMotion.m.

```
    axis square
    pause(dt)
    drawnow
end
```

The program AnimateCircularMotion2.m adds several more lines to the plotting to show the projection of the position on the *x* and *y* axes. It's very helpful at this point to examine each line in the plot command and see how it makes the corresponding addition to the graph. Run the program with different values of Nt, R, and dt to see the effect of each parameter.

```
% AnimateCircularMotion2.m
%    move a particle in a circle
%    add radius line and projection on axes
%        Author: Delwyn Quight

%% set parameters
Nt=100;        % Number of time steps
R=1;           % radius of circle
T=1;           % period of motion (assume time goes from 0 to 1)
dt=0.06;       % time step in seconds—change to vary speed
```

```
%% initialize arrays
t=linspace(0,1,Nt)
x=zeros(1,Nt);
y=zeros(1,Nt);
```

```
%% calculate circular motion
for it=1:Nt
    x(it)=R*cos(2*pi*t(it)/T);
    y(it)=R*sin(2*pi*t(it)/T);
end
```

```
%% animate circular motion with trailing line
for it=1:Nt
    line([-R R],[0 0]);
    plot(x(1:it),y(1:it),'r',...       % plots curve
         x(it), y(it),'ro',...         % plots point
         1.2*[-R, R],[0, 0],'k',...        % x-axis
         [0, 0],1.2*[-R, R],'k',...        % y-axis
         [0, x(it)],[0, y(it)],'k',...   % radius
         [0, x(it)],[0, 0],'b',...         % x-projection
         [0, 0], [y(it), 0],'b',...,       % y-projection
         [x(it), x(it)],[0, y(it)],':b',... % y-drop
         [0, x(it)], [y(it), y(it)],':b')    % x-drop

    axis(1.2*R*[-1, 1, -1, 1]);
    axis square
    pause(dt)
    drawnow
end
```

6.2 Animating function plots

It is often helpful to animate not just the motion of a point, but also how an entire function changes in time. As an example, we animate the motion of a sinusoidal wave with spatial wavelength λ and temporal period T.

$$y(x, t) = A \cos (kx - \omega t)$$

The quantity k is called the wavenumber k, and ω is the angular frequency; they are simply related to the wavelength and period.

$$k = 2\pi/\lambda$$

$$\omega = 2\pi/T$$

The strategy is to construct a spatial grid (an x array) and a time grid (a t array), and then loop through the time. For each value of t, the whole curve is calculated and plotted, y as a function of x.

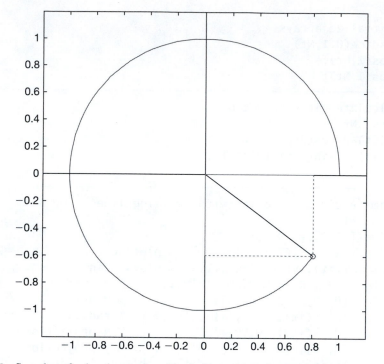

FIGURE 6.2 Snapshot of animation produced by `AnimateCircularMotion2.m`.

```
%% AnimateSine.m
% plot moving sine wave
%     Author: Japonica Fenway

%% set parameters
Nx=200;
Nt=200;
lambda=1;        % spatial wavelength
T=1;             % period
A=1;             % amplitude
xmax=3*lambda ;
Tmax=4*T ;
tpause=0.02;     % controls animation speed

k=2*pi/lambda ;   % wavenumber
omega=2*pi/T ;    % angular frequency

%% initialize arrays
x=linspace(0, xmax, Nx);
t=linspace(0, Tmax, Nt);
```

```
%% at each time, calculate curve and plot
for it=1:Nt
    y=sin(k*x-omega*t(it));
    plot(x,y);
    xlabel('x')
    ylabel('y')
    title('Traveling wave')
    pause(tpause)
    drawnow
end
```

(The `drawnow` command is not strictly necessary here, since the `pause` statement also flushes the event queue.) Try changing the sign of the wavevector (so $k = -2\pi/\lambda$) and see the result in the motion of the wave.

Because the entire curve is plotted for each value of t, we can rely on autoscaling and don't need to insert an `axis` command. Increasing the value of `tpause` slows the animation. Setting `tpause` to 0 will make redrawing the screen happen as fast as possible. If one needs to speed the animation up even further, we should plot fewer waves, that is, use fewer values of t. Accomplish this by changing the controlling `loop` to:

```
for it=1:Nstride:Nt
```

where `Nstride` is an integer greater than 1 (it will have to be set earlier in the program). Fewer waves will be drawn, but each one will have all Nx points plotted, and the animation will still appear smooth if `Nstride` isn't too large.

In general, if one is calculating a dynamical quantity in time, it is often easier to calculate the entire temporal evolution and then animate its display, rather than animating while the calculation is occurring. The latter is harder; one doesn't know how to scale the graph because later results are not yet available.

The following example illustrates the process. First, the time evolution of the x and y coordinates of the particle is calculated. Then the motion is animated in a second loop. In this case, each frame of the animation includes the particle's position, its path up to that point in time, and a line from the origin to the current position.

```
% AnimateEllipse.m
%    demonstrate animation technique for elliptical
%    motion x(t)=a cos(omega*t +phi), y(t)= b sin(omega*t-phi)
%    Author: Petunia Leeway

%% set parameters
a=1;
b=1.25;
T=1;    % period of the motion in time (get omega from this)
Np=4;   % number of periods to plot
```

```
Nt=500;
Nstride=2; % speeds up plotting if >1
phi=pi/8;  % relative phase shift

%% compute parameters and initialize arrays
Tf=Np*T;                    % final value of time
omega=2*pi/T;               % omega calculated from period
t=linspace(0, Tf, Nt);
x=zeros(1, Nt);
y=zeros(1, Nt);

%% compute motion
for it=1:Nt
    x(it)=a*cos(omega*t(it)+phi);
    y(it)=b*sin(omega*t(it)-phi);
end

%  find extremes of motion
xmin=min(x);
xmax=max(x);
ymin=min(y);
ymax=max(y);

%% plot motion as animation
for it=1:Nstride:Nt
    plot(x(1:it), y(1:it),...        % line to current position
        x(it), y(it), 'ro',...       % red circle
        [0, x(it)],[0, y(it)], 'r'); % red line from origin
    axis(1.2*[xmin, xmax, ymin, ymax]);
    axis equal
    title('Demo elliptical animation');
    drawnow
end
```

By choosing different options for the `axis` command, various effects can be achieved. The following example shows a stripchart recording that preserves the recent history of the function:

```
% AnimateStripchart.m
%    demonstrate animation techniques
%    Author: Lew Basnight

%% set model parameters
a=[1.2, 0.9, 0.8, 0.2];     % Fourier amplitudes
f=[1.3, 2.1, 3.2, 9.4];     % frequency ratios
```

```
Nt=2000;
T=40;                        % base period and window width
omega0=2*pi/T;
```

```
%% initialize array
t=linspace(0,6*T,Nt);
```

```
%% calculate particle path
y=a(1)*sin(f(1)*omega0*t)+...
   a(2)*sin(f(2)*omega0*t)+...
   a(3)*sin(f(3)*omega0*t)+...
   a(4)*sin(f(4)*omega0*t);
ymax=max(y);
ymin=min(y);
```

```
%% plot particle path
for it=1:Nt
    plot(t(1:it), y(1:it),...  % plots path up to now
         t(it), y(it), 'o');    % plot o at current point
    axis([max(0,t(it)-T), max(T,t(it)), ymin, ymax]);
    xlabel('t');
    ylabel('y');
    drawnow
end
```

6.3 Kinematics of motion

Animation techniques are very useful in understanding the mathematical description of the motion of physical bodies through space, a subject known as kinematics. If, for simplicity, we consider the motion of point particles, neglecting the spatial extent and rotational motion, then motion can be described in terms of three quantities: position, velocity, and acceleration. These three are connected by the idea from calculus of an instantaneous rate of change—the velocity is the instantaneous rate of change of the position, and the acceleration is the instantaneous rate of change of the velocity.

One-dimensional motion: Constant speed

Let the position of the particle be x and the velocity of the particle be v. The two are related by

$$v = \frac{dx(t)}{dt} \equiv \lim_{\Delta t \to 0} \frac{x(t + \Delta t) - x(t)}{\Delta t}$$

If Δt is small, we can approximate the velocity by a finite difference.

$$v \approx \frac{x(t + \Delta t) - x(t)}{\Delta t}$$

Solving for the new (approximate) value of position in terms of the old value of position and the velocity, we obtain:

$$x(t + \Delta t) = x(t) + v\Delta t \qquad (6.2)$$

This is an example of a "time marching" formula—by repeatedly applying it we can move from the present into the future in small steps. Time marching of one-dimensional motion with constant velocity is illustrated in the program motion1D:

```
% motion1D.m
% Animate 1D constant velocity
%      Author: Boris Badinov

%% set parameters
v0=0.1;        % m/s
x0=0;          % m
Tf=10;         % sec
deltat=0.05;   % time-step (s)

%% initialize
t=[0:deltat:Tf];   % alternative to linspace when deltat is
                   %      specified instead of Nt
Nt=length(t);
x=zeros(1, Nt);
v=zeros(1, Nt);
x(1)=x0;
v(1)=v0;

%% calculate the motion
for it=2:Nt
    v(it)=v(it-1);
    x(it)=x(it-1)+v(it)*deltat;
end

%% plot the motion
xmax=max(x);
xmin=min(x);
for it=1:Nt
    plot(x(it), 0, 'ro');
    axis([xmin, xmax, -1,  1]);
    xlabel('x (m)')
    drawnow
end
```

Let's examine the basic parts of this program.

Setting the parameters We need to set the initial position, the initial velocity, the total time of the simulation, and the length of the small timesteps (deltat represents Δt).

Initializing the arrays We set up arrays to hold the tabulated values of time, position, and velocity. In this case, since we're specifying the timestep length, the colon operator is used to form an equally spaced array of time values from 0 to Tf. The x and v arrays are filled with zeros, but the first values are then set to the values of the initial position and initial velocity.

Calculating the motion by time marching Iterating through small timesteps, we repeatedly use equation (6.2) to calculate the next value of position from the previous position and the current velocity. By assumption, for this example, the velocity is constant so we do not need to store the velocity value at each timestep. However, we do so to have a complete record of the motion and to make the code easy to extend to types of motion with a nonconstant velocity.

Plotting the motion We again loop through time and plot a symbol at the position of the object at each timestep, using the animation techniques described earlier in the chapter.

Now we can make this more interesting by adding a bounce condition. We set boundaries at $x = 0$ and $x = L$ so that if the particle's position is found to be outside those boundaries, we flip the sign of the velocity so that it will move back in. This approximates elastic collisions with hard, massive boundaries (like walls or floors). The particle's speed, by which we mean the magnitude of its velocity, is still constant. The concept of velocity includes both the magnitude and direction of the particle's motion. The direction of the velocity, and therefore its sign, changes at each bounce.

```
% motion1Dbounce.m
% Animate 1D constant velocity with bounces
%   at boundaries
%     Author: Natasha Fatale


%% set parameters
v0=0.1;        % m/s
x0=0;          % m
Tf=10;         % sec
deltat=0.01;   % time-step (s)
L=0.1;             % boundaries are at 0 and L (meters)


%% initialize
t=[0:deltat:Tf];
Nt=length(t);
x=zeros(1, Nt);
v=zeros(1, Nt);
x(1)=x0;
v(1)=v0;


%% calculate the motion
for it=2:Nt
    v(it)=v(it-1);
```

```
    x(it)=x(it-1)+v(it)*deltat;
    % bounce condition
    if x(it)>L
        v(it)=-abs(v(it)); % flip to left-moving
    elseif x(it)<0
        v(it)=abs(v(it));  % flip to right-moving
    end
end

%% plot the motion
xmax=max(x);
xmin=min(x);
for it=1:Nt
    plot(x(it), 0, 'ro');
    axis([xmin, xmax, -1,  1]);
    xlabel('x (m)')
    drawnow
end
```

This can be extended to two-dimensional bounded motion, so-called "billiard problems." The equations of motion for $x(t)$ and $y(t)$ are separable.

$$v_x = \frac{dx(t)}{dt}$$

$$v_y = \frac{dy(t)}{dt}$$

The corresponding time-marching equations are very similar.

$$x(t + \Delta t) = x(t) + v_x \Delta t \tag{6.3}$$

$$y(t + \Delta t) = y(t) + v_y \Delta t \tag{6.4}$$

To describe two-dimensional motion, we need to create arrays to keep track of $x(t)$, $y(t)$, $v_x(t)$, and $v_y(t)$. A simple rectangular billiard would include bouncing off walls at $x = 0$, $y = 0$, $x = L_x$, and $y = L_x$. This challenge is in one of the programming problems at the end of the chapter.

Motion with constant acceleration

The time derivative of the velocity is the acceleration. If the velocity has units of meters/second, the acceleration has units of meters/second^2. Here we consider the case where the acceleration is constant.

$$a = \frac{dv(t)}{dt} \tag{6.5}$$

$$v(t) = \frac{dx(t)}{dt} \tag{6.6}$$

As before, we can use the definition of the derivative and then use a finite time difference instead of going all the way to the the limit of an infinitesimal time difference.

$$a = \frac{dv(t)}{dt} \equiv \lim_{\Delta t \to 0} \frac{v(t + \Delta t) - v(t)}{\Delta t} \tag{6.7}$$

$$\approx \frac{v(t + \Delta t) - v(t)}{\Delta t} \tag{6.8}$$

So the time-marching equations for the one-dimensional constant acceleration case would be:

$$v(t + \Delta t) = v(t) + a\Delta t \tag{6.9}$$

$$x(t + \Delta t) = x(t) + v\Delta t \tag{6.10}$$

But which value of v should we use in equation (6.10)? The velocity is changing during the interval from t to $t + \Delta t$. Using the velocity at the beginning of the interval would give us $x(t + \Delta t) = x(t) + v(t)\Delta t$, an approximation that results in a time-marching technique known as *Euler's method*. This turns out not to be a very good approximation for this problem (energy won't be conserved). A much better approximation can be obtained by substituting for v in equation (6.10) the average value of v over the interval. That is, simply take the sum of $v(t)$ and $v(t + \Delta t)$ and divide by two. This approach is called the *improved Euler's method*, and works very well for constant acceleration.

$$x(t + \Delta t) = x(t) + \frac{1}{2}[v(t + \Delta t) + v(t)]\Delta t \tag{6.11}$$

We obtain the desired one-dimensional time-marching equations:

One-dimensional constant acceleration time-marching equations (improved Euler's method)

$$v(t + \Delta t) = v(t) + a\Delta t \tag{6.12}$$

$$x(t + \Delta t) = x(t) + \frac{1}{2}[v(t + \Delta t) + v(t)]\Delta t \tag{6.13}$$

In two dimensions, we specify the particle's position by $x(t)$ and $y(t)$. The velocity now has two components, $v_x(t)$ and $v_y(t)$, as does the acceleration a_x and a_y. The time-marching equations (6.12) and (6.13) apply to each component separately.

Two-dimensional constant acceleration time-marching equations (improved Euler method)

$$\vec{r} = (x, y) \tag{6.14}$$

$$\vec{v} = (v_x, v_y) \tag{6.15}$$

$$\vec{a} = (a_x, a_y) \tag{6.16}$$

$$v_x(t + \Delta t) = v_x(t) + a_x \Delta t \tag{6.17}$$

$$v_y(t + \Delta t) = v_y(t) + a_y \Delta t \tag{6.18}$$

$$x(t + \Delta t) = x(t) + \frac{1}{2}[v_x(t + \Delta t) + v_x(t)]\Delta t \tag{6.19}$$

$$y(t + \Delta t) = y(t) + \frac{1}{2}[v_y(t + \Delta t) + v_y(t)]\Delta t \tag{6.20}$$

The following program `motion2DconstAccel` illustrates how these equations can be straightforwardly implemented in MATLAB.

```
% motion2DconstAccel.m
% Animate 2D constant accleration
%     Author: Cpt. Peter Peachfuzz


%% set parameters
g=9.81;  % m/s^2  acceleration due to gravity
ax=0;
ay=-g;
x0=0;      %m
y0=0;
vx0=1;     %m/s
vy0=10;
Tf=5;      %s
Nt=1000;


%% initialize
t=linspace(0, Tf, Nt);
x=zeros(1, Nt);
y=zeros(1, Nt);
vx=zeros(1, Nt);
vy=zeros(1, Nt);
x(1)=x0;
y(1)=y0;
vx(1)=vx0;
vy(1)=vy0;
```

```
%% time march to calculate motion—bounce at y=0
for it=1:Nt-1
    vx(it+1)=vx(it)+ax*deltat;
    vy(it+1)=vy(it)+ay*deltat;
    x(it+1)=x(it)+0.5*(vx(it+1)+vx(it))*deltat;
    y(it+1)=y(it)+0.5*(vy(it+1)+vy(it))*deltat;

    if (y(it+1)<0)                  % bounce condition
        vy(it+1)=abs(vy(it+1));
    end
end

%% plot results animating motion
xmax=max(x);
xmin=min(x);
ymax=max(y);
ymin=min(y);
for it=1:Nt
    plot(x(it),  y(it),  'ro',...
         x(1:it), y(1:it), 'r');
    axis(1.1*[xmin, xmax, ymin, ymax]);
    xlabel('x(m)');
    ylabel('y(m)');
    drawnow
end
```

Time-marching dynamics: Nonconstant force

We frequently encounter situations in which the force on a particle is not constant as the particle moves. A simple but important example is the motion of a mass on a spring. Assume one end of the spring is attached to a mass m at position x, with the other end of the spring fixed at $x = 0$. The spring is assumed to have a zero unstretched length and a spring constant k. According to Hooke's law (which applies if the spring isn't stretched too far), the force on the mass due to the spring is

$$F = F(x) = -kx \tag{6.21}$$

Since the position x varies with time, the force varies—it is greater when the spring is stretched more.

We could use the Euler method to calculate the new velocity in each timestep using the force at the beginning of the interval, and the improved Euler method to calculate the new position.

$$v(t + \Delta t) = v(t) + (F(t)/m)\Delta t \tag{6.22}$$

$$x(t + \Delta t) = x(t) + (1/2)(v(t + \Delta t) + v(t))\Delta t \tag{6.23}$$

We would like to do better than this and use the improved Euler method for the velocity as well, replacing $F(t)$ in equation (6.22) with the average of $F(t)$ and $F(t + \Delta t)$, but there is a problem. We don't know how to evaluate the force at the end of the interval, because it depends on the position $x(t + \Delta t)$ (and the position depends on the velocity which we're trying to calculate).

There are a number of sophisticated ways of approaching this problem. A common technique is to use a method called *fourth-order Runge-Kutta*. We will employ a simpler but quite useful method that is easier to understand. The method is called the *Verlet* method and is commonly used in molecular dynamics calculations as well as computer gaming. The idea is to proceed as follows:

1. Use the force at the beginning of the timestep to calculate the velocity half a timestep later.

2. Use the half-step velocity to calculate the new position at the end of the interval.

3. With the new position, calculate a new value for the force at the end of the timestep.

4. Finally, use the new force to calculate the velocity forward from the half-way point to the end of the interval.

The method is stated mathematically in four steps:

Time-marching equations (Verlet) for nonconstant force

$$\text{Step 1:} \quad v_{1/2} = v(t) + \left[\frac{F(v(t), x(t), t)}{m} \right] \frac{\Delta t}{2} \tag{6.24}$$

$$\text{Step 2:} \quad x(t + \Delta t) = x(t) + v_{1/2} \Delta t \tag{6.25}$$

$$\text{Step 3:} \quad F_{new} = F(v_{1/2}, x(t + \Delta t), t + \Delta t) \tag{6.26}$$

$$\text{Step 4:} \quad v(t + \Delta t) = v_{1/2} + \left[\frac{F_{new}}{m} \right] \frac{\Delta t}{2} \tag{6.27}$$

When realized as a MATLAB program, the key part of the calculation for the simple harmonic oscillator looks something like this:

```
...
for it=1:Nt-1
    Fold= -k*x(it);
    vhalf=v(it)+(Fold/m)*deltat/2;
    x(it+1)=x(it)+vhalf*deltat;
    Fnew= -k*x(it+1);
    v(it+1)=vhalf+(Fnew/m)*deltat/2;
end
...
```

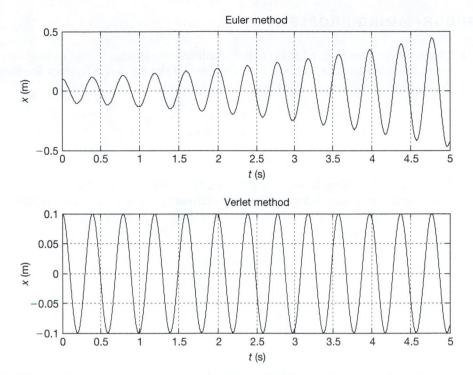

FIGURE 6.3 Simple harmonic motion as calculated by the Euler method (top) and the Verlet method (bottom). The solution given by the Euler method, equations (6.22) and (6.23), steadily increases in amplitude, an unphysical result.

Figure 6.3 compares the results of a calculation of simple harmonic motion using the improved Euler method [equations (6.22) and (6.23)] with a calculation using the Verlet method. The Euler approach fails to conserve energy so the oscillations increase in amplitude—clearly not what actually happens.

The Verlet method is useful for a large range of problems, including ballistic problems with lossy bounces or with aerodynamic drag. Any force $F(x, v, t)$ can be included. For motion in three dimensions, tabulate x, y, z, v_x, v_y, v_z, and time march with all six, evaluating the three components of the vector force F_x, F_y, and F_z, separately.

Looking ahead

Animation techniques will prove invaluable in creating the MATLAB GUI tools that will be described in Part II. Before we can build the tools, two topics remain. The first topic is writing your own MATLAB functions, described in the next chapter. GUI Tools will be constructed from many interacting functions. Functions are also enormously useful in breaking up large problems into many smaller problems. The second topic will be defining a few more data classes and data structures—more ways in which we can aggregate many pieces of information in one container. That is of general use, but for our purposes we need only a few nuggets to equip us for tool building.

PROGRAMMING PROBLEMS

1. **Circle.** Write a program, `plotcirc.m`, that animates the plotting of the following parametrically defined motion with period T. In addition to plotting the circle, plot a line from the center of the circle to the point, for each point plotted.

$$r = r_0$$
$$x = r\cos(\omega t)$$
$$y = r\sin(\omega t)$$

2. **Decaying circle.** Write a program, `plotdecay.m`, that animates the plotting of the following parametrically defined motion characterized by T and τ. In addition to plotting the motion, plot a line from the origin to the point, for each point plotted.

$$r = r_0 e^{-\frac{t}{\tau}}$$
$$x = r(t)\cos(\omega t)$$
$$y = r(t)\sin(\omega t)$$

3. **Ellipse.** Write a program, `plotellipse.m`, that animates the plotting of the following parametrically defined motion characterized by T and ϕ.

$$x = r\cos(\omega t)$$
$$y = r\sin(\omega t + \phi)$$

4. **Lissajous.** Write a program, `plotLJ.m`, that plots the following parametrically defined motion characterized by T, a, b, and ϕ.

$$x = r\cos(a\omega t)$$
$$y = r\sin(b\omega t + \phi)$$

Add the option to animate the motion (`animateON=true or false`) in a second figure (see help `figure` in the Command window) after pausing 2 seconds to see the complete graph.

5. **Random walk in one dimension.** Write a program, `rw1d.m`, that generates and plots random walks in one dimension. Let the walker start at $x = 0$ and move a unit step to the right or left, depending on a random number generated with `r=rand`. If $r <= 0.5$, the walker steps one unit to the right; if $r > 0.5$, the walker steps one unit to the left. Its position after each step depends on the previous position and the value of r.

The key data structure is an array x. Let `x(istep)` be the position of the walker after `(istep-1)` steps. Initialize the x array to N zeros (start with $N = 100$ and let it get bigger). Create an array of step numbers, `steps=(1:N);`. Use a `for` loop to calculate the position after each step.

- Since the walker starts at the origin, $x(1) = 0$.

- A step to the right means `x(istep)=x(istep-1)+1;`.

- A step to the left means `x(istep)=x(istep-1)-1;`.

- Calculate the entire x array without plotting. Then plot and animate the motion and path of the walker.

Write the program in well-structured blocks:

  a. *Header.* File name, description, author.

  b. *Set walk parameters.* (e.g., number of steps)

  c. *Set program parameters.* (*x* array, steps array)

  d. *Calculate walk.*

  e. *Plot and animate walk.*

6. **Roulette.** Write a program, `roulette.m`, that simulates betting red (or black, or even, or odd) each time for *N* spins of a roulette wheel. The wheel has 38 positions: 18 red, 18 black, 0 and 00 (green). Describe the game using a vector `cash`; `cash(ispin)` is the amount of cash you have after `ispin-1` spins.
   - The probability of winning on any spin is 18/38 = 47.37%.

   - Start with `cash(1)=100` dollars.

   - Set a fixed amount to bet each time, `betAmount`. If you have at least that much cash left, bet C dollars on the spin.

   - Payout is 1:1, so if you win, you add `betAmount` to your cash; if you lose, subtract it.

   - You can't bet money you don't have. If you don't have `betAmount` dollars left, you must bet 0 until the game ends. (Or use a `while` loop to play only until you're broke.)

   Plot cash as a function of spin number. As in the previous problem, calculate all *N* spins first, then animate the results, plotting the current value of your cash and the history of your bankroll.

7. **Epicycles.** Write a program, `epicycles.m`, to draw circular motion with one epicycle, as illustrated in Figure 6.4.

   The object moves around the origin with a period T_1 and around the center of the epicycle with a period T_2. The radius of the primary orbit is *R* and of the epicycle is *r*. The angular frequency of each orbit is:

$$\omega_1 = \frac{2\pi}{T_1} \qquad \omega_2 = \frac{2\pi}{T_2}$$

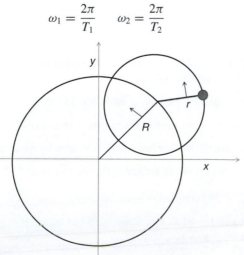

FIGURE 6.4 Epicycles.

The x and y coordinates of the motion are given by (convince yourself of this):

$$x(t) = r\cos(\omega_1 t) + r\cos(\omega_2 t)$$

$$y(t) = r\sin(\omega_1 t) + r\sin(\omega_2 t)$$

Let $R = 5$ and $r = 2$ initially. Let $T_1 = 1$ and $T_2 = T_1/\texttt{tratio}$. Start with `tratio = 9.25`. Let the number of large cycles be `Nc` (initially 10, say). Let the number of time points per cycle be `Ntpc` (initially 200). The total time is `Nc*T1` and the total number of times for which you calculate the position is `Nt=Nc*Ntpc`. Calculate the frequencies `omega1` and `omega2`. For each time in the interval `[0,Tf]` (say loop index `it` goes from 1 to `Nt`), calculate `x(it)` and `y(it)`. Plot the position of the object and a line tracing its path from the beginning to its present position.

a. Try various values of `tratio`. Try integers, simple rational numbers (e.g., 9.25) and non-simple numbers (e.g., 9.277).

b. Experiment with different r and R. What if $r > R$? Play around.

c. Add a logical switch, `doAnimation`, which lets you choose between an animation and a plot of the whole trajectory at once.

8. **A random walk in two dimensions.** Write a program, rw2d.m, to describe a walker making a random walk with unit steps in the x-y plane. The walker starts at the origin. Represent the walkers N positions using MATLAB arrays `x` and `y`. A good value to start with would be 1×10^3.

The walk starts with `x(1) = 0`, `y(1) = 0` (initialize both arrays to zero). Use a `for` loop to calculate the walker's moves. At each step the walker uses a random number to decide whether to take a step.

- North (y increases by 1; x stays the same).

- South (y decreases by 1; x stays the same).

- East (x increases by 1; y stays the same).

- West (x decreases by 1; y stays the same).

The walker always takes a step of length 1.

Notes:

a. Note that one can generate a random number in the set $\{1, 2, 3, 4\}$ by using the command `idirection=randi(4);`.

b. Animate the plot by plotting at each step `istep`.

   i. The starting position at the origin as an asterisk.

   ii. The path the walker has taken up to now by a curve.

   iii. The position of the walker at the present as an "o." E.g.,

```
plot(0, 0, 'r*', ...
        x(1:k), y(1:k), ...
        x(k), y(k), 'ro');
axis equal
draw now
```

c. Write the program in structures blocks labeled:

```
%% set walk parameters
...
%% set program parameters and
initialize arrays
...
%% calculate walk
...
%% plot walk
...
```

9. **Vertical motion and energy.**   If an object is shot upward with an initial vertical velocity v_0, its height at any time t can be calculated by the equation:

$$h(t) = h_0 + v_0 t - \frac{1}{2} g t^2$$

where h_0 is the initial height of the object, and $g = 9.8 \ m/s^2$, the acceleration due to gravity. The object's potential energy PE (its energy due to its position above the ground), kinetic energy KE (the energy associated with its movement) and total mechanical energy TE (potential energy + kinetic energy) can also be calculated at each time t, using the following equations:

$$PE = mgh$$
$$KE = 1/2mv^2$$
$$TE = PE + KE$$

where m is the mass of the object, and v is the vertical velocity of the object. The vertical velocity of the object is the derivative of the height with respect to time, dh/dt.

Write a program, verticalMotion.m, for a 58 g tennis ball that is hit upward from an initial height of 0.8 m at a speed of 60 mph ($\approx 17.8 \ m/s$), which computes for Nt=500 timesteps and Tfinal $= 4$ s.

a. The height, h, of the ball.

b. The ball's vertical velocity, dh/dt.

c. Its potential energy (PE), kinetic energy (KE) and total energy (TE).

Using the subplot command (use doc subplot to get information on the subplot command) to plot and animate (with Nstride=20) the following three graphs:

a. The height, h, of the tennis ball.

b. The vertical velocity, dh/dt, of the ball vs. time.

c. The PE, KE, and TE of the ball vs. time. Use the legend command to create a legend that distinguishes the graphs from one another.

Each plot should be titled and each axis should be labeled.

Note: After the plot is complete, the legend can be dragged using the cursor to get a better view of the energy plot.

10. **Two-dimensional billiards.** Write a program `billard.m` that calculates and displays the motion of a point particle moving in two dimensions, x and y, with constant speed. The x-component of the velocity is v_x and the y-component is v_y. The velocities remain constant, so $v_x(t + \Delta t) = v_x(t)$ and $v_x(t + \Delta t) = v_x(t)$, unless there is a bounce off one of the walls at $x = 0$, $x = L_x$, $y = 0$, and $y = L_y$. Implement the bounce condition as follows:

    - If $x(t + \Delta t) < 0$, flip the sign of $v_x(t + \Delta t)$ so that it is positive (moving to the right).

    - If $x(t + \Delta t) > L_x$, flip the sign of $v_x(t + \Delta t)$ so that it is negative (moving to the left).

    - If $y(t + \Delta t) < 0$, flip the sign of v_y so that it is positive (moving up).

    - If $y(t + \Delta t) > L_y$, flip the sign of v_y so that it is negative (moving down).

    Start the particle at $x = x_0$, $y = y_0$, $v_x = v_{x0}$, and $v_y = v_{y0}$. You will need to experiment with different time steps and simulation times.

    a. Animate the path of the particle as a circle with a trailing line.

    b. Set the playback speed using an animation stride, as in `AnimateEllipse.m`.

    c. Change the program to accept an initial speed v_0 and an initial angle θ (with respect to the x-axis).

11. **Handball (a two-dimensional billiard with gravity).** Extend the previous program `billard.m` by adding a constant acceleration due to gravity, $a_y = -9.8$ m/s^2, $a_x = 0$. Call the new program `handball.m`. The equations of motion are given by equations (6.14) through (6.20). Good values for the parameters to start your explorations are $(x, y) = (0, 0)$, $(v_x, v_y) = (1.123, 3.8)$ m/s, `Tf=12` s, `Nt=12000`, and a stride value of 7.

    a. As with the `billard.m` program, animate the motion with a trailing line.

    b. Assume the mass of the particle is 0.05 kg. Calculate and plot, as functions of time, the kinetic energy, $\frac{1}{2}m(v_x^2 + v_y^2)$, the potential energy, mgy, and the total energy. The units of energy are joules.

Writing Your Own MATLAB Functions

A mathematical function, like $y = \sin(x)$, can be thought of as a machine that takes a numerical value x as an input and returns a numerical value y as an output. The precise algorithm it employs to calculate the value is out-of-sight. MATLAB functions can be thought of in analogy with built-in mathematical functions like sine and cosine, but in fact, MATLAB functions operate more generally and play a much greater role. In computer programming, functions are the principal tools for managing complexity. They allow a complicated program to be broken up into many simpler parts, parts that are easier to understand, easier to write, and easier to test.

Functions can have inputs and outputs. Inputs are the values of variables that are sent to the function. There can be several inputs and they can be of any MATLAB class— real numbers, vectors, matrices, arrays, strings, and more. Functions can even take other functions as inputs (such a function is called a function function). Similarly, the output of the function can be any number of values of any class.

In addition to calculating the outputs based on the inputs, a function can have *side-effects*, that is, it can make something happen beyond assigning values to its outputs. We have seen a number of such functions already. The `disp` function takes a string as an argument and produces no output, but has the side-effect of making the string appear in the Command window. The `plot` function can take a variety of inputs, and causes a graph to appear in a Figures window. The function `beep` causes a beep sound to be sent to the speaker. Functions can have any number of inputs, including no input, any number of outputs, and any number of side-effects.

Breaking down a complicated task into several smaller tasks and implementing those with functions is an important conceptual skill. If the decomposition is done badly it obfuscates the overall problem-solving strategy; if it is done well, the strategy is made clear. Well-designed functions can often be reused in future programs. The golden rule of functions is: a function should do one thing and do it well.

After mastering the material in this chapter you should be able to:

- Create MATLAB functions that take a single input and produce a single output.

- Create functions that have multiple inputs and multiple outputs.

- Write a program that employs several functions, each of which resides in its own file.

- Write programs that are comprised of a main function and several subfunctions, all in one file.

- Use nested functions, functions that are defined within other functions, so that a function can access variables in the workspace of its calling function.

- Create short *anonymous* functions that make simple repetitive tasks clearer and easier.

7.1   MATLAB function files

MATLAB has many built-in functions, such as $sin(x)$, $abs(x)$, $exp(x)$, $plot(x)$, $xlabel('x')$, and $num2str(x)$. You can extend the MATLAB language by writing functions of your own.

Let us suppose that, for some reason, you often need to evaluate the following mathematical function.

$$y(x) = 3.5x^2 + 2.1x + 0.2$$

To automate this, you can create a MATLAB function dedicated to the task. Open the MATLAB editor and enter the following file.

```
function y=myfun(x)
%   y=myfun(x) returns the value of
%       y(x)= 3.5 x^2 +2.1 x +0.2

a=3.5;
b=2.1;
c=0.2;
y= a*x.^2 + b*x + c;
```

Save the file into a file named myfun.m (click on "Save|Save As ..." on the EDITOR tab). Always make sure that the file name and the function name declared in the first line of the file are identical, including capitalization.

Now you can invoke the function from the command line, just the way you would any other MATLAB function.

```
>> myfun(0)
ans =
    0.2000
>> vinit=myfun(1)
```

```
vinit =
    5.8000
>> t=linspace(-1, 1, 200);
>> plot(t,myfun(t))
>> help myfun
   y=myfun(x) returns the value of
       y(x)= 3.5 x^2 +2.1 x +0.2
```

The file must have the same name as the function and should be in the current folder.

Declaring MATLAB functions

The first line of a function must be the function declaration. The function declaration has the form:

```
function <return variable>=funcname(<input arguments>)
```

Unlike a script, the first line of the file holding the function should always start with the word "function." The return variable on the left side of the equals sign declares the name of the variable that will be assigned a value by the function. For example:

```
function  y=hermite(x, n)
%    returns the value of the nth hermite polynomial evaluated
%    at x (which can be a vector)
...

function Tc=f2c(Tf)
%    returns the temperature in celcius given the
%    temperature Tf in Fahrenheit
...

function isleap=isLeapYear(year)
%    true if year is a leap year, false otherwise
...

function  y=bessel(x, n)
%    returns the Bessel function of order n
...
```

Functions help break up long programs into smaller subunits. Each function should do one thing and do that one thing well. Functions can call other functions.

7.2 Function inputs and outputs

Inputs are passed to MATLAB functions through the arguments of the function, also known as the "calling parameters." For example, consider the following main program and function.

```
% file main.m
x1=9;                    % line 1
a=1;                     % line 2
b=9;                     % line 3
x=gmean(a, b);           % line 4
disp(x)                  % line 5
```

```
(A separate file named gmean.m)

function y=gmean(x1, x2) % line 1
% geometric mean         % line 2
a=sqrt(x1*x2);           % line 3
y=a;                     % line 4
```

Line 4 of `main.m` calls the function `gmean`, passing the current values of `a` and `b` to the function. The function stores the values received in the variables `x1` and `x2`. So before line 3 of `gmean.m` is executed, `x1` holds the value 1 and `x2` holds the value 9. This is called "passing by value." The function `gmean` will not alter the values of `a` and `b` in the calling program.

The function declaration (line 1 of `gmean`) declares the name of the return value of the function to be `y`. This means that the function must set a value for the variable `y`, and this value will be returned to the calling program. In this case, the function stores the value 3 in the variable `y`, which is then returned to the calling program. The right-hand side of the assignment statement (main line 4) evaluates to 3, which is then stored in the variable `x` in the main program.

7.3 Local workspaces

Each function has its own private workspace of variables. Variables in the *function workspace* are distinct from those in the *main workspace* even if they have the same name. In the previous example, the variable `x1` in line 1 of `main` has nothing to do with the local variable `x1` in the function `gmean`. Neither one affects the other. The fact that functions have their own workspaces is a huge help. It means that when writing a function *one does not need to worry about the names of variables outside the function*. The function interacts with other code only through the function inputs and outputs. One result is that, once you get a function written and debugged, you can use it in many other programs without having to alter it at all. A really useful function could follow you around for many years.

7.4   Multiple outputs

A MATLAB function can have any number of inputs and any number of outputs. The inputs are specified as the arguments of the function, e.g., `myfunc(x1,a,b,str)`. Inputs and outputs can be any MATLAB data structure—numbers, vectors, strings, Boolean variables, handles, etc. Multiple outputs are specified in the function declaration by naming the output variables and inclosing them in square brackets. For example:

```
function [x,y,strout]=myfunction(a, b, str)
```

Here the function must set values for the variables `x`, `y`, and `strout` by the time it completes. The output variables can be treated as optional by the calling program, though it must respect the order of the outputs. Thus, given the previous function, a calling program could invoke the function in any of the following ways.

```
myfunction(1.2, c, mystr);
x1=myfunction(r, theta, stry);
[x1, y]=myfunction(x, z, name);
[xinit, yinit, bill]=myfunction(a2, b2, last);
```

7.5   Function files

Each function must be in a separate file (exceptions are mentioned in the next section) and the name of the function should match the name of the file exactly. Thus, the function declared by `function y=gmean(x1,x2)` should be in a file called `gmean.m`. Make the first line of the file the function declaration and follow it by comments describing the function.

```
function y=bessel0(x)
% returns the sperical bessel function of order 0
%       y=bessel0(x)
y=sin(x)./x;
```

Typing `help bessel0` will return the comments following the function declaration so that other users can see what the function does and how to use it.

7.6   Other functional forms

The most general and accessible way to write functions is to keep each function in a separate file, with the file name identical to the function name. There are other ways to organize functions that can be very useful, however.

Subfunctions

One file can contain a primary function (whose name is the same as the file's name) and also several other functions that are listed after the primary function. The functions listed after the primary function are called *subfunctions* and are accessible only from the primary function or from others subfunctions in the same file. If this particular group of functions are all meant to work together on the task of the primary function, this has the advantage of keeping them all in a single file. Rather than having a folder (directory) with many, perhaps small, function files, they're all together in one place.

A primary function and a group of subfunctions are often used to break down a lengthy calculation into manageable parts. Each part can be checked and debugged separately before assembling the whole. The following program illustrates this.

The basic problem is this: given a location on the Earth specified by latitude and longitude, and a specific time, find the position of the sun in the sky. The sun's position is specified by its altitude (in degrees) above the horizon, and its azimuthal compass angle (degrees east from north). To calculate the position, the code proceeds through several steps, each invoking a particular function. In this case, the sun's position is calculated for each day of a year at the same time of day. The resulting figure-eight shape is called an analemma.

One value of this rather lengthy example is that it illustrates how the calculation can be seen in the main function, PlotAnalemma, as consisting of just a few clear steps. Each step in turn corresponds to a function call that has a simpler, well-defined, and often reusable task. For example, the function calcGHA finds the Greenwich hour angle (GHA) for a celestial object, given its right ascension (which is tabulated for most objects) and the GHA of the first point of Aries (a reference point on the celestial sphere). This function can be used for other tasks, for example, finding the location of a star in the sky. The function calcGHA itself calls other utility functions, like d2dm, which changes decimal degrees into whole degrees and decimal minutes.

```
function [AltSun, AzSun]=PlotAnalemma(y,m,day,EST_hour,minutes,
                                      seconds,... Lon,Lat)
% [AltSun, AzSun]=PlotAnalemma(y,m,day,EST_hour,minutes,seconds,
%                                      longitude,latitude)
%    plots the position of the sun (altitude and azimuth) in
%    degrees at the same time each day through a calendar year
%                           Author: C. Lent
%  Time of starting observation
%   y            year (e.g. 2013)
%   m            month (e.g. 10 for October)
%   EST_hour     integer hour EST (e.g 13 for 1:00 pm)
%   minutes      integer minutes
%   seconds      seconds
%
%  Position of observer:
%   Lon          longitude in degrees
```

```
%                   (+ for northern hemisphere, - for southern)
%   Lat     latitude in degrees
%                   (- for west of Greenwich, + for east of Greenwich)
%
%  Example:
%    plot analemma starting Oct 25th at 1:47 pm for an observer
%       at 86.2218 deg W and 41.6754 deg N
%    PlotAnalemma(2013,10,25,13,47,0,-86.2218,41.6754);

% minimum and maximum Azimuth
AzMin=90;
AzMax=270;

% scan through year
d=[day:day+365];

% find the time since 1/1/2001 12:00:00
[T,hUT]=Tcelestial(y,m,d,EST_hour,minutes,seconds,'EST');

% find the right ascension and declination of sun
[RA,Dec]=solarRADEC(T);

% find Greenwich hour angle of the first point of Aries
[GHAaries,d,m]=calcGHAaries(T,hUT,minutes,seconds);

% find Greenwich Hour Angle of the sun
[GHAsun,d,m]=calcGHA(RA,GHAaries);

% find local hour angle (LHA) and meridian angle t
[LHAsun,tsun]=calcLHA(GHAsun,Lon);

% find altitude  and azimuth of the sun
[AltSun, AzSun]= AltAz(Lat,Lon,Dec,LHAsun);

% plot azimuth vs. altitude
plot(AzSun,AltSun,AzSun(1),AltSun(1),'ro')
grid on
axis([AzMin AzMax 0 90])
xlabel('Degrees from North');
ylabel('Altitude (degrees)');
title('Analemma')


%=================================================
function [T,hUT]=Tcelestial(y,month,day,hour,minute,second,
                                          TimeZone)
%  T=Tcelestial(y,month,day,hour,minute,second,TimeZone)
```

```
%    find time in decimal days since Jan 1 2000 12:00:00 UT
% hUT =decimal hour in Universal Time
%
%      y,    month, day, hour, minute, second
% e.g.  2005   10    27    13    55      0  Oct. 27, 2005 1:55pm
%
% TimeZone ='EST','CST','MST','PST'
%           'EDT','CDT','MDT','PDT'
%           based on http://www.celnav.de/

switch TimeZone
    case 'EST'
        deltaUT=+5;
    case 'CST'
        deltaUT=+6;
    case 'MST'
        deltaUT=+7;
    case 'PST'
        deltaUT=+8;
    case 'EDT'
        deltaUT=+4;
    case 'CDT'
        deltaUT=+5;
    case 'MDT'
        deltaUT=+6;
    case 'PDT'
        deltaUT=+7;
end
% find UT (e.g.12.5125)  Universal Time in decimal hours
hUT=hour+deltaUT;
mUT=minute;
sUT=second;
UT=hUT+(mUT/60)+(sUT/(60*60));

term1=367*y;
term2=-floor(1.75*(y+floor((month+9)/12)));
term3=floor(275*month/9)+day+UT/24 - 730531.5;
T=term1+term2+term3;


%======================================================
function [RA,Dec]=solarRADEC(T)
%    [RA,Dec]=solarRADEC(T)
% find solar right ascension and declination
% T= time in decimal days since Jan 1 2000 12:00:00 UT

% mean anomaly of the sun (degrees)
```

```
g=0.9856003*T-2.472;
g=norm360(g);

% mean longitude of the sun
Lm=0.9856474*T-79.53938;
Lm=norm360(Lm);

% true longitude of the sun
Lt=Lm+1.915*sind(g)+0.02*sind(2*g);
Lt=norm360(Lt);

% obliquity of the Sun
epsilon=23.439-4*T*1e-7;

% declination of the sun
Dec=asind(sind(Lt).*sind(epsilon));
[d,m]=d2dm(Dec);

% right ascension of the sun
RA=2*atand( (cosd(epsilon).*sind(Lt))./(cosd(Dec)+cosd(Lt)));
RA=norm360(RA);


%====================================================
function [GHAaries,d,m]=calcGHAaries(T,hUT,minutes,seconds)
%     GHAaries=calcGHAaries(T,hUT,minutes,seconds)
% Greenwich Hour Angle of the 1st point of Aries [0,360] deg
% T= time in decimal days since Jan 1 2000 12:00:00 UT
% hUT current integer hour time at Greenwich
% minutes and seconds of current time
%
% also returns GHAaries in integer degrees (d) and
%                         real minutes (m)

% find current Universal Time in decimal hours
UTh=hUT+minutes/60+seconds/(60*60);

% compute GHA of 1st point of Aries
%  based on http://www.celnav.de/

GHAaries=0.9856474*T + 15*UTh + 100.46062;
GHAaries=norm360(GHAaries);
[d,m]=d2dm(GHAaries);


%====================================================
function [GHA,deg,mins]=calcGHA(RA,GHAaries)
%  [GHA,d,m]=calcGHA(RA,GHAaries)
%  Greenwich hour angle for object (deg) [0 360]
```

```
% also returns integer degrees (deg) and
% real minutes (mins)

GHA=GHAaries-RA;
GHA=norm360(GHA);
[deg,mins]=d2dm(GHA);


%=========================================================
function [LHA,t]=calcLHA(GHA,Lon)
%   [LHA,t]=calcLHA(GHA,Lon)
% local hour angle and meridian angle
% GHA is the current Greenwich hour angle (degrees)
% Lon is longitude of observer in degrees (W neg; E pos)
%
% LHA is angle between meridian and
%            object in degrees (0,360)
% t is angle from meridian
%    t<0 pre-meridian
%    t>0 post meridian

LHA=GHA+Lon;
LHA=norm360(LHA);

% meridian angle of the sun (hour angle)
t=GHA+Lon;    % t=H is [-180,180] from local meridian
for k=1:length(t)
    if t(k)>180
        t(k)=t(k)-360;
    elseif t(k)<-180
        t(k)=t(k)+180;
    end
end


%=========================================================
function y=norm360(x)
% map to range [0,360]
y=360*((x/360)-floor(x/360));


%=========================================================
function [Alt, Az]= AltAz(Lat,Lon,Dec,hour)
% [Alt, Az]= AltAz(Lat,Lon,Dec,hour)
%
%           all angles in degrees
%    Lat    Latitude of observer
%    Lon    Longitude of observer
%    Dec    Declination of object—angle from equator
%    hour   Local hour angle—angle of object from local meridian
```

```
%
%    Alt    Altitude, angle from horizon
%    Az     Azimuthal angle (0 to 360) east from north

Alt=asind(sind(Lat).*sind(Dec)+cosd(Lat).*cosd(Dec).*cosd(hour));
x=-cosd(Dec).*sind(hour);
y= (cosd(Lat).*sind(Dec)-sind(Lat).*cosd(Dec).*cosd(hour));
Az=norm360(atan2(x,y)*180/pi);


%=========================================================
function [d,m]=d2dm(dd)
% [d,m]=d2dm(dd) decimal degrees to degrees and minutes
% dd decimal degrees
% d  integer degrees
% m  decimal minutes

sgn=sign(dd);
dd=abs(dd);
d=sgn.*floor(abs(dd));
remainder=dd-abs(d);
m=remainder*60;
```

Nested functions

The basic function paradigm, emphasized in a previous section, is that each function has its own workspace, completely independent from the workspace of the program (or function) that invoked it. A *nested function* departs from that paradigm in a way that is sometimes useful. For one function to be nested inside another, each must have a terminating **end** statement. The structure of the nesting is shown schematically as follows:

```
function y=myfunc1(a, b, c)
    ...

    function  z=myfunc2(x)
        ...
    end


    ...
end
```

The **end** statements are, in this case, not optional, but rather essential to establish that one function is nested within the other function.

The key feature is that a nested function, in addition to having its own local workspace, inherits the workspace of the function in which it is nested. This means that variables defined in the outer function can be used in the nested function without having to formally pass them in through the function's arguments. This is shown in a simple example:

```
function E=func1(r)
    a=1.2;
    b=sqrt(2)/2;
    E1=(a+b)*r^2;
    E2=myfunc2(r);

    function  z=func2(x)
       kbar=7.3;
       z=a*sin(2*pi*x)+b*cos(2*pi*x)+kbar*x.^2;
    end

    E=E1+E2;
end
```

In this example, the nested function func2 has a purely local variable kbar, and uses the variables a and b defined in the outer function func1.

It's not usually a great idea to use nested functions. They make it harder to figure out which program is changing which variable. But, as we will see, nested functions do come to the rescue in a big way when using ordinary differential equation solvers and other functions that operate on functions.

Anonymous functions

Anonymous functions are one-line functions that can be defined within a script or another function. The purpose of using anonymous functions is to avoid having many individual function files with just one line of actual code in each of them.

The syntax for defining an anonymous function named aFunc, which is a function of one variable (here called x), is:

```
aFunc = @(x) <expression>;
```

The name to the left of the equals sign acts as the name of the function. The assignment statement actually creates a *function handle* variable named aFunc. Function handles are another MATLAB data type (like double or logical). The construction @(x) declares that the argument of the function here is x. The expression then must be a single MATLAB expression that evaluates the function in terms of the variable x. The variable x is local to the function definition, so it does not conflict with another variable with the same name elsewhere in your program. Both the value returned by the function and the argument to the function may be arrays.

```
% define spherical Bessel function of order 1
sBesselOne = @(x) sin(x)./x.^2-cos(x)./x;
```

```
%% plot the function
x=linspace(0, 12*pi, 200);
plot(x,sBesselOne(x))
grid on
```

If a function of two variable was needed, one would write @(x,y).

```
sinc2D= @(x,y) sin(sqrt(x.^2+y.^2))./sqrt(x.^2+y.^2);
```

For more information about anonymous functions, including how to pass the function handles as arguments or store them in arrays, see the MATLAB documentation.

Looking forward

For everything but short programs, one should be looking for ways to break up the problems into appropriate functions. This takes some skill and practice. It helps to keep a bird's-eye view of the problem, and to be thinking about future problems and little calculations that might recur several times. It's also important to keep an eye on the fundamental data structures that represent the problem you're solving and the algorithm you're using to solve it.

MATLAB GUI tools, introduced in Chapters 9 and 10, are comprised of one main function and many other functions, most of which are tied to events on the interface (like the user clicking a button or moving a slider). The main strategy will be to create a "primary model function" that represents your computational model. Certain user interface events will invoke the model function, which in turn can call other functions to calculate the model performance. To understand how various GUI tool functions communicate with each other will require familiarity with some new classes of data structures, to which we turn in the next chapter.

PROGRAMMING PROBLEMS

Example function:

```
    function Tc=f2c(Tf)
    % returns temperature in Celsius
        given
    % temperature in Fahrenheit
    Tc=(5/9)*(Tf-32);
```

Write MATLAB functions for the following:

```
    function y=yfmby(year)
1.  % returns the difference between
        given year and
    % my (your) birth year
```

2.
```
function Tf=c2f(Tc)
% returns temperature in
    Fahrenheit given
% temperature in Celsius
```

3.
```
function rv=reverse(v)
% reverses vector or string
% example:
% >>reverse([4 5 6])
% >> 6 5 4
```

4.
```
function [x, y]=pol2rect(r, theta);
% given circular coordinates
    r and theta
% returns rectangular
    coordinates x and y
```

5.
```
function vout=shuffle(vin)
% returns vector in random order
% (uses Matlab function randperm)
```

6. Write a program named `test1.m` that uses the function `fymby`, from Problem 1, and a `for` loop to produce a tabular output of your age in the years from 2009 to 2050. Output should look like this:

```
%
...
In 2015 I will turn 22.
In 2016 I will turn 23.
In 2017 I will turn 24.
In 2018 I will turn 25.
In 2019 I will turn 26.
In 2020 I will turn 27.
...
```

7. Write a program named `test2.m` that uses the function `c2f`, from Problem 2, and a `for` loop to produce a tabular output of temperatures in Celsius and Fahrenheit for T_c from 32° to 44° in steps of 2°Celsius. Output should look like this:

```
T(C)       T(F)
0          32
2          35.6
4          39.2
6          42.8
8          46.4
...
```

(Advanced) Try using the MATLAB function `sprintf` instead of `num2str` to make the tabular output look better.

8. Write and test a MATLAB function for simulating a roll of two dice:

```
function [die1, die2, resultstr]=rolldice;
% function [dice1,dice2,resultstr]=rolldice;
%    simulates roll of two fair dice
%   returns
%    die1    an integer in the range [1,6]
%    die2    an integer in the range [1,6]
%    resultstr   string with result (sumd=die1+die2)
%             'snake eyes'  sumd=2
%             'ace-deuce'   sumd=3
%             'yo'          sumd=11
%             'boxcars'     sumd=12
%             'natural'     sumd=7
%             'hard six'    3 3
%             'hard four'   2 2
```

This function should not write anything to the screen. Now write a MATLAB program `playdice` that does the following:

a. Set the number of throws, N, and a logical variable `printresults`.

b. Initialize the random number generator using `rng('shuffle')`.

c. (Optional, Advanced) Initialize an array `roll sums=zeros(1,12)` that will hold the number of times each possible outcome (from 2 to 12) occurs.

d. In the "calculate games" section, play N throws of the dice using a `for` loop. Play each throw using the `rolldice` function. Print out the results (one roll per line) like this:

```
..
Player rolls a 2 and a 5 : natural
Player rolls a 6 and a 2 :
Player rolls a 2 and a 1 : ace-deuce
Player rolls a 1 and a 4 :
Player rolls a 2 and a 6 :
Player rolls a 2 and a 2 : hard four
Player rolls a 6 and a 3 :
Player rolls a 3 and a 2 :
Player rolls a 3 and a 3 : hard six
Player rolls a 4 and a 1 :
Player rolls a 1 and a 3 :
Player rolls a 6 and a 6 : boxcars
...
```

e. (Optional, Advanced) Turn off the printout (`printresults=false`) and play N=1e5 times to collect statistics on how many times each result (from 2 to 12) occurs in `rollsums(2:12)`. At the end, make a bar chart of the percentages for each result using the `bar` command.

9. Solve the *birthday problem* by Monte Carlo simulation. The question to be answered is: given a group of N_{people} people, what is the probability that at least two of them will have birthdays on the same day? The goal of this program, `birthday.m` is to calculate this probability for N_{people} in the range [2, nPeopleMax].

Break the problem up into three programs: the main program `birthday.m`, a function `nRowsWith Match(M)`, and another function `vectorHas Match(v)`.

The function `hasMatch=vectorHasMatch(v)` takes a vector argument and returns a value of true if the vector has as least one pair of identical elements. (Hint: Use the MAT-LAB function `sort` to first sort the vector, and then search it for *adjoining* elements that are identical.)

The function `m=nRowsWithMatch(M)` takes a matrix as an argument and returns an integer that is the number of rows of the matrix with at least one pair of identical elements. (Hint: Use the MATLAB function `size` to get the number of rows and columns of the matrix, then loop through each row and call `vectorHasMatch` to determine if that row has a match.)

The main program `birthday` should use `randi` to set up an Nsets × Npeople array of integers between 1 and 365. The number of sets (once the program is debugged) should be larger than 5000. For each such array, find nM, the number of rows with at least one match. The probability of a birthday match is then just nM/Nsets. Tabulate that probability for the various values of `Npeople` in the given range and plot the results. Try plotting using the `bar` command.

10. **Ticker text.** Write a function `tickerText(s,iwidth, dt)` that displays the string `s` scrolling through a text window with width `iwidth`. The parameter `dt` gives the length of the pause after piece of text is displayed. For example, the following would be displayed scrolling across the Command window (here shown at each snapshot in time).

```
>> tickerText('Sic transit gloria mundi!', 8, 0.1)
       s a
      Si
    Sic
   Sic
  Sic t
  Sic tr
  Sic tra
 Sic tran
 ic trans
 c transi
  transit
 transit
 ransit g
 ansit gl
 nsit glo
 sit glor
 it glori
```

```
t gloria
 gloria
gloria m
loria mu
oria mun
ria mund
ia mundi
a mundi!
 mundi!
mundi!
undi!
ndi!
di!
i!
!
```

11. **Rotation cypher.**   Characters are represented internally in MATLAB by the standard integer ASCII code. The `char` and `double` functions will convert back and forth between the alphanumeric character and its associated ASCII code.

```
>> v=double('Hello!')
v =
    72   101   108   108   111   33
>> s=char(v)
s =
Hello!
```

The 72 corresponds to "H," 101 to "e," etc. Here we will use the 94 codes for printable ASCII characters from 32 (space) up to 125 ("]") to make a rotation cipher. Think of the numbers from 32 to 125 on a circle:

$$[\ldots 32, 33, 34, \ldots, 124, 125, 32, 33, \ldots] \qquad (7.1)$$

The cipher consists of replacing each character with ASCII code N with the character corresponding to the code 47 steps to the right around the circle. Write a function `so=rot47(si)` that returns the input string encrypted in this way. Using the function again should decrypt the string.

```
>> s=rot47('Abort mission.')
              % plaintext
s =
p3@CEO>:DD:@?] % cyphertext
>> rot47(s)
ans =
Abort mission.
              % decoded cyphertext
```

12. **Josephus problem.** The Josephus problem takes its name from a historical incident in the Jewish revolt against the Romans. Flavius Josephus was a Jewish military leader who, with his men, became trapped in a cave by the Romans. Rather than surrender, they were determined to kill themselves and Josephus suggested the following technique. They formed a circle and starting with the first man, selected the third man to be killed by his neighbor. The next two live men were skipped and the third killed, and so on around the circle until only one man is left alive. This turned out to be Josephus. He decided to surrender to and aid the Roman forces, and subsequently went on to write the important book *The Jewish War*, chronicling the destruction of the Jewish state. The Josephus problem is motivated by the suspicion that Josephus could have done the math and selected just the right initial position in the circle to assure his survival.

   a. Consider the problem of N people arranged in a circle, initially all in the "live" state. Moving around the circle set the state of the kth live person to "dead." Continue until one person, whose initial position was j, survives. Write a MATLAB function `j=Josephus(N, k)`, which returns the survivable position. [Check: `Josephus(10, 2)` should return 5].

   b. Extend the function to return an $N \times N$ array M of ones and zeros, representing alive and dead, encoding the history turn by turn. The first row of M should be all ones, the last row has a single one in the jth column. The syntax should be `[j, M]=Josephus(N, k)`. Write a program that calls the function to get M and devise a graphical display of the deadly history.

13. **Clipping a vector.** Write a function `vout=clipVec(v, vmin, vmax)` that copies the input vector `v` to the output vector `vout`, except if a value is greater than `vmax` or less than `vmin`. Values greater than `vmax` are set to `vmax` and values less than `vmin` are set to `vmin`.

   Check by running this test, which should plot a sine wave clipped level at the tops and bottoms.

   ```
   x=linspace(0, 3, 300);
   y=sin(2*pi*x);
   plot(x,clipVec(y, -0.9, 0.9));
   axis([0, 3, -1, 1]);
   ```

14. **Swap.** Write a function that returns the values of the two inputs in reversed order: `function [a,b]=swap(x, y)`. To use it to swap the values of two variables simply write `[v1,v2]=swap(v1,v2)`.

15. **Check if sorted.**

   a. Write a function `tf=isSortedAscending(v)` that returns true if each element of the vector `v` is greater than or equal to the preceding element.

   b. Write a function `tf=isSortedDescending(v)` that returns true if each elements of the vector `v` is less than or equal to the preceding element.

   c. Write a function `tf=isSorted(v)` that returns true if `v` is sorted in either ascending or descending order.

16. **Boggle sort.** Write a function `vout=boggleSort(v)` that uses the following terrible algorithm: repeatedly rearrange the elements of `v` randomly until they are sorted. Use the `isSortedAscending` function you've already written, and the MATLAB function

randperm(n), which will generate a vector with a random permutation of the first *n* integers. The expression v=v(randperm(length(v))) randomly rearranges v. Test by sorting nine random integers. (Only try this method on short lists—it's terribly slow.)

```
bogglesort(randi(100, 1, 9))
```

To boggle sort a deck of cards, one would first check to see if the cards are already sorted, then repeatedly throw the cards into the air, randomly pick them back up, and see if they're sorted yet.

17. **Guess sort.** Write a function vout=guessSort (v) that sorts the input vector in ascending order by the following algorithm. Randomly pick two elements of the vector, and if the left element (lower index) is greater than the right element, swap the two elements. Repeat until the vector is sorted. This method is better than a boggle sort, but is still very slow.

18. **Bubble sort.** A respectable sorting method is the bubble sort. Examine in turn each element of the vector and it's neighbor to the right. If they're in the wrong order, swap them. Continue going repeatedly through the vector in this way until the whole vector has been traversed once with no swaps.

   a. Write a function vout=bubbleSort(v) that sorts a vector by this method.

   b. Write a function vout=bubbleSortVisualized(v) that creates a visual representation of the bubble sort in progress. The visualization doesn't need to work for really long vectors.

19. **Vector utilities.**

   a. Write a function vout=vInsertAfter(v, x, k) that inserts the value x into the vector v after the k*th* entry.

   b. Write a function vout=vDelete(v, k) that deletes the k*th* entry of the vector v, returning a shorter vector.

20. **Insertion sort.** An insertion sort corresponds to the way people often sort a hand of cards. Given a vector *v* to sort, make a new vector *vout*. Copy each element of *v* into the appropriate position in *vout*. To determine the appropriate position, examine in order each possible insertion point in *vout*. Write a function vout=insertionSort(v) that implements this algorithm.

21. **Rotate vector.** Write a function sout=vrotate(v,k) that returns a vector (or string) circularly rotated by k spaces. If k is positive, rotate forward; if k is negative rotate backward.

```
>> vrotate('washington', 3)
ans =
tonwashing
>> vrotate('washington', -3)
ans =
hingtonwas
```

22. **Rounded step function.** Write an anonymous MATLAB function that evaluates the Fermi function.

$$f(x, \delta) = \frac{1}{1 + e^{x/\delta}} \tag{7.2}$$

Plot the function on $x = [-1, 1]$ for $\delta = [0.001, 0.01, 0.05, 0.1, 0.2, 0.4]$.

23. **Anagrams.** Write a function `dispAnagrams(s,n)` that displays n anagrams of the string `s`. Use `randperm` to generate the anagrams. (There is no guarantee that an anagram will not be repeated with this method.)

More MATLAB Data Classes and Structures

We have already seen and used several classes of MATLAB data: `double`, representing real numbers; `char`, representing character data; and `logical`, representing Boolean data. Arrays can be formed from each of these. One-dimensional arrays of `char` we call "strings."

```
v=-1.234;               % double
vec=[1, 2.2, 4];        % vector of double
M=[4, 1; 2, 1.2];       % 2D array of double = matrix

keypressed='k';         % char
myline='now go';        % 1D array of char = string
CM=[ ['a', 'b']; ['c', 'd'] ];  % 2D array of char

isDone=true;            % logical
switchIsOn=[true, false, false, true]; % vector of logical
isBig=(M>1);            % matrix of logical
```

There are several other MATLAB data classes that will prove useful. The first two are examples of *heterogenous aggregation*, that is, gathering information of different types together into one container, i.e., a MATLAB variable. Cell arrays are an extension of the by-now-familiar array idea to include different types of data as elements in the array. Structures, the class `struct`, aggregate different types of data that are labeled by names, rather than by indices. These would be more advanced topics we could differ to later but for the fact that a particular structure, called `handles`, plays a crucial role in managing GUI tool operation, as described in the next two chapters. We therefore need to have at least a nodding familiarity with structures. Cell arrays also come into play in transferring data between programs as well as handling sets of strings.

This chapter also describes the complex class, a straightforward extension of the real number `double` class. Many problems in engineering and science use complex numbers.

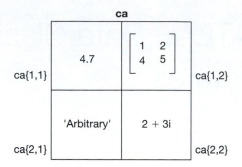

FIGURE 8.1 A cell array can contain different data types. Each element is referenced by integer indices within curly brackets.

Function handles are a class that allows a function to operate on other functions, passed to it as inputs. This is useful for several mathematical operations described in Chapter 14.

This chapter is brief because, for our purposes, a basic familiarity with these ideas will suffice.

8.1 Cell arrays

MATLAB cell arrays allow the aggregation of data of different types and sizes into a one- or two-dimensional array of elements, indexed by row and column numbers. The heterogeneous nature of the individual elements is the unique feature. For example, a 2×2 cell array could be composed of a number, a matrix, a string, and a complex number. Curly brackets are used to index the cell array elements.

```
ca{1,1}=4.7;
ca{1,2}=[1, 2; 4, 5];
ca{2,1}='Arbitrary';
ca{2,2}=2+3i;
```

This is illustrated schematically in Figure 8.1. A particular element in the cell array can be further indexed to retrieve elements of it. So, to access the (2, 2) element of the previous matrix we use cell array indexing (with curly brackets) followed by array indexing (with round brackets).

```
>>disp(ca{1,1});
      4.7000
>>disp( ca{1,2}(2,2) );
     5
>>disp( ca{2,1}(3:5) );
bit
```

Cell arrays of strings are particularly useful in that they allow us to store a set of strings that have different lengths. The alternative, a two-dimensional array of char, would require each row to be the same length. For example, the following creates a 1×4 cell array of strings called Partners and prints the listing.

```
Partners={'Warpe', 'Wistfull', 'Kubitschek', 'McMingus'};
disp(['The law partners: ']);
for ip=1:4
   disp([blanks(17), Partners{ip}])
end
```

```
The law partners:
                 Warpe
                 Wistfull
                 Kubitschek
                 McMingus
```

8.2 Structures

Arrays and cell arrays aggregate individual data elements into higher-level composite objects. The individual elements are then referenced using one or more integer indices. It is sometimes useful to aggregate different kinds of data by referring to the different components using a *name* rather than an index. The MATLAB struct class creates higher level composite objects, but allows the different components to be specified using names, here called *fields*. A specific item of data is specified by postfixing a period and field name to the name of the struct variable. For example, information about a book might include its author, copyright year, title, and number of pages.

```
myMathbook.title='Beginning Group Theory';
myMathbook.author='Albert Magus';
myMathbook.year=2002;
myMathbook.npages=482;
```

The field names here are title, author, year, and npages. There is no important ordering of these fields. The book's publication year could be displayed with the command:

```
disp(['Publication year: ', num2str(myMathbook.year)]);
```

As with other MATLAB classes, the struct's can be further aggregated into arrays. For example, several books might be put into the mybooks array of struct.

```
mybooks(1)=myMathbook;
mybooks(2).title= 'The Way of the Samurai';
mybooks(2).author='Kanji Fujimori';
mybooks(2).year=   1995;
mybooks(2).npages= 186;

mybooks(3).title= 'Physics for the Perplexed';
mybooks(3).author='Ronald Ballistic';
mybooks(3).year=   2005;
mybooks(3).npages= 827;
...
nBooks=length(mybooks);
% pick a random book
thisBook=mybooks(randi(nBooks, 1));
disp(['Book selected: ', thisBook.title]);
```

As mentioned previously, structures will play an important role in programming the graphical interface.

8.3 Complex numbers

An extension of the `double` class represents complex numbers by storing the real and imaginary parts as double-precision numbers. The variables i and j are both initialized to $\sqrt{-1}$. Thus, one can write z=1+2*i to enter a complex value. In addition, the special syntax 1+2i can be used without requiring a multiplication symbol (*). Complex numbers can thus be entered in several ways.

```
z=complex(4, 5);
z1=4+5i;                    % unique complex syntax
z2=1.2+4.1j;                % unique complex syntax
z3=7.1+2.1*i;
z4=1.2*exp(i*pi/6);         % polar form of complex number
z5=sqrt(-26);
```

Most MATLAB operators and functions work with complex arguments as well as real arguments. One exception is the `plot` function, which normally requires real-valued arguments. Some useful functions for working with complex-valued variables are listed:

`complex(a, b)`	returns the complex number $a+ib$
`real(z)`	real part of z
`imag(z)`	imaginary part of z
`abs(z)`	modulus of z
`angle(z)`	phase angle of z in radians
`conj(z)`	complex conjugate of z

8.4 Function handles

A function handle is the encoded address of a function in memory. Function handles permit one to pass a function as an argument to another function, and more generally to treat the function as a type of data. If a function myfun is defined, the handle to it can be obtained simply by writing @myfun. In the following example, the function myPlotter receives a function handle as its first argument. It can invoke the function by using the name of the handle as though it were the name of a function.

```
function myMain
figure(1)
myPlotter(@sin, -2*pi, 2*pi);
figure(2)
myPlotter(@cos, -2*pi, 2*pi);
```
```
function myPlotter(fun, a, b)
% plot function fun from a to b
Nx=200;
x=linspace(a, b, Nx)
y=fun(x);
plot(x, y)
```

This is particularly useful in creating so-called function functions, functions that take other functions as arguments. Examples discussed in Chapter 14 include functions for integrating other functions, for finding minima of functions, and for solving differential equations.

8.5 Other data classes and data structures

Several other data classes are largely beyond our scope here and we mention them briefly. Learn more from the MATLAB documentation.

Integers can be stored more compactly in memory using one of the integer classes: int8, int16, int32, int64, uint8, uint16, uint32, and uint64. The number indicates the number of bits that are used to store the information; the "u" indicates that the numbers represented are unsigned (assumed positive). Images are often stored using arrays of unsigned integers representing the strength of each color signal in each pixel.

The amount of memory required to store real numbers is also less for the single (single-precision) class than for the default double class.

Matrices that have few nonzero elements can be efficiently stored and manipulated using the sparse matrix class sparse and manipulated with an associated set of functions.

Multidimensional arrays, for example Bfield(ix, iy, iz), can also be useful. Three-dimensional arrays can be thought of as matrices, comprised of rows and columns, arranged in sheets. RGB image arrays can be stored as $N \times M$ arrays, where each of the three $N \times M$ sheets holds the red, green, and blue information.

PROGRAMMING PROBLEMS

1. Consider a (very small) class with the following students and their GPA's.

Student name	GPA
Alfonso Bedoya	3.43
Tonya Harding	2.77
Warren Harding	2.30
Warren Piece	3.25

   Write a MATLAB program, `ProcessStudents.m`, that constructs `students`, a one-dimensional array of structures with fields named `firstname`, `lastname`, and `gpa`. It should then loop through each element in the array and call a function `DisplayStudentRecord(theStudent)` (which you also need to write) that displays data for each student on the screen. This function should take a single student structure as an argument.

   ```
   function DisplayStudentRecord(theStudent)
   % function Display_StudentRecord(theStudent)
   % displays theStudent.firstname, theStudent.lastname,
   %          and theStudent.gpa
   ```

2. Write a MATLAB program, `ShowPoem.m`, that constructs `poemlines`, a one-dimensional cell array of strings. Use an appropriate brief poem or part of a poem of your choosing. It should call a function (which you also need to write) `DisplayCellText` that displays the poem on the screen. The function should take a single-cell array of strings as an argument.

   ```
   function DisplayCellText(castring)
   % function DisplayCellText(castring)
   %      input castring is a cell-array of string
   %      the function displays each line of castring
   %        to form a block of text on the screen
   ```

3. **Magic 8Ball.** A Magic 8Ball uses an icosahedral die floating in a dark liquid to randomly produce an answer to a yes-or-no question. Write a program `MagicEightBall.m` that simulates this. Use a cell array of strings to store the twenty possible responses shown as follows and randomly select an answer to display to the user.

It is certain	It is decidedly so	Without a doubt
Yes—definitely	You may rely on it	As I see it, yes
Most likely	Outlook good	Yes
Signs point to yes	Reply hazy, try again	Ask again later
Better not tell you now	Cannot predict now	Concentrate and ask again
Don't count on it	My reply is no	My sources say no
Outlook not so good	Very doubtful	

4. **Break into words.**   Write a function `wordsca=breakIntoWords(s)` that returns a cell array of strings containing the words in the given string. Words are here defined as any set of non-blank characters separated by blanks. You may want to use the built-in function `strtrim` that removes leading and trailing white space.

5. **Reverse words.**   Write a function `sout=reverseWords(s)` that returns a string containing the words in the original string in reverse order, separated by blanks.

6. **Scramble words.**   Write a function `sout=scrambleWords(s)` that returns a string containing the words in the original string in random order, separated by blanks. (Use the function `randperm`.)

Building GUI Tools

Building a Graphical User Interface

The graphical user interface development environment (GUIDE) enables the rapid creation of a graphical user interface (GUI) for a MATLAB program. In this chapter we will introduce the GUIDE program and describe how to use it in basic GUI deployment. GUIDE is used to build the GUI, which can then be connected to a program, through a process we will describe in the next chapter. The GUI is contained in two files, a figure file with the suffix `.fig`, which contains graphical layout information, and an m-file with suffix `.m`, which contains the main GUI function and a number of subfunctions. This latter file is written in template form by GUIDE, and can be edited to add functionality and connect with other functions.

This chapter and the chapter that follows are very tutorial. Much of the information to be conveyed is visual and procedural. The goal is to provide a fairly complete and detailed explanation of the process of GUI creation. A perhaps unfortunate side-effect of this level of detail is that it can leave the reader with the impression that the process is more complex than it is in reality. It actually is not that hard; just a few concepts and processes suffice.

9.1 Getting started with GUIDE

To start GUIDE, type `guide` (no capitals) at the command prompt in the Command window.

```
>> guide
```

The GUIDE Quick Start window will appear, as shown in Figure 9.1.

Choose the default option, "Blank GUI" by pressing "OK" or the [Enter] key. The GUIDE window will then appear with the window name "untitled.fig" as shown in Figure 9.2.

The window has three areas: (a) on the top are the menus and the menu bar, (b) the left side has buttons to select particular GUI objects, and (c) the main figure-design area starts as a blank panel with grid marks on it. This panel is where the various GUI objects will be placed.

147

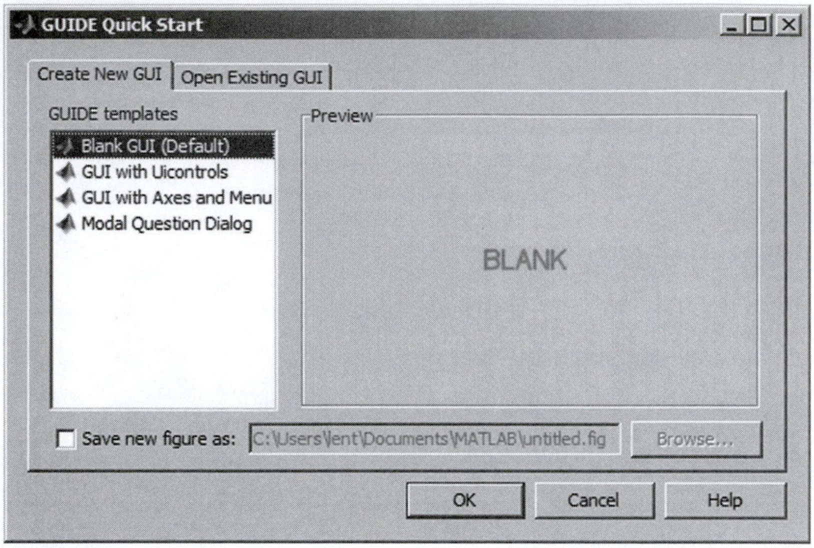

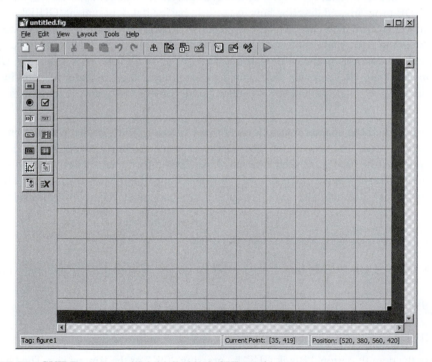

FIGURE 9.1   The GUIDE Quick Start window.

FIGURE 9.2   GUIDE window with initially blank GUI panel.

The GUIDE window can be resized by grabbing the lower right corner with the mouse and stretching. The GUI figure panel inside can be sized by clicking and dragging on the black square in the lower right corner. Individual controls can be positioned on the figure by clicking on an icon button on the left and dragging a GUI element into position. Try it

Push button		Slider
Radio button		Checkbox
Edit textbox		Static textbox
Pop-up menu		Listbox
Togglebutton		Table
Axes		Panel
Button group		ActiveX control

FIGURE 9.3   Selection of GUI objects in GUIDE.

out—drag several items over and position them on the main figure area. A GUI is designed by positioning and setting the properties of these GUI elements. Most of these GUI objects are instances of a MATLAB class called `uicontrol` (user interface controls).

The GUI objects you can create using the buttons on the left panel of GUIDE are:

- push button – A button that activates when the user clicks the mouse on it.
- slider – Enter a real number by adjusting the position of the slide.
- radio button – Changes its state from unselected to selected and back.
- checkbox – Changes state from selected (checked) to unselected (unchecked).
- edit textbox – Allows the user to input information by typing text into the window.
- static textbox – Displays some text; useful for labeling items or reporting the results of a calculation.
- pop-up menu – Gives the user a list of options from which one may be selected.
- listbox – Presents a list of options that can be scrolled. Several items can be selected at the same time.
- toggle button – Pressed once, it stays down until it is pressed again.
- table – Displays data in a tabular form.
- axes – A surface on which to display two-dimensional and three-dimensional graphics.
- panel – Groups controls together visually.
- button group – Groups a set of radio buttons or toggle buttons so that they act together with the result that only one at a time is selected.
- activeX control (Windows) – allows the insertion of an ActiveX control made by another program. (Only use these if you really know what you're doing; improperly configured controls can crash MATLAB.)

You can adjust the size of a GUI object by clicking on it once to make it the current object, and then dragging the sizing handles, which appear when it's selected. You can make small adjustments in the position of the object using the arrow keys. It is a good idea to experiment

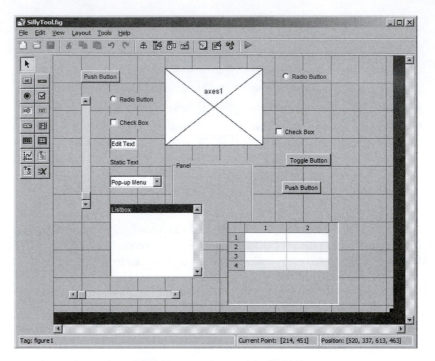

FIGURE 9.4 Arranging various GUI objects on the panel in GUIDE.

with this by dragging several items onto the figure. The GUI objects won't yet respond and the tool you construct won't be useful, just experimental.

Saving the GUI to a file

Name and save the GUI you have made by selecting File|Save As and entering the name—here enter "SillyTool" (don't type the quotes) and press Save or [Enter]. It is a *very* helpful practice to name each GUI file with the suffix "Tool" to distinguish the sort of code it contains.

> *NOTE: This convention may seem unnecessary but experience proves it to be very very helpful. I urge you to follow it. Choose names for GUI-based programs of the form* <Name>Tool.

At this point GUIDE does two things, each wonderful in its own way.

1. GUIDE saves all the information you have designed into the GUI, i.e., all the geometric information and all the properties of every GUI object you put in the frame, into a file named SillyTool.fig.

2. GUIDE also creates a file called SillyTool.m, stores it in the current MATLAB folder, and loads it into the MATLAB editor. This file contains the program that creates and executes the GUI tool you have made.

Look in the Current Folder window (you may need to click the Current Folder tab) and notice that these two files have been created: SillyTool.fig and SillyTool.m. The figure file (*.fig)

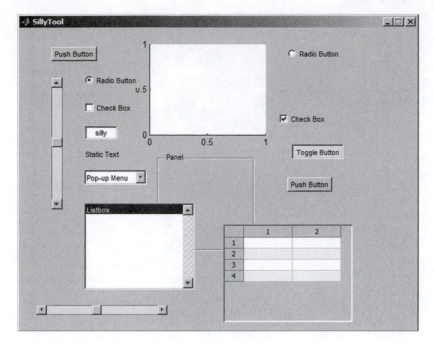

FIGURE 9.5 SillyTool running.

is not directly human-readable. It is a binary file that encodes the information about your GUI design. Such a figure file is meant to be edited only by using the GUIDE program. The file SillyTool.m is, by contrast, just MATLAB code that GUIDE has generated and which, when executed, will launch and run the tool. It is comprised of a series of functions, most of which are just stubs to be filled in later.

You may notice that MATLAB took control and put you into the main MATLAB window with the file `SillyTool.m` loaded in the editor. We won't explore the file `SillyTool.m` at this point—it's chock-full of interesting things but is likely a little mystifying and potentially overwhelming right now. Ignore it. But do run the file by pressing the green Run button on the EDITOR tab.

When you do, you should see your SillyTool running in its own window. Play with each of the graphic elements and see how they perform. Many won't be very impressive just yet; you will learn how to configure them so they do useful things. But notice the basic behavior of the push button compared to the toggle button, the checkbox, the radio button, etc. When you are done, exit SillyTool by clicking on the "close button" at the top corner of the panel (red x on the top right for Windows, red circle on the top left for Mac). Close the GUIDE window similarly.

9.2 Starting an action with a GUI element

One way in which GUI elements allow the user to interact with the code is familiar to everyone—click a button. This is an example of a general pattern: The user activates a specific GUI element, usually by a mouse click over the element, and this initiates some

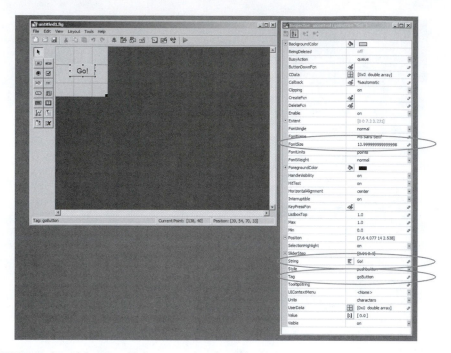

FIGURE 9.6 A push button with its properties altered in the Property Inspector.

action on the part of the program. Let's explore how that works by making a very simple GUI, consisting of a single button.

Launch GUIDE again from the Command window by typing "guide" at the prompt. In the GUIDE Quickstart panel, select the option to create a blank GUI (rather than to open an existing GUI file). When the GUIDE window appears, select the push button icon from the panel of uicontrols on the left, and drag a push button onto the panel surface.

The button initially says "Push Button" on it. Let's alter this, so the button's label will be different. This is an example of editing the Properties of a uicontrol. To change a property of the button, or any object, double-click on it and the Property Inspector window will pop up. All of the properties of the specific GUI object appear in this window and can be edited. The name of each property is listed in the left column and the value of each property is listed in the corresponding row of the right column.

At this point we'll change three properties:

1. Slide down to the Tag property and change its value from "pushbutton1" to "goButton." Tag names are very important, so be careful to name it this way exactly (no quote marks, no spaces, capitalization just as shown).

2. Edit the String property and change its value from "Push Button" to "Go!".

3. Edit the FontSize property and change its value from 10.0 to 14.

The button now has a new label and a new name. The label on the button is determined by the value of the String property, which in this case is now "Go!". The value of the Tag

FIGURE 9.7   StartTool running in its own window.

property is a string (with no spaces) which uniquely identifies this particular object and constitutes the name of the object. The name of the button is now `goButton`. The Tag property should be chosen carefully and with consistency.

Close the Property Inspector. Now resize the panel using the black square in the lower right-hand corner. Save the .fig file in GUIDE with the name `StartTool`. Run the tool this time by typing the name of the GUI m-file at the command prompt.

```
>> StartTool
```

StartTool should now appear in its own window.

The tool works, in the very limited sense that the button behaves appropriately when clicked, but it's fairly unsatisfying in that pressing the button accomplishes nothing. To make it accomplish something, we need to edit the file `StartTool.m`, which is already loaded into the editor.

In the MATLAB Editor window, scroll through the StartTool.m code that GUIDE has generated. It consists of four functions:

- `StartTool` – This is the main function; it creates the tool itself.
- `StartTool_OpeningFcn` – This executes when the function is started up. This is the place to put many different kinds of initialization steps. Right now it can be ignored.
- `StartTool_OutputFcn` – This function is for more advanced uses. Ignore it now and for a long time.
- `goButton_Callback` – This function is executed when the goButton is pressed and released.

Our focus now is on the `goButton_Callback` function. Callback functions are associated with particular GUI objects and are executed when an object is activated. A button like `goButton` is activated when the user presses and releases it. Every time that happens, the function `goButton_Callback` is executed. Notice that GUIDE created the name of the callback function based on the name of the object (i.e., the value of its Tag) with which it's associated. Since this button is named goButton, the callback function that GUIDE made is named goButton_Callback.

Right now the function goButton_Callback does nothing. To make it more interesting, we need to add code to the body of the function. In the Editor, add one line to the function as follows:

```
% ──── Executes on button press in goButton.
function goButton_Callback(hObject, eventdata, handles)
% hObject     handle to goButton (see GCBO)
% eventdata   reserved - to be defined in a future version
    of MATLAB
% handles     structure with handles and user data (see GUIDATA)
disp('Go, go, go, world!');  % <── inserted this line
```

In the Editor, save the file. The tool itself should still be running (it should be running in its own window, not being edited in GUIDE; if it is not, restart it by pressing the green Run button on the EDITOR tab). Now press the goButton button again, and you should see the results appear in the Command window.

```
>> Go, go, go, world!
>>
```

Any set of commands you put in the callback function (and save) will be executed when the button is pressed. Try it out and write some code in the callback function, then save the file and press the button. Note that you do not need to relaunch the tool (StartTool.m) each time you make a modification. The callback function is a significant factor in the power of GUI tools. You can give the user the ability to make choices through a graphical interface and the program will respond.

The body of the callback function can, of course, include the invocation of other functions. This is most often what you will want to do. If you make your own function, stored in a separate file myFunction.m, you can make it run when the button is pressed by inserting a call to it in the body of the button's callback function.

9.3 Communicating with GUI elements

In the previous section we learned how to make the GUI object activate other program components through the mechanism of the *callback function*. Now we want to examine how to operate from the other side—how a program can (a) get information from a GUI object, and (b) how it can change the properties of the GUI object dynamically.

Building SliderTool

Close all other GUI tools and GUIDE. Make a new folder in your MATLAB folder called SliderTool and navigate to it in MATLAB so it becomes the current folder.

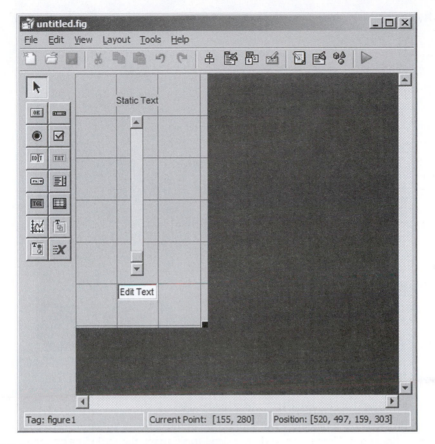

FIGURE 9.8 Laying out SliderTool GUI in GUIDE.

You can do this from within the Current Folder browser by pulling down the menu on the right of the browser tab and selecting "New Folder." Start GUIDE and open a new GUI panel. Drag a slider, an edit textbox, and a static textbox onto the panel and adjust the panel size to be appropriate. It should look something like Figure 9.8.

The next step is to change some of the properties of these three objects using the Property Inspector. Double-click on an object to view the table of properties and the value of each property in the Property Inspector. Each property has a specified value, which may be of any MATLAB class: a string, a number, a vector of numbers, a cell array, or a function handle, and may be restricted in the values it can take. The concept of specifying the *state* of an object by a series of *property-value* pairs is an important one. The notation here will be to capitalize the name of the specific property that is being discussed: String, Tag, Min, Max, etc. Some objects, such as sliders, have a property named Value, so it's sometimes necessary to refer to the value of the Value property.

You can find out more information about a specific property, and which values it may take, by right-clicking (command-click for Macs) over the property name in the Property Inspector and then clicking on the "What's this?" button that appears. There are also full descriptions of the properties associated with the objects of various classes in the MATLAB

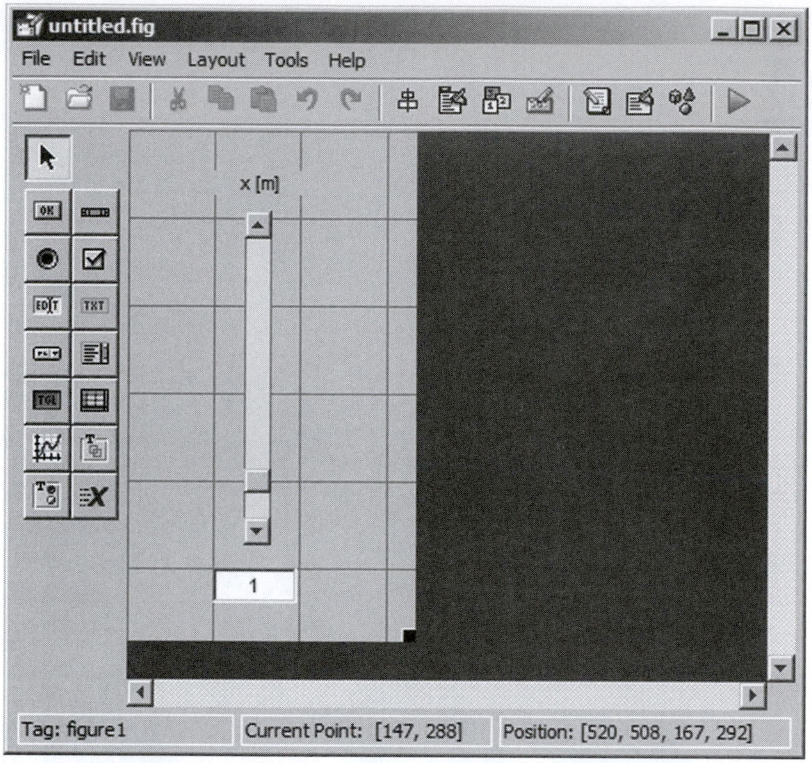

FIGURE 9.9 SliderTool GUI in GUIDE with edited properties.

online Product Help. For example, search for: uicontrol properties, axes properties, uimenu properties, uibuttongroup properties, etc. These are very helpful references.

Using the Property Inspector, make the following changes to the objects:

- Set the value of the Tag for the slider to "xSlider."

- Set the value of the Value property of the slider to 1.0. Because the Value property for many objects can be a vector, it is set using a pop-up panel activated by clicking the icon to the right of the word "Value' in the property list. This will pop up the Value Panel, which allows you to edit the value. Click on the present value (0) and change it to 1; then press OK.

- Change the Max property, which sets the maximum value of the slider, from 1.0 to 10.

- Set the value of the Tag property of the edit text object to "xText."

- Set the value of the String property of the textbox to "1."

- Set the value of the String property of the static text object to "x[m]." We suppose that we are going to use this slider to allow the user to set the value of a physical position x, given in units of meters. The user will be able to adjust the value of x to be between 0 and 10.

Close the Property Inspector.

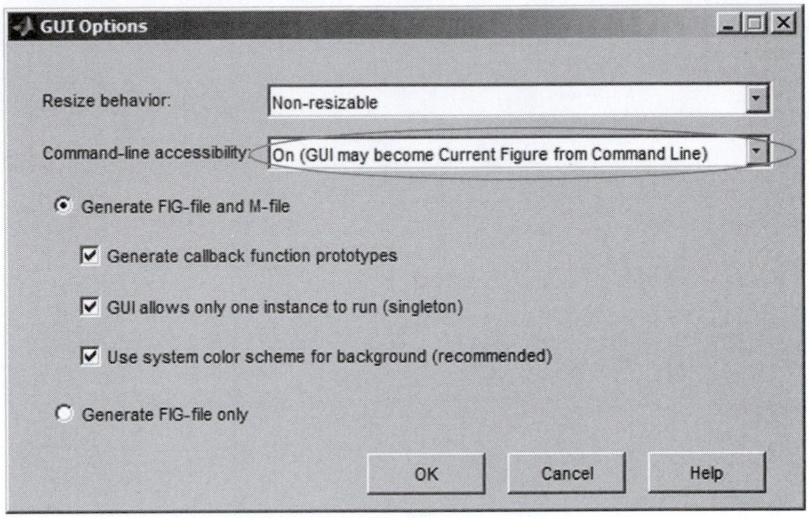

FIGURE 9.10 Changing the GUI Options panel.

We will refer to setting the value of the Tag property of an object as "naming the object" because the value of the Tag functions as the unique name of each object. The value of each object's Tag should be unique to that object and should not include spaces or punctuation. Pick names of this form: xSlider, xText, v0Slider, KinitialText, recalibrateButton, energyAxes, pressureSlider, etc. The first part of the name describes the quantity or variable being represented or input; the second part of the name reflects the class of the object and is capitalized. Following this convention consistently prevents many errors. God gave humans the authority to name things—use it wisely.

In this case we did not bother to name the static text object because it was being used simply as a label. In some cases, a static text object is used to output information from the program to the user by setting its `String` property. In that case, it is important to name it appropriately.

Communicating with GUI elements from the command line

In order to communicate with a GUI object, we need to know the *handle* of the object. A handle is the address of the object in the computer's memory, encoded by MATLAB as a real number. To create GUI tools, GUIDE will provide a convenient mechanism for obtaining the handle of each GUI object (through the `handles` structure discussed in the next chapter). It is useful for pedagogical purposes to get the handle directly at the command line. To do that, we are going to take an unusual step that won't normally need to be done. On the GUIDE menu bar select "Tools|GUI options." When the GUI Options panel appears, change the "Command-line accessibility" setting to "On (GUI may become Current Figure from Command Line)."

Then press OK. Making changes in the GUI Options panel is not usually necessary because we don't normally need to communicate with the GUI objects from the MATLAB Command window.

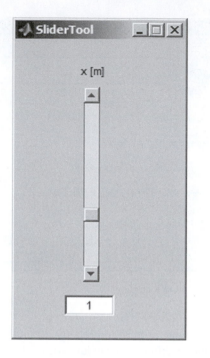

FIGURE 9.11 SliderTool.

Save the figure file (with "File | Save As . . .") under the name SliderTool.

Run the program by pressing the green Run button on the EDITOR tab. The running tool should look something like Figure 9.11.

Communicating with the slider

We would like to experiment with getting information to and from GUI elements. For this experiment, undock the Command window by clicking on the menu button at the top right corner of the Command window and selecting "Undock." It will pop out of the MATLAB IDE.

Minimize the IDE and arrange your desktop so that the Command window and SliderTool are right next to each other, as in Figure 9.12.

To communicate with the slider, we need to get its handle. This can be done interactively using the findobj command, which searches for an object with a specific property-value pair. The general syntax is:

```
h=findobj(<Property>, <Value>);
```

The findobj command returns a handle to the object whose <Property> matches the specified <Value>. If more than one object satisfies the match criterion, a vector of handles is returned. If no object matches, an empty matrix is returned. Since we want to communicate

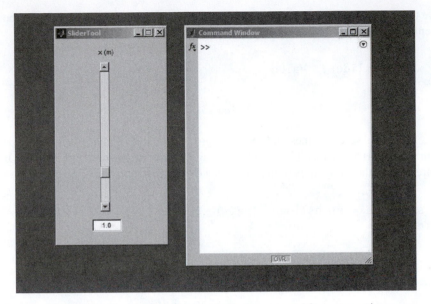

FIGURE 9.12   SliderTool and undocked Command window prepared for conversation.

with the slider, we'll use the Tag property and look for a match with "xSlider." Type the following in the Command window (with no terminating semicolon).

```
hslider=findobj('Tag', 'xSlider')
```

If this is successful, you should see a real value returned in the variable `hslider`.

```
>> hslider=findobj('Tag', 'xSlider')
hslider =
   177.0017
```

The specific value you obtain may be different than this. The actual value of the handle can vary from MATLAB session to session. If the value of the `Tag` specified in the `findobj` command does not match *exactly* with the one you assigned in GUIDE, you will get an empty matrix.

```
>> hslider=findobj('Tag', 'xslider')
hslider =
    Empty matrix: 0-by-1
```

With the handle to the slider in hand (so to speak), one can ask the slider to report on its state. This is accomplished with the `get` command. Often the thing we most want to know about the slider is its value, that is, where the slide is positioned along its length. (There is potential for confusion here because "Value" is the name of a particular property of the slider— the value of the Value property is a number representing the position of the slider.)

Move the slider to an arbitrary position and then use the `get` command to inquire about the present value of Value as follows.

```
>> x=get(hslider, 'Value')
x =
    6.8966
```

Move the slider several times and redo the `get` command (perhaps using the up-arrow command recall) to see that it is indeed returning the present position of the slider. One can inquire about other properties of the slider as well, for instance, the Max property.

```
>> sliderMax=get(hslider, 'Max')
sliderMax =
    10
```

The general form of the `get` command is:

```
<var>=get(<handle>, <Property name>);
```

Having the handle of the slider allows one to address that particular slider. A colloquial interpretation of the `get` command is something like:

```
get(hslider, 'Max')      "Hey slider, what is is the value of your Max property?"
get(hslider, 'Min')      "Hey slider, what is is the value of your Min property?"
get(hslider, 'Value')    "Hey slider, what is is the value of your Value property?"
```

We can also tell the slider, or any other GUI object, to *change* the values of its properties. And it will obey if we do it correctly. The general form of the `set` command is:

```
set(<handle>, <Property name>, <Property value>);
```

Try setting the value of the slider using the `set` command repeatedly and watch it change its state:

```
>> set(hslider, 'Value', 0.5)
>> set(hslider, 'Value', 1)
>> set(hslider, 'Value', 10)
>> set(hslider, 'Value', 9)
```

Try setting the slider's value to a number greater than its Max value (here set to 10). It becomes invisible and leaves a message that it will reappear only when its Value is back in the range [Min, Max]. The slider does not want to mislead you. Set the value back in the acceptable range and it will become visible again.

Communicating with the edit textbox

Let's talk with the edit textbox. We first obtain its handle using the `findobj` command, as before.

```
>> htext=findobj('Tag', 'xText')
htext =
    3.0020
```

Again, note that the spelling must be exact and that the precise handle value is irrelevant. We can now ask the textbox to report on the value of its various properties. For a textbox the most important of these is often the String property, which holds the string displayed in the box itself.

```
>> xstring=get(htext, 'String')
xstring =
1
```

Note that this is returning the *string* `'1'` not the number 1. Other properties of the textbox could be inquired about, for example, the `FontName`.

```
>> get(htext, 'FontName')
ans =
MS Sans Serif
```

Suppose we want to set the string Property of the text so it displays the number stored in the variable `xfirst`. We first convert the number to a string using `num2str` and then use the `set` command to set the string Property of the textbox.

```
>> xfirst=5.23;
>> set(htext, 'String', num2str(xfirst));
```

9.4 Synchronizing information with a GUI element

The SliderTool we've made is a little unsatisfying because one can move the slider to set the value of x, but we're not seeing the value reflected in the textbox underneath. We can now change that by editing the callback functions in the file `SliderTool.m`. Examine the program in the MATLAB editor. You will see that there are now, in addition to the usual `SliderTool`-related functions, two functions associated with the slider and two functions associated with the textbox.

```
function xSlider_Callback(hObject, eventdata, handles)
function xSlider_CreateFcn(hObject, eventdata, handles)
function xText_Callback(hObject, eventdata, handles)
function xText_CreateFcn(hObject, eventdata, handles)
```

Only the callback functions concern us here. Each callback function has the `handles` structure passed to it as an argument. The very important `handles` structure is conveniently constructed so that each fieldname in the structure is the Tag of an object in the GUI (this information is stored in the `SliderTool.fig` file and read in by `SliderTool.m`). Thus, within the callback function we have access, without the need of `findobj`, to the handle for each object in the GUI tool. For example, in the present case:

`handles.xSlider`   contains the handle to the slider with Tag "xSlider"

`handles.xText`   contains the handle to the textbox with Tag "xText"

Let's think through what we want to happen. When the user moves the slider and releases it, a new value of the parameter x is represented by the position of the slider and we'd like to update the textbox to reflect that. The moment the user releases the slider, the function `xSlider_Callback` is executed. So we want to edit that function to do the following:

1. Get the new value of the slider's position from its Value property. This will be a number we can store in the variable x.

2. Make a string representing the number x.

3. Set the value of the String property of the textbox to this new string.

We can achieve these three things that by putting the following three commands in the function `xSlider_Callback`.

```
function xSlider_Callback(hObject, eventdata, handles)
% GUIDE generated comments omitted
x=get(handles.xSlider, 'Value');
xs=num2str(x);
set(handles.xText, 'String', xs);
```

The slider now automatically updates the textbox to reflect its position each time it's moved. Just what we wanted. You should also now be able to see clearly some aspects of standard slider behavior. Clicking the small arrows at the end of the slider moves the slider in small steps that are one-hundredth (0.01) of its total range (between Min and Max). Clicking on the space between the slide and the ends moves the slider in large steps that are one-tenth (0.1) of the range. The size of the small steps and large steps can be changed by altering the values of the slider's SliderStep property. The value of SliderStep is a vector `[smallStepSize, largeStepSize]`; its default setting is `[0.01, 0.1]`.

It's probably clear by now that we'd like one more feature to connect the editbox with the slider. Sometimes we'd like to be able to type a specific value for x in the textbox (it might be challenging to manage to move the slider to exactly that position). We'd like to be able to type in the value of x in the textbox and have the slider change to that value.

Let's think through what we'd like to happen. When the user types a number in the textbox, that represents the new value for x and we'd like to update the slider position to reflect that. At the moment the user presses <Enter>after typing in the textbox, or clicks somewhere else in the frame, the function `xText_Callback` is executed. So when the callback function for the textbox is executed we'd like it to do the following:

1. Get the new string from the String property of the textbox.

2. Find the number represented by that string.

3. Set the value of the Value property of the slider to this updated number.

We can achieve these three things by putting the following three commands in the function `xText_Callback`.

```
function xText_Callback(hObject, eventdata, handles)
% GUIDE generated comments omitted
xs=get(handles.xText, 'String');
x=str2double(xs);
set(handles.xSlider, 'Value', x);
```

(The use of `str2double` is preferred over `str2num` because of the way it handles some special cases.)

9.5   Key points from this chapter

GUIDE The GUIDE program within MATLAB is used to construct the graphical user interface (GUI). It produces two files of the form: `MynamedTool.m` and `Mynamed-Tool.fig`. The file `MynamedTool.fig` is a binary file that contains the layout and properties of each GUI object. The file `MynamedTool.m` consists of a main function `MynamedTool`, and several other subfunctions, including callback functions.

Properties Each GUI object has a lengthy set of properties appropriate for that specific class of object. Each property has a specific value, which may be of any MATLAB class (e.g., number, string, vector, matrix, cell array, etc.). Most properties can be edited using the Property Inspector.

Tags The Tag property is very important because it functions as a uniquely specified name for each particular GUI object.

Callback functions When a GUI object is activated by a user action, the callback function associated with the object is executed. GUIDE constructs the name of the callback function associated with each object using the Tag you assigned to the object. For example, if the object has the Tag "zminSlider," its callback function is named `zminSlider_Callback`.

Handles The handle to a GUI object is a coded version of its address in the computer's memory. It is used to communicate with the object, principally through the `get` and `set` commands. Inside a callback function the handles of all the objects in the tool are available through the MATLAB structure `handles` (of class `struct`). GUIDE creates the fields of the `handles` structure to be the same as the Tags of the GUI objects. For example, the handle for an object with Tag `zminSlider` is `handles.zminSlider`.

get To ask an object to report the value of a specific property, use the `get` command and the `handles` structure. For example, to retrieve the value of the FontSize property of the textbox with Tag `zminText`, the command:

```
fsize=get(handles.zminText, 'FontSize');
```

returns the numerical value of the font size and stores it in the variable `fsize`.

set To tell an object to change the Value of a specific property, use the `set` command and the `handles` structure. For example, to order the textbox with Tag `zminText` to change the value of its FontSize property to the value stored in the variable `fsize`, use the following command:

```
set(handles.zminText, 'FontSize', fsize);
```

Transforming a MATLAB Program into a GUI Tool

10.1   Creating a GUI tool step by step

10.2   Further GUI design considerations

Let's suppose we have developed a model for a system we want to study. The system could be a physical system modeled by the relevant physical laws, e.g., Newton's second law of motion, the Schrödinger equation, Kirchoff's circuit laws, Maxwell's equation, or chemical reaction-rate equations. It could also be a financial, sociological, or economic system model. In any case, the model needs to be expressed in a mathematically precise form. The model will consist of mathematical relations—these could be algebraic equations, differential equations, matrix algebra, and so forth. The model will also have some parameters that characterize the specific characteristics of a particular system, e.g., masses, voltages, concentrations, spring constants, or initial velocities.

The first task is to capture the mathematical model in a computational model expressed as a MATLAB program. This can often be a MATLAB script or function, which may call other user-written functions. Going from a model expressed mathematically to a computational model is itself challenging and involves some careful thinking about what one knows at the outset, what one doesn't know, and how the relevant mathematics can be used to connect the two. The mathematical model must be transformed into a computational *algorithm*—a series of well-defined steps that proceeds from known quantities to find the desired unknown quantities. It also involves constructing the appropriate MATLAB data structures (e.g., numbers, arrays, strings, logical variables) to represent relevant quantities. One must make at least preliminary decisions about how the calculated results are to be displayed to the user. This could be a single number, a set of plots, or an animation. Often, the model performance can be compared to experimental data, a comparison that may allow refinement, or rejection, of the model.

The previous several chapters have been designed to enable you to make such a computational model. It takes a reasonable amount of practice to get good at it. Proficiency is also helped by experience in solving problems in several domains.

The purpose of this chapter is to describe how, given a successful (debugged) program—we will assume it's in the form of a MATLAB script—one can construct a graphical user interface (GUI) and connect it to the program. The result of this process we call a MATLAB GUI tool. The tool allows the user to change both the parameters of the the model, and the way in which the results are displayed. The user can interact with the model through graphical objects like sliders and textboxes, and see the results in accessible and revealing graphical representations. A well-designed tool makes it easy for the user to *explore* the system behavior, gaining intuition and insight into the way the modeled system behaves.

This is the purpose of the GUI tool; it's a tool built to enable exploration that increases understanding.

In the last chapter we introduced the GUIDE program for making GUIs, and learned how to communicate with GUI objects using the `get` and `set` commands. In this chapter we will describe a step-by-step procedure for transforming an existing MATLAB script into a GUI tool using GUIDE. The procedure described here does not cover every type of GUI tool that could be built. It will go a long way, however, and it will enable you to build a variety of very useful tools to explore the behavior of rather sophisticated computational models in a great variety of problem domains. We will, of course, start simply and add gradually.

It is helpful to state the structure of the approach at the outset. The basic steps are shown below.

Step 0: Write and debug the program that realizes the computational model as a MATLAB script file.

Step 1: Plan the GUI. Design the layout and determine which variables are set through the GUI and how they are presented to the user. Design the output display.

Step 2: Create the GUI with GUIDE. This will result in the GUIDE-generated `*.fig` and the GUI tool `*.m` files.

Step 3: Transform the program into an appropriate function, called the "primary model function," which will be invoked from within the GUI tool code.

Step 4: Connect the function to the GUI. Add calls from the GUI tool code to the primary model function and synchronize the GUI objects.

10.1 Creating a GUI tool step by step

Step 0: Write and debug the program

In the interest of making the basic process clear, we consider a very simple model that consists of simply evaluating a mathematical function and plotting it appropriately. The following program will serve as our initial model program.

```
%% plotDampedEfield
%    plot a damped sinusoidal electric field
%         with skin depth a
%         domain is 0 to 10 microns

%% set parameters
a=3;        % skin depth (microns)
E0=12;      % magnitude of  field at x=0 (V/micron)
lambda=1;   % period of oscillation (microns)
xmin=0;
xmax=10;
Nx=200;
```

```
%% initialize arrays
x=linspace(xmin, xmax, Nx);
E=zeros(1,Nx);

%% calculate field
k=2*pi/lambda;
E=E0*cos(k*x).*exp(-x/a);

%% plot results
plot(x,E);
axis([xmin, xmax, -E0, E0]);
xlabel('x (microns)');
ylabel('E(V/micron)');
grid on
```

The program above models the exponential damping of an electric field in a slightly con-ductive dielectric medium. (It doesn't matter whether or not you know exactly what that means—the key here is the structure of the program.) Mathematically, the model amounts to simply tabulating the values of an exponentially damped sinusoid on a grid of x-values. We are keeping it simple to focus on the structure of the process rather than the physics or algorithms involved in the model. We've chosen to represent the function using two MATLAB vectors, x and E, as the key data structures.

Notice that the program is broken up into four sections. There are clear blocks for (a) setting input parameters, (b) initializing arrays, (c) performing the calculation, and (d) displaying the results. Throughout this text, pulling numerical parameters up to the front of the program has been encouraged by admonition and example. This practice is all the more helpful when attaching the GUI to form a tool.

Step 1: Plan the GUI

The first step in actually making a GUI tool is planning the GUI. This is a process of design, which means there is not a single right answer and it's okay to start with one design and decide to improve or alter it later.

The key decision is which parameters to expose in the GUI. Looking at the program above, notice that there are six parameters set in the first executable section of the code: a, E0, lambda, xmin, xmax, and Nx. Which of these does one want the user of the tool to be able to alter through the graphical interface? Of course, one could decide that all should be GUI-exposed, but typically the purpose of the GUI is to allow the user to explore some of the parameter space of the problem but not necessarily all of it. The downside of exposing too much is a cluttered interface and the opportunity for the user to wander into a confusing part of parameter space.

Notice that the parameters here naturally separate into two classes: the physical parameters a, E0, and lambda, and computational parameters xmin, xmax, and Nx. The latter change how the output is displayed, while the former reflect the underlying physics of the problem. Frequently one wants to select good computational parameters, and not expose them in

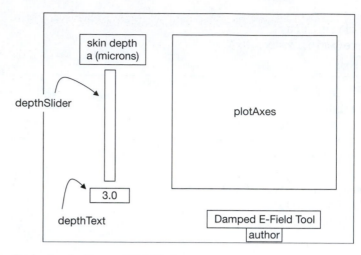

FIGURE 10.1 Basic plan for DampedEfieldTool.

the GUI, so the user can focus on the model's behavior and not be concerned with its implementation.

For this example we decide to expose only the skin depth a that controls the strength of the exponential damping and leave the other numbers fixed by the program. That means that we want the user to be able to easily change a and see the result. We'll choose a common GUI motif and use a synchronized slider and textbox to let the user control a, and an `axes` object on which to plot the resulting damped field. It's often a good idea to actually sketch out the rough layout for the tool we want to build, before even starting up GUIDE.

We decide on the name of the tool file, `DampedEfieldTool`, and include a more readable name on the tool, as well as credit for the author. It's very helpful to decide on the Tag names for the GUI objects, and keep to the convention that the names have the form recommended in the preceding chapter:

<quantity name><ObjectClass>

The "quantity name" should express either the variable associated with the element or the physical quantity itself. The "ObjectClass" is just a shorthand for precisely the sort of object it is. Examples of good Tag names are: `xinitText`, `vinitSlider`, `animationCheck-box`, `methodPopup`, `plotPopup`, `componentListbox`, or `velocityOutputText`. The most common error in this process is inconsistently spelling the Tag names. It is *hugely* helpful to stick to a naming convention, and this has proven to be a good one.

More planning notes might include: what exactly is going to be plotted, the plotting domain (here the interval $x = $ [xmin, xmax]), the minimum and maximum for each slider, and the initial value each parameter will have. Here we decide that initially the skin depth a will be set to 3 and widthSlider will go from 0 to 20 (Min and Max).

Step 2: Create the GUI with GUIDE

Now we can use GUIDE to lay out the graphical objects we need. Drag objects from the palette and position and size them according to the planned GUI layout. The initial layout is shown in Figure 10.2 for this example.

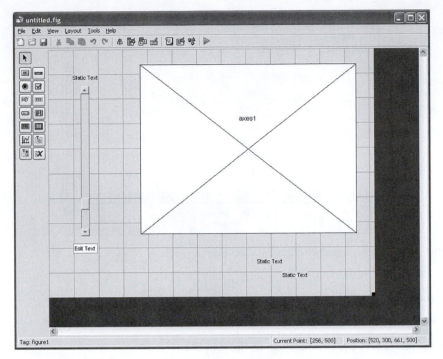

FIGURE 10.2 Initial layout for DampedEfieldTool in GUIDE.

Next, set properties for each object using the Property Inspector. Double-click on each object in turn to edit its properties. For this example,

Edit the slider label static text object:

- Change FontSize to 12.
- Click on the edit text icon near the String property and enter a two-line label: "skin depth <Enter> a (microns)." See Figure 10.3.
- Adjust the size of the object for readability.

Edit the slider:

- Change the Tag to "depthSlider."
- Change Max to 20.
- Change Value to 3.

Edit the textbox under the slider:

- Change the Tag to "depthText."
- Change FontSize to 12.
- Change String to "3" to match the value of the slider.
- Adjust the size of the object (with the mouse) for readability.

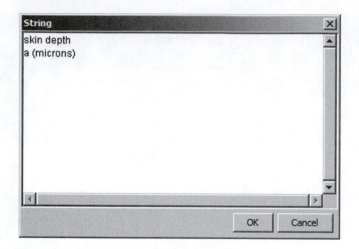

FIGURE 10.3 Entering a multiline label as the String property.

Edit the axes object:

- Change the Tag to "plotAxes."

Edit the static text which functions as the tool title:

- Change FontSize to 30.

- Change String to "Damped E-Field Tool."

- Adjust the size of the object for readability.

Edit the static text for the tool author:

- Change String to your name.

- Adjust the size of the object for readability.

There is no need to set meaningful Tag names for objects that simply serve as labels. The objects that are crucial in this example are the slider, the associated textbox, and the axes object. Each will need to be addressed by the program, so we want to make sure they have clear Tag names, which will end up as field names in the `handles` structure.

In GUIDE, save the GUI as `DampedEfieldTool`; GUIDE will generate the figure file `DampedEfieldTool.fig` and the m-file `DampedEfieldTool.m`, which will automatically be loaded into the Editor. The m-file will be edited in Step 4 below.

Step 3: Transform the program into an appropriate function.

a. **Transform the script into a function.** Load the working script file into the MATLAB editor and save the file under a new name that ends with the letter "F" (for "function"). In this example, the program was named `plotDampedEfield`, so it should be saved as a file with the name `plotDampedEfieldF`. This is the primary model function.

Edit the first line of the new file so that it becomes a function declaration with the argument `handles`. In this example that means the first line should be:

```
function plotDampedEfieldF(handles)
```

b. **Replace the assignment statements for those variables that should be exposed in the GUI with appropriate `get` commands.** For this example, the plan is to expose the skin depth a. So the existing assignment statement

```
a=3;
```

should be replaced by a command that gets the value from the Value property of the `depthSlider` object.

```
a=get(handles.depthSlider, 'Value');
```

Here it can be assumed that the slider has the up-to-date value of a. Synchronization of the slider value with the value in the textbox will be the responsibility of the GUI code (here `DampedEfieldTool.m`), which will be edited later.

c. **Direct graphical output to the appropriate axes object.** By default, `plot` statements and related graphical statements will direct MATLAB to do the plotting on the current figure. This may or may not have the desired result. To assure that the plotting happens on the axes object of the GUI tool, add the handle of the axes object to the argument list of the plotting command. Most plotting-related commands will take the handle to an axes object as the first argument. For example, the command in the original program

```
plot(x,E);
```

should be replaced by

```
plot(handles.plotAxes, x, E);
```

For brevity, it is often easier to store the handle in a variable with a shorter name. So, for example, one might do the following.

```
hax=handles.plotAxes;
plot(hax, x, E);
axis(hax, [xmin, xmax, -E0, E0]);
xlabel(hax, 'x (microns)');
ylabel(hax, 'E(V/micron)');
grid(hax, 'on');
```

Although in this example there is only one axes object, frequently it's helpful to have two or more axes objects in the GUI and direct the appropriate commands to each. A hypothetical example in a different context—plotting position on one axes object and energy on a second axes object—is shown as follows:

```
hax=handles.positionAxes;
haxe=handles.energyAxes;

%%  plot the position as a function of time on one axes
plot(hax, t, x);
axis(hax, [tmin, tmax, xmin, xmax]);
xlabel(hax, 't (seconds)');
ylabel(hax, 'x(m)');

%%  plot the Energy as a function of time on another axes
plot(haxe, t, E);
axis(haxe, [tmin, tmax, Emin, Emax]);
xlabel(haxe, 't (seconds)');
ylabel(haxe, 'E(J)');
```

Back to the task of transitioning from a working program to a GUI tool. We started in the current example with the program `plotDampedField` shown on page 166. We've made three types of changes: (a) changed it from a script into a function, (b) changed the assignment statement for the variable `a` so that it gets the value from the slider, and (c) directed the plotting statements explicitly to the axes object. The result is the following function; the altered lines are shown in bold.

```
function plotDampedEfieldF(handles)
%      plot a damped sinusoidal electric field
%            with skin depth a
%            domain is 0 to 10 microns
%      Author: T.A. Edison

%% set parameters
% skin depth (microns)
a=get(handles.depthSlider,'Value');
E0=12;       % magnitude of  field at x=0 (V/micron)
lambda=1;  % period of oscillation (microns)
xmin=0;
xmax=10;
Nx=200;

%% initialize arrays
x=linspace(xmin, xmax, Nx);
E=zeros(1, Nx);
```

```
%% calculate field
k=2*pi/lambda;
E=E0*cos(k*x).*exp(-x/a);

%% plot results
hax=handles.plotAxes;
plot(hax, x, E);
axis(hax, [xmin, xmax, -E0, E0]);
xlabel(hax, 'x (microns)');
ylabel(hax, 'E(V/micron)');
grid(hax, 'on');
```

Step 4: Connect the function to the GUI

The main GUI tool code is the file DampedEfieldTool.m, which was generated automatically by GUIDE and is loaded in the Editor (if not, please open it in the Editor). Run the program as-is by pressing the green Run button on the EDITOR tab. All the parts work but don't accomplish anything useful. This program now needs to be edited to accomplish three things:

a. Synchronize the slider and the associated textbox with each other.

b. Execute primary model function plotDampedEfieldF(handles) whenever the user moves the slider or changes the number in the textbox.

c. Execute the primary model function when the tool is first run.

Examine the file DampedEfieldTool in the Editor. It consists of the following seven functions, only three of which will need to be changed.

```
function DampedEfieldTool
function DampedEfieldTool_OpeningFcn        CHANGE
function DampedEfieldTool_OutputFcn
function depthSlider_Callback               CHANGE
function depthSlider_CreateFcn
function depthText_Callback                 CHANGE
function depthText_CreateFcn
```

Altering the slider callback

When the user moves the depthSlider and releases it, the function depth-Slider_Callback is executed. The function has several arguments, including the handles structure, which we will use to communicate with GUI objects. Since the user has just changed the value of the slider, this function's tasks are two: update the string shown in the depthText textbox, and then invoke the primary model function plotDampedEfieldF(handles).

Updating the string in the textbox is the same process as was described on page 162. We add a fourth step to automatically invoke the primary model function with the new value.

- Get the value of the slider.

- Create the corresponding string.

- Then set the String property of the textbox to this newly created string.

- Finally, execute the function `plotDampedEfieldF(handles)` to recalculate and replot using the new value. Recall that within `plotDampedEfieldF` the new value of the width will be obtained (using `get`) from the `widthSlider`.

The fully filled-out callback function for the slider now looks like this:

```
function depthSlider_Callback(hObject, eventdata, handles)
% <GUIDE-generated comments omitted>
a=get(handles.depthSlider, 'Value');
astr=num2str(a);
set(handles.depthText, 'String', astr)
plotDampedEfieldF(handles);
```

Altering the textbox callback

When the user edits the text in `depthText` and either presses <Return>or clicks somewhere else, the function `depthText_Callback` is executed. Since the user has just changed the string in the textbox, this function's tasks are two: update the value of the `depthSlider` object to reflect the new value, and then invoke the function `plotDampedEfieldF(handles)`.

Updating the value of the slider is the same process as was described on page 163. Again, we add a fourth step to automatically invoke the primary model function with the new value.

- Get the String of the textbox.

- Create the corresponding number, using `str2double`.

- Set the Value property of the slider to this newly calculated number.

- Finally, execute the function `plotDampedEfieldF(handles)` to recalculate and replot using the new value.

The fully filled-out callback function for the textbox now looks like this:

```
function depthText_Callback(hObject, eventdata, handles)
% <comments omitted>
astr=get(handles.depthText, 'String');
a=str2double(astr);
set(handles.depthSlider, 'Value', a);
plotDampedEfieldF(handles);
```

Altering the opening function

The function `DampedEfieldTool_OpeningFcn` is executed when the GUI tool is first run, just before the tool is made visible. If no change is made to this function, the tool will work just fine. The drawback is simply that the user will need to move the slider or type a value into the text window before the plot will appear. So it's a nice touch to simply add one line to the end of the function invoking the primary model function.

```
plotDampedEfieldF(handles);
```

This assures that, when the tool is executed, the plot appears right away.

Note that the opening function, unlike callback functions, is not just an empty stub. Make sure that the call to your function is inserted at the *end* of the function, after the command `guidata`.

The modified tool file

By making these changes, the primary model function `plotDampedEfieldF` has now been attached to the GUI code in `DampedEfieldTool`. Each of the additions to `DampedEfieldTool` has been described earlier, but for convenience the complete listing is given as follows. Boldface indicates the added code that synchronized the slider with the textbox and connected the GUI to the primary function. Most comments are omitted.

```
function varargout = DampedEfieldTool(varargin)
% Begin initialization code - DO NOT EDIT
gui_Singleton = 1;
gui_State = struct('gui_Name',       mfilename, ...
                   'gui_Singleton',  gui_Singleton, ...
                   'gui_OpeningFcn', @DampedEfieldTool_
                                        OpeningFcn, ...
                   'gui_OutputFcn',  @DampedEfieldTool_
                                        OutputFcn, ...
                   'gui_LayoutFcn',  [] , ...
                   'gui_Callback',   []);
if nargin && ischar(varargin{1})
    gui_State.gui_Callback = str2func(varargin{1});
end
if nargout
    [varargout{1:nargout}] = gui_mainfcn(gui_State, varargin{:});
else
    gui_mainfcn(gui_State, varargin{:});
end
% End initialization code - DO NOT EDIT
```

```
function DampedEfieldTool_OpeningFcn(hObject, eventdata,
 handles, varargin)
handles.output = hObject;
guidata(hObject, handles);
plotDampedEfieldF(handles)
```

```
function varargout = DampedEfieldTool_OutputFcn(hObject,
 eventdata, handles)
varargout{1} = handles.output;
```

```
function depthText_Callback(hObject, eventdata, handles)
astr=get(handles.depthText, 'String');
a=str2double(astr);
set(handles.depthSlider, 'Value' ,a);
plotDampedEfieldF(handles);
```

```
function depthText_CreateFcn(hObject, eventdata, handles)
if ispc && isequal(get(hObject,'BackgroundColor'),
 get(0,'defaultUicontrolBackgroundColor'))
    set(hObject,'BackgroundColor','white');
end
```

```
function depthSlider_Callback(hObject, eventdata, handles)
a=get(handles.depthSlider, 'Value');
astr=num2str(a);
set(handles.depthText, 'String', astr);
plotDampedEfieldF(handles);
```

```
function depthSlider_CreateFcn(hObject, eventdata, handles)
if isequal(get(hObject,'BackgroundColor'),
 get(0,'defaultUicontrolBackgroundColor'))
    set(hObject,'BackgroundColor',[.9 .9 .9]);
end
```

The GUI tool is now complete. It consists of three files:

> DampedEfieldTool.m, the main tool file
> DampedEfieldTool.fig, the GUI layout information file
> plotDampedEfieldF.m, the primary computation function

The tool is launched by running DampedEfieldTool.m. Figure 10.4 shows the tool immediately after launch. Note that the initial value of the skin depth (3 microns) was determined when the Value property of the slider was set in GUIDE using the Property Inspector. The String property of the textbox was similarly set at that point. Try using the tool and exploring the effect of changing the skin depth by using the slider and by typing values in the textbox.

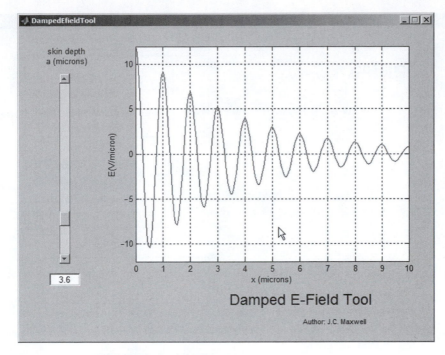

FIGURE 10.4   DampedEfieldTool after initial startup.

10.2   Further GUI design considerations

A GUI tool named XpultTool, shown in Figure 10.5, illustrates some features of a more complex calculation and somewhat more complicated GUI than DampedEfieldTool. XpultTool models the behavior of a small rubber-band-powered catapult, which launches Ping-Pong balls. The launch angle is set to one of several discrete positions by a metal pin. The shooter pulls back the catapult arm and can read off the pull-back angle in degrees. Other parameters that characterize the launch are entered through textboxes: the mass of the ball, the ball diameter, the height of the floor relative to the catapult axis, the number of rubber bands, the simulation time, the number of timesteps in the simulation, the spring constant of each rubber band, the coefficient of restitution of the ball hitting the floor, the aerodynamic drag coefficient of the ball, and an animation stride parameter. The pullback angle is set by using a synchronized slider and textbox. The launch angle is set by clicking one of the radio buttons, which are mutually exclusive. The user sets these parameters and then starts the model simulation by pressing the Start button. The motion of the ball in space is calculated in two steps. First, energy balance equations are solved for the boost phase, when the ball is being accelerated by the catapult. For the ballistic phase, when the ball is being acted on by gravity and the drag force of the air, Newton's second law of motion is solved to obtain the position, velocity, and energy of the ball at each point in time. The position of the ball moving in time is then animated in the upper graphics panel (axes object), and the energy (kinetic, potential, and total) is plotted synchronously in the lower panel. Using the popup menu above the lower panel, the user can choose to view the energy or the velocity of the ball as each changes in time. The calculated distance between the catapult axis and the first bounce is displayed at the bottom of the frame, using a static textbox.

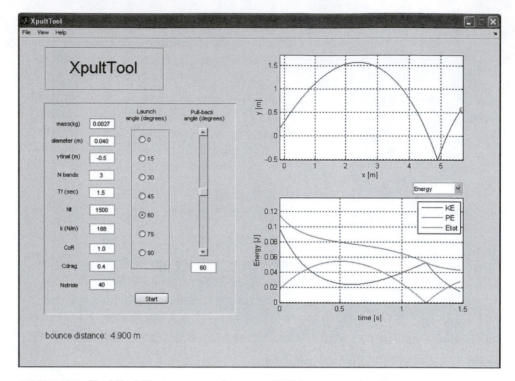

FIGURE 10.5 XpultTool illustrates several common GUI design considerations.

Multiple graphics windows

A useful motif for many problems is to have at least two axes objects. Then two curves can be plotted simultaneously and the user can see the comparison between them. In XpultTool the user can see, in both the animation and the completed plots, the way the energy shifts between potential and kinetic energy as the ball is in flight. Being able to simultaneously view a computational model through multiple lenses can be very valuable in enhancing insight into the science on which the model is based. A popup menu allows the user to change lenses.

For a tool with multiple axes objects it is important to be sure that every graphics command is targeted at the appropriate axes. We have seen (page 171), that many high-level MATLAB graphics commands can be directed to output to a particular axes by including the handle to the axes object as the first argument:

```
plot(handles.firstAxes, ...)
```

This also works for plot3, xlabel, ylabel, grid, title, axis, box, polar, hold, rotate3d, loglog, semilogx, semilogy, legend, area, bar, pie, hist, surf, and rotate3d. Not all of these commands have been discussed here; many will be described in Chapters 12 and 13.

Low-level graphics commands do not clear the current figure but rather just add another graphical component to the axes. These include rectangle, line, patch, surface, text, hgtransform, and image (again, these are discussed in Chapters 12 and 13). These commands do not take an axes object handle as their first argument. Rather, one needs to set the Parent property to the appropriate axes handle. This can be done when the object is created.

```
%      create square green patch
patch([0, 1, 1, 0, 0],[0, 0, 1, 1, 0], 'g', ...
        'Parent',handles.animAxes);
```

It can also be done after the object is created using the object handle.

```
hline=line([0, 1.4], [0, 1.4]);
set(hline, 'Parent', handles.animAxes, 'LineWidth', 2,
  'Color', 'k');
```

The annotation command creates annotation objects of various types: line, arrow, double-arrow, textbox, ellipse, or rectangle. It takes the handle to a figure as the first argument.

Longer calculations and animations

The length of time a calculation takes to run on the computer has an impact on how one designs the GUI. In the tool DampedEfieldTool, the actual calculation of the damped sinusoid took very little time on a modern computer. It was therefore natural to redo the calculation each time the user changed an input value. This often has a payoff in allowing the user to immediately see the effect that changing a particular parameter has on the result. Sometimes, however, the calculation to be performed takes some time, perhaps several seconds or longer. In XpultTool, it is the animations that, by design, take some time to run. In a case like that, one doesn't want to have the calculation start every time an input value is changed. It makes more sense to let the user adjust the input values, perhaps several of them, and then start the calculation by pressing a pushbutton object. In this case one need only invoke the primary model function from the pushbutton's callback function. It is not then desirable to invoke the primary model function in the tool's OpeningFcn.

Displaying a result in a static textbox

Although a graphical plot conveys a lot of information, it is often useful to also report to the user particular numbers that are the result of the calculation. In a MATLAB script, one typically does this using the disp command, for example:

```
disp(['Mean velocity (m/s): ',num2str(vmean)]);
```

This can be accomplished in a GUI tool by creating two static text objects. The first simply displays a label to communicate the nature of the information being displayed. In this case the String property of the label text object would be set in GUIDE to be "Mean velocity (m/s): ." The second static text object holds the string representing the numerical output and should have a meaningful name (Tag), for example, "vmeanText." The disp statement is then replaced in the primary model function by the following statement:

```
set(handles.vmeanText,'String',num2str(vmean));
```

Mean velocity (m/s):   0.342

FIGURE 10.6   Numerical output displayed in a textbox within the GUI tool.

This results in the string displayed at the appropriate part of the GUI tool changing to reflect the new value. In XpultTool, for example, the distance to the first bounce is reported in a textbox at the lower left of the panel.

A textbox can contain other types of information besides numbers. The result of the calculation could also be simply a string, for example "Convergence obtained," "Target acquired," or "You lose!" A textbox could also contain information or instructions for the user, for example "Calculating, please wait ...," "Please enter valid date MM/DD/YYYY," or "Using stiff ODE solver."

PROGRAMMING PROBLEMS

1. Write a MATLAB GUI Tool extending the program plotdamped.m, which plots the following function:

$$f(x) = e^{-x/a} \cos\left(2\pi\frac{x}{\lambda}\right)$$

Plot for $x \in [-5, 5]$, $a \in [0.05, 50]$, and $\lambda \in [0.05, 20]$. Vary the parameters a and λ with synchronized sliders and editable text. Use static text to label the sliders.

2. Write a program, plotlogistic.m, which plots the following function:

$$p(y) = \frac{1}{1 + e^{-\left(\frac{y-y_0}{a}\right)}}$$

Transform the program into a MATLAB GUI tool named LogisticTool. Choose an appropriate domain for the function and vary the parameters y_0 and a with synchronized sliders and text. Experiment with the plot and set an appropriate range for the parameters (you're trying to let the user see the way the function varies its shape as you change the parameters). Use static text to label the sliders.

(Advanced) Calculate the derivative of the function and add a pull-down menu to let the user choose between plotting the function or its derivative.

3. **Lissajous.** Write a MATLAB program plotLJ.m, which plots the following parametrically defined curve characterized by $T = 1, a, b,$ and ϕ.

$$x = \cos(a\omega t) \qquad (10.1)$$

$$y = \sin(b\omega t + \phi) \qquad (10.2)$$

where

$$\omega = 2\pi/T$$

Let $t \in [0, T]$, $a, b \in [0, 10]$ and $\phi \in [0, 2\pi]$.

Transform the program into a MATLAB GUI tool named LJTool. Vary the parameters a and b, and ϕ with synchronized sliders and text.

4. **CounterTool.** Using GUIDE, develop a MATLAB program with a GUI that implements a simple counter with two buttons, one to increment the count and the other to reset the count to zero. The GUI should contain the following elements:

   • a textbox with tag countText to display the current count

   • a button with tag countButton to increment the count

   • a button with tag resetButton to reset the count

   • a textbox with your name

5. **IntegralTool.** The following script tabulates and plots a sine function from 0 to 2 and shades the area under the curve from xleft to xright.

```
% demoFill.m
%    Author: Rene Decartes

%% tabulate function for plotting
xmin=0; xmax=2*pi; Nx=100;
x=linspace(xmin, xmax, Nx);
y=sin(x);

%% tabulate function on finer grid
  for integration and filling
Nf=300;
xleft=0.3;
xright=2*pi/3;
xf=linspace(xleft, xright, Nf);
yf=sin(xf);

%% plot curve with area defined
  by (xf,yf) shaded
plot(x,y)
holdon
fill([xf(1), xf, xf(Nf), xf(1)],
  [0, yf, 0, 0], 'r',... 'Parent',
  gca);
holdoff
gridon
xlabel('x')
ylabel('y')
```

   (a) Write a MATLAB script named `calcIntegral.m` that extends `demoFill.m` to include a calculation of the approximate value of the integral of the sine function from `xleft` to `xright`. To do this, break the region into trapezoids bounded by the tabulated values in the `xf` and `yf` arrays and sum the areas of all the trapezoids. The area of each small trapezoid is:

$$A_k = \frac{1}{2}(y_{k+1} + y_k)\Delta x$$

where $\Delta x = x_2 - x_1 = x_{k+1} - x_k$ and the integral can be approximated by:

$$I = \int_{xleft}^{xright} f(x)dx \approx \sum_{k=1}^{N-1} A_k$$

A code fragment that would accomplish this is:

```
deltax=xf(2)-xf(1);
Integ=0;
for ix=1:Nf-1
    Integ=Integ+0.5*(yf(ix+1)
     +yf(ix))*deltax;
end
```

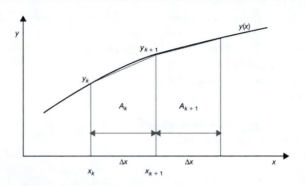

FIGURE 10.7 Trapezoidal integration.

(b) Make a GUI tool that uses the positions of two sliders to set the limits of integration, xleft and xright, calculates the integral and displays it numerically, and graphically shows the area under the curve using the previous fill method. It should look something like Figure 10.9.

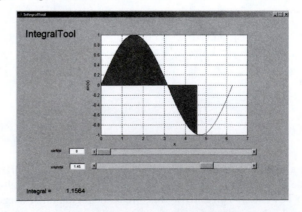

FIGURE 10.8 Possible layout for IntegralTool.

6. **RPSTool: A rock-paper-scissors GUI.**
   (a) Write a MATLAB script named processRPS.m, which does the following:
      i. sets a variable iHumanPlay to 1, 2, or 3, representing choices rock, paper, or scissors

   ii. picks the computer's choice, represented by `iComputerPlay` using randi

  iii. decides who won based on the usual rules and sets a string variable `gameResult` to either humanWon, computerWon, or tie

  iv. calls a function, which you also write, with the function declaration

```
function showGame(iComputerPlay, iHumanPlay, gameResult)
```

The function `showGame` should report to the Command window what happened in the game in a well-formatted way.

(b) Make a GUI version called `RPSTool` using GUIDE that includes the following:
    i. buttons for the user to choose rock, paper, or scissors

   ii. static text objects that report (a) what the human and the computer each chose, (b) who won the game, and (c) the current number of human wins, computer wins, and ties

  iii. a reset button to restart the game

  iv. Modify `processRPS.m` and `showGame.m` and save them under new names `process RPSF.m` and `showGameF.m` with these declarations:

```
function processRPSF(handles, iHumanPlay)
functionshowGameF(handles, iComputerPlay, iHumanPlay,
gameResult)
```

Set the callbacks to each of the buttons appropriately. For example, the button labeled Rock should call `processRPSF(handles,1)`.

The function `showGameF`, which is called by `processRPSF`, should change the text objects on the GUI to reflect the last play and current game statistics.

OPTIONAL: You can add an axis component to the GUI to display the result of the game or the current leader with images. The buttons themselves could have images on them also.

FIGURE 10.9   Possible layout of RPSTool.

7. **BallisticTool.** Write a GUI tool that models a ping-pong ball (diameter 40 mm) launched at a given angle with a specified initial speed. Let the user input both with synchronized textbox and slider pairs.

(a) During flight the ball is acted on by gravity

$$\vec{F}_g = -mg\,\hat{y}$$

and a velocity-dependent aerodynamic drag force

$$\vec{F}_D = -\frac{1}{2}C_d A \rho v^2 \hat{v}$$

where C_d is the drag coefficient (≈ 0.5 for a sphere), ρ is the air density, A is the cross-sectional area of the ball, and $\hat{v} \equiv \vec{v}/\|\vec{v}\|$ is the unit vector in the direction of the velocity. This will require the Verlet method to solve.

(b) Describe bounces of the ball using the coefficient of restitution β of the ball on a hard floor surface. Assume ball bounces off the floor with the y-component of its velocity flipped to the positive direction and reduced in magnitude, $v_y^{fin} = \beta|v_y^{init}|$, and the x-component v_x unchanged. Regulation ping-pong balls must have a coefficient of restitution of 0.4.

(c) Place a target for the user to hit with the ball; you can use random numbers to generate variety. If the ball hits the target, it should stop and some onscreen celebration should occur. Keep score of shots and hits.

(d) Advanced: Use the techniques described in Section 12.8 to make it possible for the target to be repositioned by dragging.

8. **Magic8Tool.** Make a GUI version of the Magic 8-ball described in the problem on page 142. Advanced: Use images as describe in Section 13.5.

9. **JosephusTool.** Make a GUI tool illustrating and animating the Josephus Problem described on page 134.

10. **BuffonTool.** Make a GUI version of the Buffon's needle problem described on page 93. Let the user set a number of needles to throw randomly on the floor with each button press. Accumulate the number of needle crossings and generate an approximation to π that improves as the number of needles increases.

Modeling random walks. The random motion of one walker or many walkers is a useful model in a variety of physical systems: diffusion of molecules in a fluid or impurities in a semiconductor, the motion of a photon from the center of a star out to its surface, electrons moving in solids, Brownian motion of small particles in air, and many more. The next few problems examine different variations of random walks.

11. **Random walk in two dimensions.** Create a GUI tool modeling the motion of a random walk on a square lattice. Start by writing a MATLAB script RandomWalk2D modeling the motion of a walker that starts at the origin and at each timestep moves randomly one unit in either the north, east, south, or west direction. Use the function randi to generate an integer $(1, 2, 3, 4)$ for each timestep and move the walker in the appropriate compass direction ($+y$ is North, etc.). Calculate the complete motion first, then animate the motion with another loop through time.

Plot the position of the origin with a "+" sign and the position of the walker with a circle. At each timestep in the animation loop, plot a line representing the path of the walker's entire history up to the current time. We are interested in seeing motion over hundreds or thousands of steps. You may find it interesting to experiment with the axis scaling and the `axis equal` command. Turn the script into a GUI tool named `RandomWalk2DTool`. Give the user the option of seeing the whole path at once or an animation of the motion.

12. **Continuous random walk in two dimensions with drift.** Create a GUI tool modeling the motion of a random walk in the plane.

    (a) Write a MATLAB script `RandomWalkC2D`. The walker starts at the origin $(x_1, y_1) = (0, 0)$, and at each step takes a unit step ($r_{step} = 1$) in a random direction. Choose the direction of each step by randomly picking an angle $\theta \in [0, 2\pi]$ using `rand`. Then

$$x_{k+1} = x_k + r_{step} \cos(\theta_k)$$

$$y_{k+1} = y_k + r_{step} \sin(\theta_k)$$

    Calculate the complete motion first, then animate the motion with another loop through time. Plot the position of the origin with a "+" sign and the position of the walker with a circle. At each timestep in the animation loop, plot a line representing the path of the walker's entire history up to the current time. We are interested in seeing motion over hundreds or even thousands of steps.

    (b) Add a drift component to the motion by adding a small positive shift $(\Delta x_{drift}, \Delta y_{drift})$ at each timestep.

$$x_{k+1} = x_k + r_{step} \cos(\theta_k) + \Delta x_{drift}$$

$$y_{k+1} = y_k + r_{step} \sin(\theta_k) + \Delta y_{drift}$$

    This provides a simple model of the motion of an electron in a semiconductor crystal, which is both scattering off impurities and being driven by an applied electric field.

    (c) Turn the script into a GUI tool named `RandomWalkC2DTool`. Give the user the ability to change the drift magnitude and direction, and the option of seeing the whole path at once or an animation of the motion.

13. **Continuous random walk in three dimensions.** Create `RandomWalk3DTool`, which extends the previous problem to a walk in three dimensions.

14. **Many random walkers in one dimension.** Create a GUI tool modeling the motion of Nw random walkers on a regular one-dimensional lattice. At each timestep, each walker steps to the right or left along the x-axis with equal probability. All walkers start at the origin. Store the trajectories in a matrix $x(Ns, Nw)$; each column represents the history of one walker's position. Calculate the trajectory of the walkers for Ns timesteps and then have a second loop for animating the display of the trajectories. A typical value for Ns might be 1000. The number of walkers might be anywhere from 1 up to perhaps 10^4 (you may be limited by the computer's memory).

Display the results graphically in (at least) two ways. Animate a plot of the walkers' paths with time increasing in the vertical direction and x along the horizontal direction. At each timestep in the animation loop, plot a line representing the path of the walker's entire history up to the current time. You may want a nonzero animation stride to keep the display from slowing down.

Make another plot that shows at each timestep a histogram of number of walkers at position $x = m$. In the limit of very large Nw, the number of walkers a distance m from the origin at timestep n_t approaches a Gaussian with width $\sqrt{n_t}$.

$$N_{m,n_t} = 2N_w \frac{1}{\sqrt{2\pi n_t}} e^{-m^2/(2n_t)}$$

Superimpose this curve on the histogram of the simulation for each timestep to compare the finite model to the limiting case (see `normHist2` on page 000). (The leading factor of 2 in this expression is due to the fact that at any time the walkers will all be on even-numbered sites or all on odd-numbered sites.)

The histogram and trajectory plots should be on different axes objects so the user can see both at the same time.

SPEED HINT: Ensemble random walk models like this are much faster if MATLAB vector operations are used to evolve the whole array (ensemble) of walkers at once rather than having a loop over the walkers in addition to a loop over time. The position changes for each walker at each timestep can be calculated at the beginning with a single call to `rand`.

```
deltax=sign(rand(Ns,Nw)-0.5);
```

Then the whole array of walker positions at timestep `istep` can be calculated in one vector operation.

```
x(istep,:)=x(istep-1,:)+
deltax(istep,:);
```

15. **Many random walkers in two dimensions.** Create a GUI tool named `RandomWalkers2DTool`, modeling the motion of N_w walkers on a two-dimensional grid. Animate the motion of the walkers without the trail of their history as was done in the previous problems. In addition to animating the motion of the walkers, let the user plot a dynamic histogram (at each timestep) of the walker's x-positions or distances from the origin. Compare the histogram of N_w walkers' x-positions with the following expression for the number of walkers at a distance m from the origin at timestep n_t.

$$N_{m,n_t} = N_w \frac{1}{\sqrt{\pi n_t}} e^{-m^2/n_t}$$

Add in the possibility of drift (see Problem 12(b)).

16. **Random Walk: 3D with multiple walkers.** Create `RandomWalkers3DTool`, which extends the previous problem to three dimensions.

17. **Tilted billiard table with pockets.** Write a GUI tool that extends the billiard problem on page 116 in the following ways:

   (a) Let the user choose the initial position of the ball and its initial speed and angle. The user should also choose the angular tilt of the table in both the x and y directions.

   (b) The user should input the coefficient of restitution, $\beta \le 1$, of the bumpers. The ball bounces off a bumper with the perpendicular component of its velocity flipped in direction and reduced in magnitude, $v_\perp^{fin} = -\beta v_\perp^{init}$, and the parallel component unchanged.

(c) Position pockets appropriately around the table. If the ball's position is within the pocket, it stops moving and the user has scored a win.

(d) If there is no drag, one can use an improved Euler method for the motion between bounces. Add a drag force proportional to the velocity (let the user set the coefficient) and upgrade the solver to use the Verlet method.

(e) Advanced: Use the techniques described in Section 12.8 to make it possible for the ball to be initially positioned by dragging.

18. **High-speed ballistics.** In an episode of *Law & Order: Criminal Intent*, a victim is killed by a gunshot, which could only have come from a position more than a mile away.[1] The detective announces that the weapon must have been a CheyTac M-200 long-range sniper rifle. He comments to his partner that to achieve accuracy at such a range the sniper would have had to take into account the rotation of the Earth. Construct a GUI tool that models ballistic motion appropriate for a high-speed projectile fired from a long-range sniper rifle. One goal is to assess the effects of drag, wind, and the Earth's rotation.

Let the origin be the end of the barrel and v be the muzzle velocity. The projectile is fired at an angle θ degrees from the horizontal and toward the compass direction with azimuthal angle ϕ (degrees east from north). The latitude of the firing station is *Lat*, and the target is down range in the x direction a distance $d = 2000$ m. Take the y-axis to be pointing positive upward, and the positive z direction points to the shooter's right. Assume a flat terrain.

The .408 CheyTac bullet has a mass of 19.8 grams, a diameter of 10.4 mm, a muzzle velocity of 1067 m/s (Mach 3.1), and an aerodynamic drag coefficient $C_d = 0.21$.

Your calculation should include the following:

(a) Gravity. The primary force on the bullet is the gravitational force:

$$\vec{F}_g = -mg\,\hat{y}$$

(b) An aerodynamic drag force. This is given by:

$$\vec{F}_D = -\frac{1}{2}C_dA\rho v^2\hat{v}$$

where C_d is the drag coefficient, ρ is the air density (1.225 kg/m^2), A is the cross-sectional area of the bullet, and $\hat{v} \equiv \vec{v}/\|\vec{v}\|$ is the unit vector in the direction of the velocity.

(c) A wind force. The wind is characterized by a velocity $\vec{W}$, which is usually stated as a magnitude W (in mi/hr) and a compass direction of origin, in degrees east from north. The wind force acts just as the aerodynamic drag force but the direction of the force is in the same direction as the wind.

$$\vec{F}_W = \frac{1}{2}C_dA\rho W^2\hat{W}$$

where $\hat{W} \equiv \vec{W}/\|\vec{W}\|$ is the unit vector in the direction of the wind velocity.

---

[1] *Law & Order: Criminal Intent*, Season 6, Episode 13 "Albatross," Marsha Norman and Warren Leight, writers, Dick Wolf, producer.

(d) The Coriolis pseudo-force. The effect of the rotation of the Earth is to create a velocity-dependent acceleration on the bullet, relative to the frame of reference fixed to the Earth. This can be expressed as a fictional Coriolis force $\vec{F}_c$ with components given by the following expression:[2]

$$[\vec{F}_c]_x = 2m\Omega[-v_y \cos(Lat)\sin(\phi) \\ - v_z \sin(Lat)]$$

$$[\vec{F}_c]_y = 2m\Omega[v_x \cos(Lat)\sin(\phi) \\ + v_z \cos(Lat)\cos(\phi)]$$

$$[\vec{F}_c]_z = 2m\Omega[v_x \sin(Lat) \\ - v_y \cos(Lat)\cos(\phi)]$$

Here $\Omega = 7.292 \times 10^{-5}$ radians/sec is the angular velocity of the Earth's rotation about the polar axis (one rotation per sidereal day).

Solve Newton's second law:

$$\vec{F} = m\vec{a} = \vec{F}_g + \vec{F}_D + \vec{F}_W + \vec{F}_c$$

for the bullet's flight from the muzzle to the target plane using the Verlet method.

The GUI tool should represent the flight of the bullet in three dimensions, and also the point where it crosses the target plane, a y-z plane through $x = d$. Design the tool so that the computation is completed before the graphics are rendered (you may want a waitbar—see Section 12.1). Design the tool so that it's easy for the user to change the azimuthal and elevation angles, and see where the bullet hits. Use checkboxes to separately include the effects of drag, wind, and Earth's rotation.

Further questions: What is the maximum range? What is the maximum range for which the bullet is still supersonic? If the bullet strikes a target at $x = 2000$ m, $z = 0$, $y = 0$, what is the maximum height it achieves along its path? How much of a targeting error could result from neglecting the Earth's rotation? Was the TV detective correct?

Advanced: Use the minimization techniques of Section 14.4 to enable the tool to calculate the optimum aim (θ and ϕ) for a given target position. The CheyTac is equipped with a handheld computer and weather station so the spotter can input air density, latitude, wind speed, and wind direction.

---

[2] Robert L. McCoy, *Modern Exterior Ballistics* (Schiffer, Atglen, PA, 1999), p. 178.

GUI Components

This chapter provides a brief overview of the basic GUIDE-generated GUI objects and how they can be used in common motifs. A lengthy description of all the object properties for each class can be found in the online MATLAB documentation.

11.1 | INITIATING AN ACTION: THE PUSHBUTTON OBJECT

Description: The user presses and releases a pushbutton to initiate an action by executing the callback function associated with the button.

Class name: uicontrol, Style=pushbutton

Primary property: String

Also of potential interest are properties controlling the look of the string on the button. These include FontName, FontSize, FontWeight, and FontAngle. To see a listing of available fonts on your system, type listfonts in the Command window. Beware of using wacky fonts or too many fonts (yielding a ransom note appearance).

The ForegroundColor property determines the color of the text label on the button (set by the String property). The BackgroundColor property sets the color of the body of the button. Each can be modified by using the color chooser tool in the Property Inspector.

Colors can be modified dynamically using the set command, in which case you should set the color to be either (a) a three-element vector of RGB values between 0 and 1, e.g., light blue is [0.8, 0.8, 1], or (b) a string naming the color (see doc colorspec for a table of possible values), e.g., "g" or "green" indicates green.

Good advice: *Don't go crazy with color.* The default gray shades usually yield a more professional appearance.

11.2 | SETTING A NUMBER: THE SLIDER OBJECT

Description: The user moves and releases the slide to set a real value between Min and Max.

Class name: uicontrol, Style=slider

Primary properties: Value, Min, Max

Example:

```
% get value of vinit from GUI slider
vinit=get(handles.vinitSlider, 'Value');
```

The value can also be adjusted by clicking on the arrows at the end of the slider, to change the value in small increments, or by clicking on the channel regions (the troughs) on either side of the slide, in order to change the value in larger increments. The size of each increment is determined by the SliderStep property, which is a vector of length 2 of the form [MinorStepSize, MajorStepSize]. The default is [0.01, 0.1], which means the small increments are 0.01 (Max-Min) and the large increments are 0.1(Max-Min).

11.3 | SETTING A LOGICAL VALUE: THE CHECKBOX OBJECT

Description: The user can check or uncheck a labeled box. This expresses a binary decision and is often used to set the value (true or false) of a logical variable.

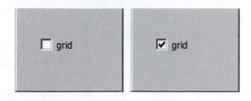

Class name: `uicontrol`, Style=checkbox

Primary properties: Value, String

The Value property is set to `true` or `false` (1 or 0) depending on whether the box is checked or not. The String property provides the label for the checkbox.

Example:

```
% get logical value makeGrid from GUI
makeGrid=get(handles.gridCheckbox, 'Value');
...
if makeGrid
    grid(handles.plotAxes, 'on');
end
```

11.4 | SETTING A STRING: THE EDIT TEXTBOX OBJECT

Description: The user can enter a string into the textbox by clicking on the box and then typing in the value. The String property of the textbox holds the information itself, which could represent a number or an alphanumeric quantity such as a name.

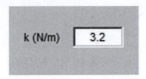

Class name: `uicontrol`, Style=edit

Primary properties: String

Example:

```
% get value of spring constant k
(in N/m) from textbox
kstr=get(handles.gridText, 'String');
k=str2double(kstr);
```

The properties related to the font of the text or the color are the same as discussed for pushbutton objects discussed on page 190.

11.5 | DISPLAYING A STRING: THE STATIC TEXTBOX OBJECT

Description: The static textbox is used to display a string on the GUI that cannot be edited by the user.

Total energy is 4.23 Joules

Class name: uicontrol, Style=text

Primary properties: String

Example:

```
% report value of Etot with object energyText
estring=['Total energy is ', num2str(Etot), ' Joules']);
set(handles.energyText, 'String', estring);
```

Static textboxes are frequently employed simply as labels for other GUI elements or for the Tool itself. As such, it's not necessary to assign meaningful Tag names to them.

They can also be used to output information to the user by constructing a string that has the necessary information and then setting the value of the String property of the textbox dynamically.

One can also alter the FontName, FontSize, FontWeight, and FontAngle properties to change the appearance of the text and make it more readable. To see a listing of available fonts on your system, type listfonts in the Command window. The standard caveat against using wacky fonts or too many fonts applies.

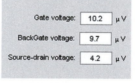

The Symbol font can be useful in making Greek letters and prefixes, e.g., $p = \pi, m = \mu, G = \Gamma$. The font must be the same for the whole textbox, however, so one may need to make more than one textbox and position them carefully together (as in the previous example).

The HorizontalAlignment property can be set to justify the text right or left, which may help. It's also helpful to use the arrow keys for making small positioning adjustments to the textbox objects, as well as GUIDE's object alignment tools (Tools | Align Objects . . .).

See the discussion of color properties on page 190.

11.6 | SELECTING A CHOICE: THE POPUPMENU OBJECT

Description: A popupmenu compactly presents the user with a set of options from which the user can select a single choice. When not activated, the current choice is represented by the string displayed on the popup.

Class name: `uicontrol`, Style=popupmenu

Primary properties: String, Value

The String property of the popupmenu determines what will be displayed as choices when the menu is activated by clicking it. The String property can be set from within the Property Inspector by clicking on the edit icon next to the property name. Enter the labels for each choice on separate lines.

Be careful to avoid entering an extra blank line which will show up as a blank option when popup is activated in the GUI.

Use the `get` function to retrieve the integer value of the Value property. The integer corresponds to the element in the list that the user has chosen. The first element on the list corresponds to a Value of 1, the second to a Value of 2, etc.

```
% Get choice of plotting the position (1),
%                            y-velocity (2),
%                   or y-acceleration (3)
iPlotChoice=get(handles.plotPopup, 'Value');
```

The String property can also be set dynamically from within the program. The value of the String property can be a cell array of strings labeling each entry.

```
set(handles.fishermenPopup, 'String',
                    {'Wynken', 'Blynken', 'Nod'});
```

The ability to dynamically set the String property means that both the menu choices and the number of menu choices offered can depend on the state of MATLAB variables at the time of execution. This allows very flexible programming of the user interface. For example, the user could enter the number of semiconductor layers in a textbox, and a popup menu can then let the user choose to examine or set the properties of each layer. The following callback function gets the total number of layers, Ntot, from a textbox and uses that number to construct an appropriate cell array of strings, which is then used to label the selection popup.

```
function NtotText_Callback(hObject, eventdata, handles)

N=str2double(get(handles.NtotText, 'String'));
for k=1:N
    popStr{k}=['Layer ', num2str(k)];
end
set(handles.iLayerPopup, 'String', popStr);
set(handles.iLayerPopup, 'Value', 1);
```

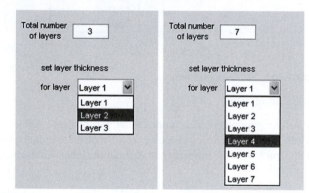

11.7 | SETTING A CHOICE: THE LISTBOX OBJECT

Description: A listbox displays a scrollable list of options from which the user may choose. It is possible to select several choices or none.

Class name: `uicontrol`, Style=listbox

Primary properties: String, Value, Min, Max

If the Min and Max Properties are set to 0 and 1 (the default), then the listbox acts like a popup menu, but with a scrollable list of options visible in the GUI. The Value property of the listbox holds an integer, which is the index of the selected element.

If Max is set to 2 (or any number greater than 1), then the user can select more than one choice. The first choice is made by clicking on the selection and subsequent choices can be added by Ctrl-clicking on choices. A second Ctrl-click deselects a choice. A contiguous group of choices can be selected by clicking the first selection and shift-clicking the last. The Value property of the listbox holds a vector of integers containing the indices of the selected elements. If no choice is selected, a zero-length vector is stored in Value.

The String property holds a cell-array of strings corresponding to the choice options. In the following example, the callback for the listbox first gets the listbox Value, a vector of the indices of the selected items (in this case [1, 3, 6]). The callback then gets the value of the listbox String property, a cell array of the choice labels (the dwarf names). It then loops through the vector of selected indices and constructs a new string composed of the currently selected names. Finally it reports this list through the String property of the static text object `dwarfText`.

Example:

```
function dwarfListbox_Callback(hObject, eventdata, handles)

dwarfChoiceVec=get(handles.dwarfListbox, 'Value');
dwarfString=get(handles.dwarfListbox, 'String');
nDwarfsChosen=length(dwarfChoiceVec);
if nDwarfsChosen>0
   commentStr=['Current dwarfs chosen: ',...
                 dwarfString{dwarfChoiceVec(1)}];
   for idwarf=2:nDwarfsChosen
        commentStr=[commentStr, ', ' ,...
                 dwarfString{dwarfChoiceVec(idwarf)}];
```

```
    end
    commentStr=[commentStr, '.'];
else
    commentStr='No dwarfs chosen.';
end
set(handles.dwarfsText, 'String', commentStr);
```

11.8 | SETTING AN EXCLUSIVE CHOICE: THE BUTTONGROUP, TOGGLEBUTTON, AND RADIOBUTTON OBJECTS

Description: The buttongroup contains several togglebuttons or radiobuttons and ensures that only one of them at a time is active.

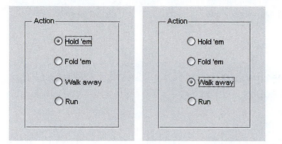

Class name: `uibuttongroup`, `uicontrol`, Style= togglebutton, `uicontrol`, Style= radiobutton

Primary property: SelectedObject

The buttongroup can be used to display a set of mutually exclusive choices, visualized as either radiobuttons or togglebuttons. Its function is very similar to a popup menu or a listbox. The choices are not in a particular order, however, and can have any geometric layout within the buttongroup. The buttongroup object manages the logic to make sure only one of the objects it contains is selected.

To determine which is the currently selected choice, one can `get` the value of the SelectedObject property, which is a handle to the selected object. With that handle, the String or Tag of the selected object can be determined and a corresponding action taken.

Callbacks for individual radiobuttons or togglebuttons are disabled. To cause an action to happen when the selection is changed, GUIDE must insert a stub for the SelectionChangeFcn, which is not done by default. To expose that callback function, select the buttongroup object in GUIDE and from the top menu bar select:

View | View Callbacks | SelectionChangeFcn.

GUIDE will then append an empty version of the SelectionChangeFcn to the tool file. Within the function, retrieving the value of the SelectedObject property of the buttongroup yields the handle of the newly selected radiobutton or togglebutton. It's often helpful to then get the Tag of that button, and decide what to do based on the Tag. The `switch` statement is convenient here, as in the following example, where the immediate action taken is simply reporting the current choice in a static textbox.

Maximum of data will be found.   Data will be smoothed.

```
hSelectedObj=get(handles.methodButtongroup, 'SelectedObject');
selectedObjTag=get(hSelectedObj, 'Tag');
switch selectedObjTag
  case 'MinTogglebutton'
    set(handles.methodText, 'String', 'Minimum of data will be found.');
  case 'MaxTogglebutton'
    set(handles.methodText, 'String', 'Maximum of data will be found.');
  case 'MeanTogglebutton'
    set(handles.methodText, 'String', 'Mean of data will be found.');
  case 'SmoothTogglebutton'
    set(handles.methodText, 'String', 'Data will be smoothed.');
  case 'IntegTogglebutton'
    set(handles.methodText, 'String', 'Integrate data.');
  case 'DerivTogglebutton'
    set(handles.methodText, 'String', 'Differentiate data.');
end
```

11.9 | VISUAL GROUPING: THE PANEL OBJECT

Description: The panel object associates a group of GUI objects visually by placing a rectangle around them.

Class name: `uipanel`

Primary properties: Title, BorderType

A set of GUI objects that are related to each other functionally can be grouped together visually by placing them in a panel together. The panel object has a Title property that is text that appears (by default) in the upper-left corner of the panel. If you don't want a title, simply set the value of the Title property to an empty string. The border appearance is altered by changing the BorderType property. A value of "beveledin" (shown) or "etchedin" is often attractive.

11.10 | TABULAR DATA: THE UITABLE OBJECT

Description: A table object presents the user with a two-dimensional array of data elements that can optionally be edited.

Sun position at solstices		
	June 21 Alt(deg)	June 21 Az(deg)
11:30 EST	65.7400	132.8000
12:00 EST	69.3200	148.2000
12:30 EST	71.4000	167.8000
13:00 EST	71.6000	189.6000

Class name: `uitable`

Primary properties: Data, RowName, ColumnName, ColumnEditable

The uitable object is useful for presenting to the user a two-dimensional table of data. The data can be of heterogenous class: numerical, logical, or string. Horizontal and vertical scroll bars make it possible to view a large array of data. Row headings and column headings can be set using cell arrays of strings. Each column can also be declared editable or not.

The value of the Data property is an array or cell array containing the contents of the table.

The table can be loaded with values and formatted in GUIDE, but it may be easier to do this within the CreateFcn. The CreateFcn for a GUI object is executed after the object is first created when the tool launches. One cannot assume that the handles structure has been created when the CreateFcn is run. The handle to the specific object (in this case, a table) is passed to the function through the argument hObject. A table of a few values of the solar analemma (the position in the sky of the sun on successive days at the same time) is shown above; the CreateFcn that initializes it is:

```
% — Executes during object creation,
% after setting all properties.
function analemmaTable_CreateFcn(hObject, eventdata, handles)
% hObject    handle to analemmaTable (see GCBO)
% eventdata reserved - to be defined
% in a future version of MATLAB
% handles    empty - handles not created until
%                    after all CreateFcns called
AnaMinMax= [...
        65.74,  132.8,  22.8,   161.9;...
        69.32,  148.2,  24.2,   169.2;...
        71.4,   167.8,  24.8,   176.7;...
        71.6,   189.6,  24.8,   184.3;...
        69.6,   209.6,  24.0,   191.8];
set(hObject, 'Data', AnaMinMax);
```

```
set(hObject,'RowName', {'11:30 EST', '12:00 EST', '12:30 EST',...
                        '13:00 EST', '13:30 EST'})
set(hObject, 'ColumnName', ...
      {'June 21 Alt(deg)', 'June 21 Az(deg)',...
       'Dec 21 Alt(deg)',  'Dec 21 Az(deg)'})
set(hObject, 'ColumnEditable', [true, true, false, false]);
```

When the user changes one of the editable values in the table, the CellEditCallback function is executed. This is a callback that has to be exposed explicity in GUIDE by choosing the menu option

View | View Callbacks | CellEditCallback.

When the CellEditCallback is invoked, the function receives, in addition to `handles`, a structure called `eventdata`, which holds information about which cell was edited, what the previous cell content was, and what the newly entered content is. The following example illustrates how to unpack this information.

```
% — Executes when cell data is changed.
function analemmaTable_CellEditCallback(hObject, event-
data, handles)
% hObject      handle to analemmaTable (see GCBO)
% eventdata    structure with the following fields (see UITABLE)
%        Indices: row and column indices of the cell(s) edited
%        PreviousData: previous data for the cell(s) edited
%        EditData: string(s) entered by the user
%        NewData: EditData or its converted form set on the Data
%                 property. Empty if Data was not changed
%        Error: error string when failed to convert EditData
%               to appropriate value for Data
%        handles: structure with handles and user data
iRowChanged=eventdata.Indices(1);
iColChanged=eventdata.Indices(2);
oldValue=eventdata.PreviousData;
newValue=eventdata.NewData;
disp(['Data at (', num2str(iRowChanged), ',', ...
      num2str(iColChanged), ')' , ' changed from ',...
      num2str(oldValue), ' to ', num2str(newValue)]);
```

The uitable can be viewed as an ordered array of static and editable textboxes. It is also possible to format the columns so they act as checkboxes or popup menus (see the MATLAB documentation).

11.11 | THE AXES OBJECT

Description: An axes object displays graphical information, such as plots (two-dimensional and three-dimensional) and images.

Class name: `axes`

Primary properties: grid, FontSize, FontWeight, FontName, LineWidth, XTick, YTick, ZTick, Box, ButtonDownFcn, CurrentPoint

Graphical information is usually put on the axes object using one of the plotting or imaging commands, e.g., `plot`, `plot3`, `surf`, `pcolor`, `image`. Often, the specific properties of the axes object are most easily set using higher-level graphics commands:

axis	sets scaling limits for x, y, and z axes and several other properties (see page 38)
xlabel, ylabel, zlabel	sets text labels for axes
title	sets string that labels graph at the top of the frame
grid	turns on and off grid lines
view	sets basic camera-related properties

Note that the LineWidth property controls the width of axes lines, not the lines of the plotted data.

When a GUI contains several axes objects, it is important to send graphics commands to the correct one. See pages 178 and 258 for discussions of how that is accomplished with high-level and low-level graphics commands.

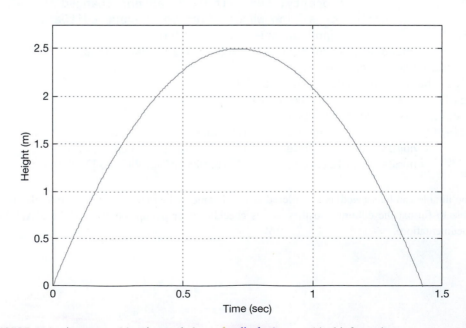

FIGURE 11.1 An `axes` object is a scaled area for displaying graphical information.

Axes objects can also be used as labels in the GUI instead of static text boxes. The advantage is that a text object displayed on the axes can be formatted using the LaTeX formatting commands. This allows Greek symbols, math symbols, subscripts, superscripts, and matix formatting, to be displayed nicely. The trick is to set up the labeling in the OpeningFcn of the tool. For each axes object that is to be used as a label, one must (a) turn the axis "off" to suppress drawing the coordinates, (b) create a text object using the text command with the Interpreter property set to "latex," and (c) make the axes object the parent of the text object. Figure 11.2 shows the GUIDE setup and the result; the corresponding code added to the OpeningFcn is:

```
% placed as last commands in MyTool_OpeningFcn
axis(handles.alphaLabelAxes, 'off');
ht=text(1, 0.5, '$\alpha/\alpha_0$', ...
        'HorizontalAlignment', 'Right',...
        'Interpreter', 'latex', 'FontSize', 14);
set(ht, 'Parent', handles.alphaLabelAxes);

axis(handles.rhoLabelAxes, 'off');
ht=text(1, 0.5, '$\rho^0_{init}$', ...
        'HorizontalAlignment', 'Right',...
        'Interpreter', 'latex', 'FontSize', 14);
set(ht, 'Parent', handles.rhoLabelAxes);

axis(handles.muLabelAxes, 'off');
ht=text(1, 0.5, '$\mu_1/\mu_0$', ...
        'HorizontalAlignment', 'Right',...
        'Interpreter', 'latex', 'FontSize', 14);
set(ht, 'Parent', handles.muLabelAxes);

axis(handles.mathLabelAxes,'off');
ht=text(1, 0.5, ...
          '$$\mu_1=\frac{1}{\eta}\int_0^\infty \chi(z) dz $$',...
        'HorizontalAlignment', 'Right',...
        'Interpreter', 'latex', 'FontSize', 14);
set(ht, 'Parent', handles.mathLabelAxes);
```

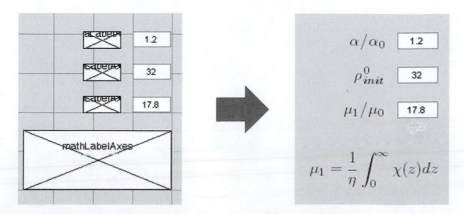

FIGURE 11.2 Axes objects can be used as labels with LaTeX formatting.

Advanced Topics

PART III

More GUI Techniques

This chapter covers several techniques you can use to make your GUI tools more interactive and helpful. Like the chapters that follow, it is meant as a resource and reference rather than a tutorial.

GUI pop-ups. MATLAB comes with a variety of small predefined GUI tools in the form of ready-to-go dialog boxes and pop-up tools. These can be added to your own GUI tools to enhance their functionality.

> **Waitbars** Waitbar pop-ups show the user how much progress has been made toward the completion of a computational task. The key MATLAB command is `waitbar`. (Section 12.1).

> **File dialogs** To save information to a MATLAB-formatted `*.mat` file, one can conveniently use a combination of the `save` command and the `uiputfile` command, which pops up a familiar file navigation tool. To read information from a file, one can use `load` and `uigetfile` (Section 12.2) Writing and reading from formatted text files is a little more complicated and can be accomplished using the commands `fopen`, `fprintf`, and `textscan` (Section 12.3).

> **Input dialogs** The pop-up produced by the `inputdlg` command allows the user to enter specific information to the GUI tool without permanently taking up space on the tool panel (Section 12.4).

> **Question dialogs** The pop-up produced by the `questdlg` command similarly allows the user to enter the answer to a simple yes/no question (Section 12.5).

Sharing information between functions. One often wants to communicate information between Callback functions. Information displayed in GUI objects is available to all Callbacks through the handles structure. It's often desirable to keep other information available as well. This can be accomplished through use of the setappdata and getappdata commands (Section 12.6).

Responding to keyboard and mouse events. Sections 12.7 and 12.8 describe how to make your program responsive to user keyboard clicks, mouse clicks, and mouse motion. This involves setting Callback functions associated with those actions by changing the value of the properties KeyPressFcn, ButtonDownFcn, WindowButtonMotionFcn, and WindowButtonUpFcn. Each of these properties takes the value of a handle to a function that is invoked when the action happens (e.g., the user moves the mouse when the mouse button is down).

Creating menus in GUIDE. A top bar of pull-down menus can be added to your GUI tool using the Menu Editor in GUIDE, as described in Section 12.9.

12.1 Waitbars

When a computation doesn't happen immediately but takes some time to complete, the user may begin to worry. Perhaps the calculation has gone seriously awry and is now in an infinite loop. Perhaps the program is waiting for the user to do something, but the user is uncertain about what to do. Or perhaps, it's just taking time to work through the calculation, in which case it would be nice to have some idea of when it will be done. To inform the user, and perhaps allay the user's worst fears, it's helpful to show the progress being made as the calculation proceeds. The waitbar command creates a thermometer-type display in a pop-up figure window that represents the progress of the calculation graphically.

The most common application is a simple one—create a waitbar that shows the progress of a for loop, usually the outermost loop in the computation. The waitbar command is invoked first, before the loop begins, in order to display zero initial progress and to store the handle of the waitbar.

```
<handle>=waitbar(0, '<message string>', 'Name', '<title>');
```

In each iteration of the loop, the waitbar command is invoked again to update the displayed state.

```
waitbar(progress, <handle>);
```

Here, progress should evaluate to a real number between 0 and 1, and <handle> is the handle to the waitbar that has already been created.

Finally, the waitbar should be deleted by the command close(handle). The following example illustrates the common pattern of waitbar use.

```
N=500;
hwb=waitbar(0, 'Calculating ...', 'Name', 'Time marching');
for k=1:N
```

FIGURE 12.1 A waitbar shows the user that progress is being made—the program is neither stuck nor is it going to last forever.

```
    % <long calculation goes here>
    waitbar(k/N, hwb);
end
close(hwb)
```

The resulting waitbar is shown in Figure 12.1.

12.2 File dialogs

Saving and loading data in .mat files

The `save` command saves the values and names of MATLAB variables. For example, to save variables x, y, and t, which could be arrays or scalars, to a file named "myData," the syntax is as follows:

```
save myData x y t
```

or

```
save('myData', 'x', 'y', 't');
```

The latter, functional, form of the command is necessary if the file name is stored in a string variable.

```
fname='myData';
save(fname, 'y', 'yinit', 'yfinal');
```

The file thus produced is named `myData.mat` and is a MATLAB-specific binary file; it is not a text file and in general cannot be read except by MATLAB. Note that the file contains not only the data, but also the name and class of each of the variables. If you do not specify a list of variables, all the variables in the current workspace are stored.

The information stored in a .mat file can be read back into MATLAB using the `load` command.

```
load myData            % loads all variables from myData.mat
load myData x y name % loads variables x, y, name from myData.mat
```

or

```
theFile='myData';
load(theFile);
load(theFile, 'x', 'y', 'name')
```

The file name can include the fully qualified path to the file, for example:

```
'C:\Documents and Settings\Alfonso\My Documents\
MATLAB\myData'.
```

The data file may be in a folder other than the current folder.

If a variable of the same name (in the previous example, say, 'x') already exists, the load command overwrites its value with the value from the file.

```
x=17;
save myvalues x
x=24;
load myvalues
disp(x)
     17
```

In the context of a GUI tool, loading the values with a load command is just the beginning. The newly loaded values will usually have to be put into the appropriate places in the GUI interface, set as textbox, slider, and checkbox values, for example. They may also be stored as generally accessible application data, as described in Section 12.6.

A GUI interface to file names using uiputfile and uigetfile

Users are accustomed to being able to find a file, name a file, and navigate directories using a standard pop-up panel. This functionality is provided with the uiputfile command, for saving files, and uigetfile, for loading files. The important feature to understand is that these tools simply provide a way to get the name of the file—they do not, by themselves, save or load information.

The syntax for uiputfile is:

```
[FileName, PathName, FilterIndex] = uiputfile(FilterSpec,...
                                    DialogTitle, DefaultName);
```

For example:

```
[fname, pname]=uiputfile('*.mat', 'Save in .mat file', 'myData');
```

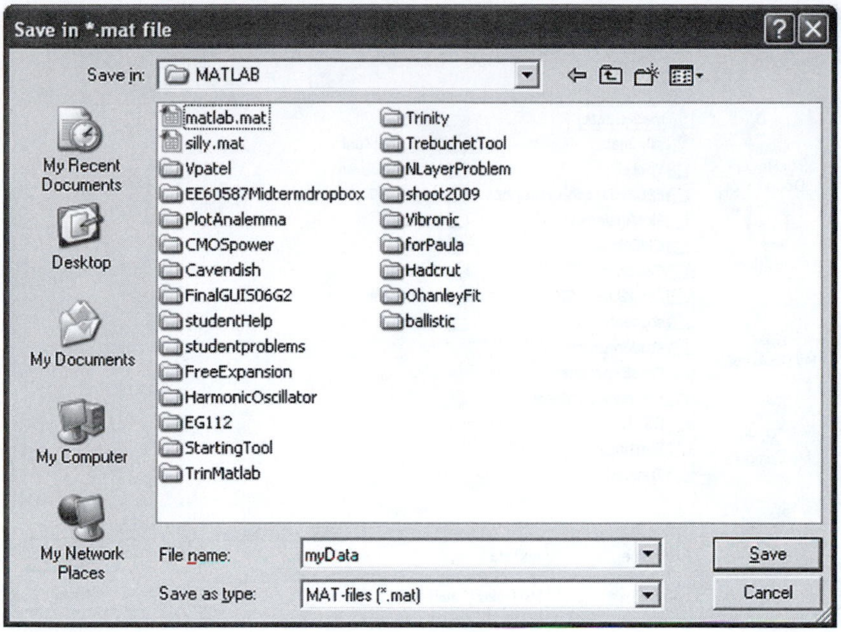

FIGURE 12.2 The dialog box produced by the `uiputfile` command.

This produces the pop-up dialog box shown in Figure 12.2. The user can navigate around the file system, create new folders, and name the file in which to save the information.

The function returns the variable `fname` containing the name of the file the user chose. The returned variable `pname` has the full path name to the chosen folder—and it's often long. For example:

```
C:\Documents and Settings\Alfonso\My Documents\MATLAB\
```

To carry through on saving the file requires a subsequent `save` command.

```
save([pname, fname], 'x', 'y', 'snoutCount');
```

The first argument is the fully qualified name of the file, including its full path name, and is formed by concatenating the strings representing the path name and the file name. Notice that in the string concatenation operation (using square brackets) the path name and file name need to be in the reverse order from that returned by `uiputfile`.

To load information into the workspace, the command `uigetfile` provides comparable functionality.

```
[FileName, PathName, FilterIndex] = ...
        uigetfile(FilterSpec, DialogTitle, DefaultName)
```

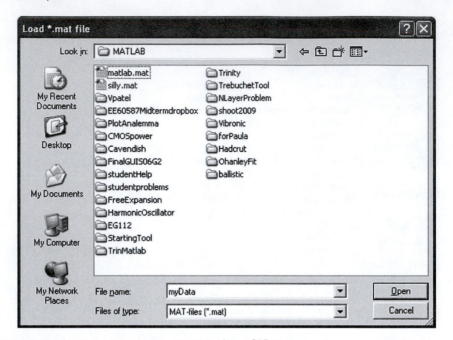

FIGURE 12.3 The dialog box produced by the `uigetfile` command.

For example:

```
[fname, pname]=uigetfile('*.mat', 'Load *.mat file', 'myData');
```

This produces the pop-up dialog box shown in Figure 12.3.

As with `uiputfile`, `uigetfile` only gets a file name and path name; it does not actually retrieve information from the file. So the common pattern is to follow it immediately by a `load` command using the string variables obtained.

```
load([pname, fname]);
```

The following example illustrates prompting the user for a file in which to save information, and prompting for a file from which to read the information.

```
% save a,b,c to *.mat file chosen by user
a=1.1;
b=2.2;
c=3.3;

[fname, pname]=uiputfile('*.mat', 'Save in .mat file');
save([pname, fname], 'a', 'b', 'c');
```

```
% set new values for a,b,c
a=10.1;
b=20.2;
c=30.3;
disp(['a=', num2str(a), 'b=', num2str(b), 'c=', num2str(c)]);

% load values from file, overwriting the current values
[fname, pname]=uigetfile('*.mat', 'Load .mat file');
load([pname, fname], 'a', 'b', 'c');

disp(['a=', num2str(a), 'b=', num2str(b), 'c=', num2str(c)]);
```

12.3   Reading and writing formatted text files

A MATLAB .mat file stores MATLAB variables and their values. An alternative is to write the information to, and subsequently read it from, a plain text file. The main advantage of storing information in a plain text file is that the data can be easily read by humans, and by many other programs. One disadvantage is that the information about the class and name of the MATLAB variables that held the information is not stored. Depending on how the text is written, there may also be a loss of precision.

Writing data to a text file can be accomplished in three steps:

1. Open the file with the fopen command; this associates an integer called the "file identifier number" with the file. The file can be opened in several different access modes (also called permissions).

2. Write data from currently defined MATLAB variables to the file using the fprintf command. The data will be written as formatted text strings.

3. Close the file using the fclose command.

The fopen command opens a file in a particular access mode and returns the file indentifier number.

```
fid=open('DataFileName.txt', '<accessString>');
```

For example, the following code creates an integer, a, two real variables, b and c, and a string, name. It then opens a file and appends a line to the file containing the values of all four variables.

```
a=randi([1, 10]);
b=7.2*sqrt(2);
c=3*pi;
name='Alfonzo';
```

```
fid1=fopen('Somedata.txt','a');
fprintf(fid1,'%d    %f    %5.3f    %s \n', a, b, c, name);
fclose(fid1);
```

This results in the following line of text being added to the end of the file Somedata.txt (if the file does not exist, it is created).

```
9    10.182338    9.425    Alfonso
```

Here the file was opened in "append" mode. Several access modes are available, indicated by the access string character in the fopen command.

Write mode 'w'. The file is open for writing new data; existing contents are discarded.

Append mode 'a'. The file is open for writing with the existing data maintained in the file; new data will be written at the end of the file.

Read mode 'r'. The file is open for reading.

The syntax for the fprintf command ("file-print-formatted") is as follows:

```
fprintf(FID, '<Format String>', Var1, Var2, ...);
```

The FID is an integer file indentifier, normally the one returned by fopen. The format string controls the way in which the values of the variables listed thereafter will appear. Special characters in the string that begin with the percent sign, '%', control where and in what format the values of the variables appear.

Without a file identifier, the command sends formatted output to the Command window.

```
fprintf('<Format String>', Var1, Var2, ...);
```

For example:

```
x=1.2;
fprintf(' Height= %f \n', x)
```

produces:

```
 Height= 1.200000
```

The '%f' in the format string indicates a floating point number; the \n inserts a new line character that ends the line.

```
>> fprintf(' Height= %g meters \n', x)
```

produces:

```
 Height= 1.2 meters
```

Both '%f' and '%g' are formats for real (floating-point) numbers; the difference is that '%g' suppresses trailing zeros for a more compact representation. Other options include '%d' for integers and '%s' for strings. For example:

```
>> fprintf('%d %18.15f %f \n   Name: %s \n', a, b, c, name)
```

produces:

```
9  6.521701946944458 9.424778
   Name: Alfonso
```

Adding numerical qualifiers to '%f' determines the total width of the formatted string produced, and the number of digits to the right of the decimal. For example, '%18.15f' means the number will be printed with a total width (number of characters including '.' and leading spaces) of 18, with 15 characters to the right of the decimal. The format '%8.5g' indicates 5 digits of precision and a total field of 8 characters.

If an array appears in the list of variables to be printed, the elements of the array are printed in column order, i.e., column by column and top to bottom. The formatting string is used repeatedly until the data ends.

```
>> A=rand(3)
A =
     0.8173    0.3998    0.4314
     0.8687    0.2599    0.9106
     0.0844    0.8001    0.1818

>> fprintf('%g \n', A)
0.817303
0.868695
0.0844358
0.399783
0.25987
0.800068
0.431414
0.910648
0.181847
```

To get three columns in the output, we use three '%f' symbols in the format string, but note that the values are taken from A in column order, but printed row-wise as the three '%f' specifiers are used repeatedly.

```
>> fprintf('%12.8f %12.8f %12.8f \n', A)
    0.81730322    0.86869471    0.08443585
    0.39978265    0.25987040    0.80006848
    0.43141383    0.91064759    0.18184703
```

Reading data from a text file can be complicated, and the way in which the file is formatted must be known in advance. For example, suppose the file 'MyRelevantData.dat' holds the following:

```
8    6.908345    9.425    Alfonso
7    0.257124    9.425    Richard
9    6.724751    9.425    Mingus
7    5.455729    7.345    Theodosius
8    2.824035    7.345    Thurston
7    1.232544    7.345    Aloysius
8    0.229196    3.787    Bob
3    0.332434    9.425    Colfax
```

To read data from a file, the file can be opened with a "read" access mode and read using textscan.

```
fid1=fopen('MyRelevantData.dat', 'r');
theData=textscan(fid1, '%d %f %f %s');
fclose(fid1);
```

The command textscan uses the same format string conventions as fprintf and returns a cell array with the data read by column. The first column of data is stored as a vector in theData{1}, the second in theData{2}, and so forth.

```
avec=theData{1};
bvec=theData{2};
cvec=theData{3};
Names=theData{4};

disp('Display last row of data')
disp(['a=', num2str(avec(end))]);
disp(['b=', num2str(bvec(end))]);
disp(['c=', num2str(cvec(end))]);
disp(['Name=', Names{end}]);
```

This produces:

```
Display last row of data
a=3
b=0.33243
c=9.425
Name=Colfax
```

Since the fourth column contains strings, it is stored in a cell array of strings.

Reading and writing to files can be done in many ways with considerable flexibility. Here, only the basics of file input and output have been addressed. See further online documentation for the commands `fopen`, `fclose`, `fprintf`, `fseek`, `fwrite`, `fread`, `ftell`, `fgetl`, `fscanf`, `fgets`, `textread`, `fileread`, and `textscan`.

Comma-delimited files can be written and read by `cvswrite` and `cvsread`. The `import-data` command will recognize many different file types, including spreadsheets, and will read the data into appropriate MATLAB data structures. A GUI wizard for importing and exporting files interactively is provided by `uiimport`, which is also accessible from the MATLAB IDE with the Import Data button on the Home tab.

12.4   The input dialog

The predefined GUI dialog box produced by `inputdlg` prompts the user for one or more values and returns the user's response in a cell array of strings. For example, the following code fragment prompts for two values. The resulting pop-up dialog panel is shown in Figure 12.4.

```
prompt={'Enter x_0 (m):',...
        'Enter v_0 (m/s):'};
name='Initial values';
numlines=1;
defaultanswer={'0.0', '1.0'};
options.Resize='on';
options.Interpreter='tex';
caStr=inputdlg(prompt,name,numlines,defaultanswer,options);
```

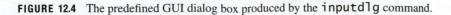

FIGURE 12.4   The predefined GUI dialog box produced by the `inputdlg` command.

The first input to the command `prompt` is a cell array of strings that contains the prompts for each value to be input. The `name` of the dialog box is displayed in the top border. If `numlines` is 1, then each input is taken to be a scalar value (see the documentation for inputting vector values). The `defaultanswer` is another cell array of strings, one for each of the values being sought. The `options` structure includes fields for making the panel resizable, and using the TEX interpreter so that here the prompt `'x_0'` is rendered as x_0 on the dialog box.

The returned cell array of strings, `caStr`, must be processed to set the values of the desired variables appropriately. If the user presses 'Cancel', `inputdlg` returns a null string (i.e., a string with length zero).

```
if length(caStr)>0
    x0=num2str(caStr{1});
    v0=num2str(caStr{2});
    disp(['x0= ', num2str(x0), '  v0=', num2str(v0)]);
end
```

12.5   The question dialog

To ask a simple binary question of the user, with an option to cancel, use the predefined GUI dialog box produced by `questdlg`. It takes two string arguments, one containing the text of the question, and one containing the title of dialog frame. The string returned is 'Yes', 'No', or 'Cancel'.

```
choice=questdlg('Do you want to sing the blues?',
  'Important  question');
wantsToSingTheBlues=false;
switch choice
    case 'Yes'
        disp('Then you gotta pay your dues.');
        wantsToSingTheBlues=true;
    case 'No'
        disp('Okay, then.');
    case 'Cancel'
        disp('Cancelled.')
end
```

This produces the dialog box shown in Figure 12.5.

It's possible to customize the three choices by including more arguments (see the documentation), but no more than three choices are possible.

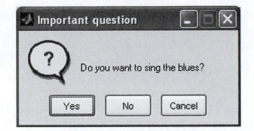

FIGURE 12.5   The predefined GUI dialog produced by questdlg gets a basic decision from the user.

12.6   Sharing application data between functions

It is sometimes desirable to share data between different MATLAB functions. We have already seen in Chapter 10 that one way to accomplish this is to have one function set the value of a property of a GUI object, such as the String property of a textbox, and have another function subsequently get the value from the object. This works well and is a natural approach for parameters that we'd like to have displayed on the GUI, but it is not suitable for other types of data. For example, one may want to store several arrays that are the result of a long calculation (e.g., x, y, t, vx, and vy) and subsequently access them in another function in order to calculate some related quantities.

The commands setappdata and getappdata operate very much like set and get, except you can make up your own property names. The data can be associated with any object provided the handle to the object is available. To illustrate, the following MATLAB code creates a figure, stores some application data in it, and retrieves the data.

```
>> hf=figure;
>> setappdata(hf, 'Combination', [1, 4, 12, 7]);
>> setappdata(hf, 'Name', 'Trillium Fortnight');
>> theCombination=getappdata(hf, 'Combination')
theCombination =
      1     4    12     7
>> Author=getappdata(gcf, 'Name')
Author =
Trillium Fortnight
```

The function gcf (get current figure) returns the handle of the current figure. In a GUIDE-generated GUI, information can be conveniently stored as application data of the figure; the figure is the window that comprises the GUI tool itself. The advantage is that the figure handle is always available using gcf.

Information can also be stored as the application data of a particular GUI element.

Application data can include structures and cell arrays so a bundle of data can be stored with a single setappdata command.

```
traj.x=xBall;
traj.y=yBall;
traj.t=t;
setappdata(gcf, 'Trajectory', traj);
```

12.7   Responding to keyboard input

It may be helpful for the user to control the action in a program by using the keyboard instead of, or in addition to, the mouse. A figure window has a property named KeyPressFcn. If the value of KeyPressFcn is set to a function handle, that function will be executed when any key on the keyboard is pressed. The keystroke-processing function should have at least two arguments. The first argument is the handle of the figure itself. The second is an event structure that has fields for the character pressed, the key pressed, and the modifiers pressed. The modifiers are the Shift, Alt, and Ctrl keys, and are coded by strings in a cell array, for example {'shift','control'}. Arrow keys and keys on the numeric keypad have distinct codes.

For the keystroke-processing function associated with the figure to be invoked, the figure window must be the active window, as determined by the operating system. This is usually done by simply clicking on the window, making it the top window.

The following program, which uses an empty figure for illustration purposes, demonstrates how to extract information about which key the user has pressed from the event structure evnt, which is passed to the keystroke-processing function. The function ca2str concatenates the strings in the evnt.Modifier cell array into a single string for display. For example, the cell array {'alt','control'} is simply converted to the string 'alt control'.

```
function DemoKeyPress
figure(1);
set(gcf, 'KeyPressFcn', @processKey);
% Note: make figure the active window by clicking on it
```
```
function processKey(src, evnt)
if length(evnt.Character)>=1
    clc;
    disp(['Character: ', evnt.Character]);
    disp(['Modifiers: ', ca2str(evnt.Modifier)])
    disp(['Key:       ', evnt.Key]);
end
```
```
function cas=ca2str(ca)
% convert 1xN cell array of strings to a single
% string with spaces separating elements
[n1, n]=size(ca);
cas='';
```

```
for k=1:n
    cas=[cas, ' ', ca{k}];
end
```

For example, when `DemoKeyPress` is run and the 'k' key is pressed with both the Shift key and Alt key held down, the following is written to the Command window.

```
Character: K
Modifiers:  shift alt
Key:        k
```

The next section includes an example of using keyboard input to move graphical objects.

12.8 Making graphic objects interactive

Graphical objects have a property called ButtonDownFcn, whose value can be a function handle. The corresponding function will then be invoked when the mouse button is clicked over the object.

When the mouse cursor is moved or the mouse button released, other functions, associated with the figure window, can be activated. By setting these appropriately, graphical objects can become more interactive.

Mouse-click response

The following program demonstrates how to set the value of the ButtonDownFcn property to create a callback that is invoked when the mouse button is clicked while the mouse cursor is over an object. In this example, for simplicity, a triangular patch object is created in a figure, without constructing a GUIDE-generated GUI. When the user clicks the mouse button over the patch, the patch color toggles between red and blue, and the position of the triangle's midpoint is displayed in the Command window.

```
function DemoButtonDown
%    makes a triangular patch that toggles its color when clicked
%              Author: Sledge Poteet

%% make axes
hf=figure(1);
hax=axes;
axis(hax, [0, 10, 0, 10]);

%% define patch vertex coordinates
x = [5, 7, 6, 5];
y = [3, 3, 5, 3];
```

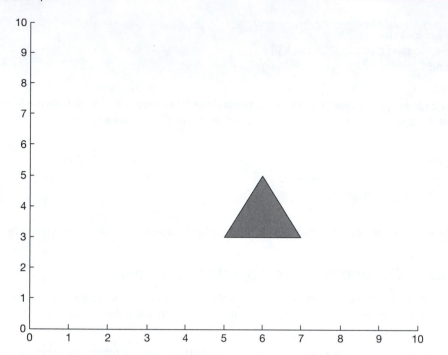

FIGURE 12.6 The program DemoButtonDown draws a triangular patch object and the ButtonDownFcn property is set so that the color toggles between red and blue when the user clicks the object. (Use your imagination here.)

```
%% create patch and set ButtonDownFcn for patch
hp = patch(x, y, 'r');
set(hp, 'ButtonDownFcn', @patch_ButtonDownFcn);


function patch_ButtonDownFcn(hObject, eventdata)
x = get(hObject, 'XData');
y = get(hObject, 'YData');
xmid=sum(x)/length(x);
ymid=sum(y)/length(y);
disp(['Object centered at x=', num2str(xmid),...
                         ' y=' num2str(ymid)])


%% toggle color from red to blue
colorVec=get(hObject,'FaceColor');
if colorVec==[1, 0, 0] % color vector is [Red, Green, Blue]
    colorVec=[0, 0, 1];
elseif colorVec==[0, 0, 1]
    colorVec=[1, 0, 0];
end
set(hObject, 'FaceColor', colorVec);
```

Mouse events and object dragging

By using a combination of callback functions associated with mouse events, graphical objects can be made draggable by the mouse cursor. Dragging an object involves these three events.

1. The user clicks the (left) mouse button when the mouse cursor is over a graphical object.

2. As the mouse cursor is moved with the button held down, the object is moved so the mouse cursor is always over the same point on the object. This motion makes it appear that the object is stuck to the mouse cursor at the point the cursor was over when the mouse button was clicked.

3. When the user releases the mouse button, the object ceases to move.

The first event is captured by setting a function handle value for the ButtonDownFcn property of the graphical object. The second and third events (mouse motion and button release) are associated with the figure window itself.

A figure window has three mouse-event-related properties. These determine the function that will be invoked when specific mouse events occur.

• WindowButtonDownFcn determines the function invoked when a mouse button is pressed anywhere in the figure window.

• WindowButtonMotionFcn determines the function invoked whenever the mouse cursor is moved within the figure window.

• WindowButtonUpFcn determines the function invoked when the mouse button is released.

By default, each property has a null value. Each type of event can be associated with an event-processing function by setting the value of the corresponding property to the function's handle. Each event-processing function should be written to take at least two arguments: the handle of the object that activated them (the figure or the graphical object within it), and an event structure (not used here). Additional arguments can be sent to the function when it is invoked by setting the property value to a cell array containing the function handle and the other values that are to be sent as arguments.

The following function dragDemo can serve as a template for making objects both draggable using the mouse, and movable using the arrow keys. The important callbacks are created using the ButtonDownFcn property of the objects, and the WindowButtonMotionFcn, WindowButtonUpFcn, and KeyPressFcn properties of the figure. The interaction between the various callbacks is a little involved and the code below rewards careful study.

```
function dragDemo
%% Demonstrate dragging patch objects
%   and manipulating with keys
%
%            Author: Dodge Flannelette
figure(1)
```

```
%% draw two patch objects
axis([0, 10, 0, 5]);
hpatch(1)=patch([1, 2, 2, 1, 1],[2.2,  2,  3.2,  3, 2.2], 'r');
hpatch(2)=patch([5, 8, 9, 5, 5],[2.2,  2,  3.2,  3, 2.2], 'g');
```

```
%% set callbacks for button down, up, and keypresses
set(hpatch(1),' ButtonDownFcn', @patchButtonDown);
set(hpatch(2), 'ButtonDownFcn', @patchButtonDown);
set(gcf, 'WindowButtonUpFcn', @ButtonUp);
set(gcf, 'KeyPressFcn', @processKey);
```

```
%% Button Functions
function patchButtonDown(hpatch, eventdata)
% when the patch is clicked, set the motion function.
%  Get the position of the patch
x=get(hpatch, 'XData');
y=get(hpatch, 'YData');

%  The offset is the difference between the lower left
%  of the object (x(1),y(1)) and the mouse position when button
%  was pushed down.
lowerleft=[x(1), y(1)];
curr_pt = get(gca, 'CurrentPoint');
offset=[curr_pt(1, 1), curr_pt(1, 2)]-lowerleft;

% set the WindowButtonMotionFcn and give it 2 additional
% arguments: the patch handle and the offset
setappdata(gcf, 'SelectedPatch', hpatch);
set(gcf, 'WindowButtonMotionFcn',...
        {@figButtonMotion, hpatch, offset});
```

```
function ButtonUp(src, eventdata);
%  when the button is released, turn off the motion function
set(gcf, 'WindowButtonMotionFcn', ' ')
```

```
function figButtonMotion(src, eventdata, hselected, offset)
%  Moves the object with handle hselected.
%  The offset is the difference between the lower left
%  of the object and the mouse position when button
%  was pushed down.

% Get position of vertices
x=get(hselected, 'XData');
y=get(hselected, 'YData');
% Find vertex coordinates relative to (x(1),y(1))
xr=x-x(1);
yr=y-y(1);
```

```
% Get the mouse cursor Location
curr_pt = get(gca, 'CurrentPoint');
% Change the position of the patch
set(hselected, 'XData', curr_pt(1,1)-offset(1)+xr);
set(hselected, 'YData', curr_pt(1,2)-offset(2)+yr);

function processKey(src, evnt)
% process arrow keys to move currently selected patch
hpatch=getappdata(gcf, 'SelectedPatch');
if length(evnt.Key)>=1
    xshift=0;
    yshift=0;
    switch evnt.Key
        case 'leftarrow'
            xshift=-0.1;
        case 'rightarrow'
            xshift= 0.1;
        case 'uparrow'
            yshift= 0.1;
        case 'downarrow'
            yshift= -0.1;
    end
    x=get(hpatch, 'XData')+xshift;
    set(hpatch, 'XData', x);
    y=get(hpatch, 'YData')+yshift;
    set(hpatch, 'YData', y);
end
```

The main dragDemo function first creates two patch objects and then sets the value of the ButtonDownFcn property of each patch to the function handle of patchButtonDown, the function to be activated when the patch is clicked. The function patchButtonDown will automatically receive as arguments the handle of the clicked patch and an event structure. The value of the figure's WindowButtonUpFcn property is set to the function handle of ButtonUp, and the value of the KeyPressFcn property is set to the function handle of the processKey function.

When the patchButtonDown function is invoked, it gets the position on the axes of the mouse cursor from the CurrentPoint property of the axes; the handle to the axes is obtained using the gca (get current axes) function. The vector offset, the difference between the cursor position and the first vertex of the patch, is then calculated. The first vertex simply serves as a reference point on the patch. A handle to the selected patch is stored as figure application data; this is used by the processKey function to determine which object should be moved when the arrow keys are pressed. Finally, the WindowButtonMotionFcn property of the figure is set to activate another function, figButtonMotion. The value of WindowButtonMotionFcn is set to a cell array that includes the handle to figButtonMotion, a handle to the active patch, and the value

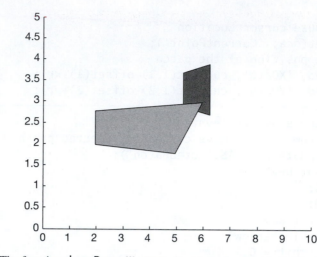

FIGURE 12.7 The function dragDemo illustrates how to make graphical objects that can be dragged with the mouse or positioned using the keyboard arrow keys. It creates these two patches that can be moved by the user by either method.

of the offset vector. This syntax indicates that these two additional values will be passed as arguments to the figButtonMotion function.

The function figButtonMotion is invoked every time the mouse cursor moves. It updates the patch's position (the values of the vertex coordinates) using the new cursor position and the offset vector.

Using these techniques, custom interactive graphical elements can be constructed that extend the ways in which the user can interact with the computational model beyond the GUI controls (buttons, sliders, etc.) already provided.

12.9 Creating menus in GUIDE

A top menu bar is a standard feature of window tools, and GUIDE provides an easy way to create them using the Menu Editor. This section will describe how to create a very simple menu—extensions to more complicated menu structures are straightforward.

Launch GUIDE from MATLAB and from the top menu in the GUIDE panel select

"Tools | Menu Editor ..."

and the Menu Editor appears.

Press the top left button on the Menu Editor toolbar (the tooltip that appears when the mouse cursor lingers over it is: New Menu) to create the first menu item. Click on that item and then click the second-from-the-left button on the toolbar (tooltip: New Menu Item). Press it three times to create three menu items that are lower in the hierarchy than the first item. You can rearrange the hierarchy using the arrow buttons on the toolbar. The red X deletes a menu item.

Select the first menu at the base of the hierarchy and fill in the Label field in the Menu Properties box at the right of the panel. Make the Label entry "File" (with no quotes). You need not alter the Tag for this item.

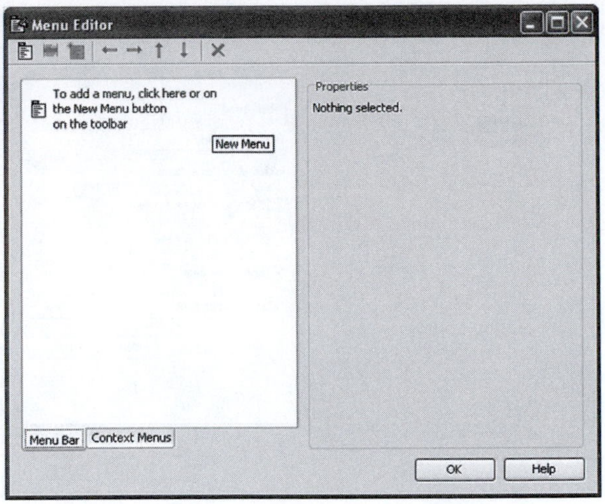

FIGURE 12.8 The GUIDE Menu Editor at startup.

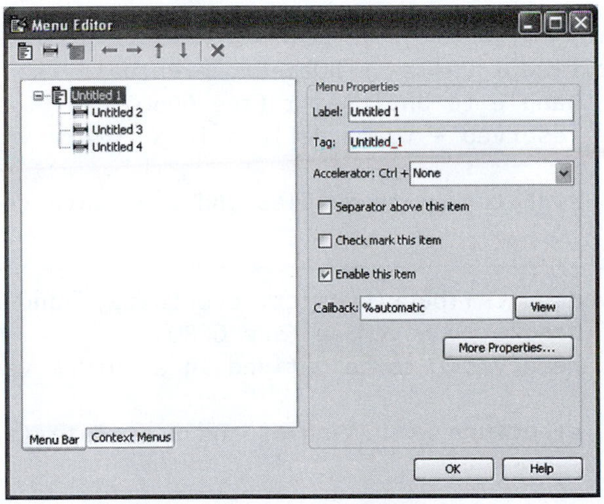

FIGURE 12.9 Menu Editor with initial setup consisting of one menu with three elements.

Select in turn each of the three menu items below the File item and add a label and a Tag for each. Make the labels: "Save", "Load", and "Quit", with corresponding Tags "saveMenu", "loadMenu", and "quitMenu". The Tags play the same role as Tags for user interface objects and it's important to have a consistent naming scheme. For the Quit menu item, check the box next to "Separator above this item." The Menu Editor should now look like Figure 12.10.

Press OK to close the Menu Editor and return to GUIDE.

Save the GUI as DemoToolMenu.fig. GUIDE will generate DemoMenuTool.m and load it into the Editor. Along with the usual other GUI functions that GUIDE generates, you will see four empty callback functions.

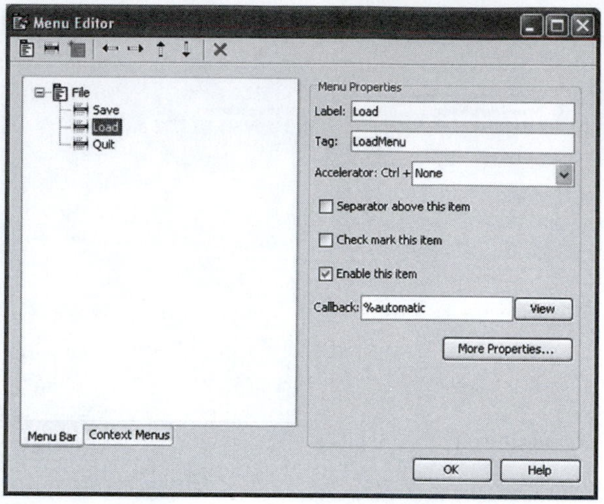

FIGURE 12.10 Menu Editor with labels and tags creating simple menu.

```
% ―――――――――――――――――――――――――――――――――
function Untitled_1_Callback(hObject, eventdata, handles)
% hObject      handle to Untitled_1 (see GCBO)
% eventdata    reserved - to be defined in a future version
  of MATLAB
% handles      structure with handles and user data (see GUIDATA)

% ―――――――――――――――――――――――――――――――――
function saveMenu_Callback(hObject, eventdata, handles)
% hObject      handle to SaveMenu (see GCBO)
% eventdata    reserved - to be defined in a future version
  of MATLAB
% handles      structure with handles and user data (see GUIDATA)

% ―――――――――――――――――――――――――――――――――
function loadMenu_Callback(hObject, eventdata, handles)
% hObject      handle to LoadMenu (see GCBO)
% eventdata    reserved - to be defined in a future version
  of MATLAB
% handles      structure with handles and user data (see GUIDATA)

% ―――――――――――――――――――――――――――――――――
function quitMenu_Callback(hObject, eventdata, handles)
% hObject      handle to QuitMenu (see GCBO)
% eventdata    reserved - to be defined in a future ver-
sion of MATLAB
% handles      structure with handles and user data (see GUIDATA)
```

The first is from the File menu item itself and can be ignored. Each of the other three is the callback function invoked when the user selects the menu item with the associated tag. These menu items behave just like push buttons; they're convenient because they're usually folded up and out of the way. Add the following line in the body of `quitMenu_Callback` to make MenuDemoTool quit gracefully.

```
close(gcf)
```

The callbacks for menu items like Save and Load often invoke predefined dialog boxes `uiputfile` and `uigetfile`. Other menu items might use `inputdlg` to get parameters from the user. The advantage of getting information when the user selects a menu choice is that then input textbox space on the GUI panel is not necessary—perhaps some values are changed infrequently. Note that the values so obtained will need to be stored somewhere or they will vanish when the callback function completes. A good solution is to store them as figure application data with `setappdata` (page 221) so they can be accessed by any other function.

Menu items also have a Checked property that takes the values "on" or "off." This allows them to be used like checkboxes. To make a menu item toggle between the checked and unchecked state, add the following code to the body of its callback.

```
if strcmp(get(hObject, 'Checked'), 'on');
    set(hObject, 'Checked', 'off')
else
    set(hObject, 'Checked', 'on');
end
```

Nested hierarchies of menus can be created using the Menu Editor. This can clean up space on the GUI tool. It is wise to be consistent with the menu system conventions for your operating system. Usually the leftmost menu item is named "File" and the rightmost is named "Help."

More Graphics

This chapter is meant to be a first reference and source of examples for creating some of the more complex graphical visualizations that MATLAB enables. The scope ranges from simple plotting commands to manipulation of aggregate graphical objects in three dimensions.

Log plots.   Section 12.1 describes the facilities for making various log and semi-log plots. The key MATLAB commands are `semilogy`, `semilogx`, `loglog`, and `logspace`.

Plotting functions on two axes.   It is sometimes helpful to plot two functions of the same independent variable on one graph, even though the functions have different units. The solution, described in Section 12.2, is to have different vertical axes on the left and right of the graph. This is accomplished using the `plotyy` command.

Plotting surfaces in three dimensions.   A function of two variables, $f(x, y)$, can be visualized as a surface over the xy–plane. Section 13.3 describes using the `surf`, `surfl`, `mesh`, and `meshgrid` commands used to create surfaces in three dimensions. Two-dimensional pseudocolor plots, using `pcolor`, and contour plots, using `contour`, are visualization alternatives.

Plotting vector fields.   A vector-valued function of two or three variables can be visualized using the `quiver` command, which creates a field of arrows indicating direction and magnitude at each point on a regular grid. See Section 13.4.

Bit-mapped images.   Bit-mapped images can be imported from many graphics formats (e.g., *.jpg, *.tif, *.gif, etc.) using the `imread` command. An image is represented by an $M \times N \times 3$ MATLAB array holding the red, green, and blue color values for each pixel. The `image` command creates an image object that can then be moved and manipulated by changing its properties. Section 13.5 describes the basics of bit-mapped image manipulation.

Creating and rotating composite graphical objects. Section 13.6 describes how one can create a composite graphical object, called an `hgtransform` object, by aggregating other graphical objects. The main advantage is that the composite object can be moved, scaled, and rotated in space easily.

The end of this chapter includes an important note about placing graphical objects on the correct axes object in a GUI tool.

13.1 Logarithmic plots

Representing functions that vary over large ranges is facilitated by constructing logarithmic plots. The MATLAB command `semilogy` functions just like the `plot` command, except that the y-axis is plotted logarithmically.

```
% DemoSemilogPlot.m
%    demonstrate semilog plot
%    Author: Pafnuty Chebyshev
%% set parameters
tau=5;  % characteristic time
alpha5=15;
Nt=50;
Tf=30*tau;

%% tabulate function
t=linspace(0, Tf, Nt);
T5=16*t.^5 -20*t.^3+5*t;
y=alpha5*T5.*exp(-t/tau);

%% plot function
semilogy(t/tau, y, 'o-')
ylabel('$y$',...
        'Interpreter', 'latex', 'FontSize', 14)
xlabel('$t/\tau$',...
        'Interpreter', 'latex', 'FontSize', 14);
title('$y(t)=\alpha_5 (16t^5-20t^3+5t)e^{-t/\tau}$',...
        'Interpreter', 'latex', 'FontSize',14)
grid on
set(gca, 'FontSize', 10)
```

This example offers an occasion to introduce the use of the LATEXinterpreter for formatting labels. By setting the Interpreter property of the title string to 'latex', mathematical formatting using the LATEX text formatting language can be applied to the display of the string. This allows subscripts, superscripts, mathematical symbols, and Greek letters to be used in axis labels, titles, and text objects. The dollar signs surrounding the text indicate it should

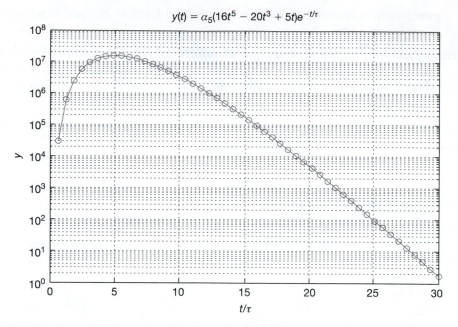

$$y(t) = \alpha_5(16t^5 - 20t^3 + 5t)e^{-t/\tau}$$

FIGURE 13.1 A semilog plot produced by `DemoSemilogPlot.m`.

be interpreted as a mathematical expression. See Appendix B for a brief summary of LaTeX commands.

Setting the FontSize property of the labels, inside the `xlabel`, `ylabel`, or `text` commands changes their size. To set the size of the axes tic mark labels, get the handle to the axes using the `gca` (get current axes) command, and set the FontSize property of the axes.

The function `semilogx` functions precisely the same way as `semilogy`, but with the logarithmic scale on the horizontal axis. The function `loglog` creates a plot that is logarithmic on both axes.

```
% DemoLoglogPlot.m
%    demonstrate loglog plot plot
%    plotting the fifth Chebyshev polynomial
%    Author: A. Lincoln
%% set parameters
Nt=30;
Tf=100;

%% tabulate function
t=linspace(1, Tf, Nt);      % linear spacing
T5=16*t.^5 -20*t.^3+5*t;

tL=logspace(0, 2, Nt);      % log spacing
T5L=100*(16*tL.^5 -20*tL.^3+5*tL);
```

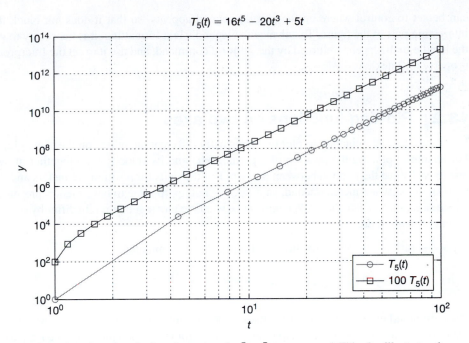

FIGURE 13.2 A loglog plot of a function using the `loglog` command. This also illustrates the use of the `legend` and `logspace` commands.

```
%% plot function
loglog(t, T5, 'o-', tL, T5L, 's-')
hleg=legend('$T_5(t)$', '$100 T_5(t)$', 'Location', 'SouthEast')
set(hleg, 'Interpreter', 'latex');
ylabel('$y$',...
       'Interpreter', 'latex', 'FontSize', 14)
xlabel('$t$',...
       'Interpreter', 'latex', 'FontSize', 14);
title('$T_5(t)=16t^5-20t^3+5t$',...
       'Interpreter', 'latex', 'FontSize', 14)
grid on
set(gca,'FontSize',10)
```

The linearly spaced grid of t-values returned by `linspace` may not be well suited to this sort of loglog representation. The `logspace(0,2,Nt)` command returns a vector of logarithmically spaced elements from 10^0 to 10^2. The difference is clear in the example, as seen in Figure 13.2. The linearly spaced set of points underrepresents the behavior for small values of the independent variable.

The legend command interprets its string arguments as labels for the curves of the recent plotting command (here `loglog`). The order in which they appear in the legend command matches the order in the plotting command. In addition, the legend's Location property can be set to control where on the plot the legend appears, so that it does not block the interesting part of the figure. To enhance the legend's text formatting, it is necessary to get the handle to the legend, returned by the `legend` command, and use it to set the Interpreter property to 'latex'.

13.2   Plotting functions on two axes

It is sometimes illuminating to plot two physically different quantities on the same graph. For example, plotting the position of a particle $x(t)$ and its velocity $v_y(t)$ together allows one to easily see the relation between the two. But the units for position are meters and the units of velocity are meters/second, so it's really not appropriate to have them represented on the same scale. Also, the two quantities one wants to plot together might differ by several orders of magnitude.

A good solution is provided by the MATLAB `plotyy` command.

```
[ha, hy1, hy2]=plotyy(t1, y1, t2, y2);
```

This command plots the vector `y1` vs. the vector `t1`, and also plots `y2` vs. `t2`. The vertical scale for the first plot is on the left axis and the scale for the second plot is on the right axis. They must share the horizontal axis to represent the values of both `t1` and `t2`; these are frequently the same.

The `plotyy` command returns three handle objects. The first, `ha` in the previous example, is a vector of handles to the two axes objects created by the command. The second and third are handles to the two curves, represented by lineseries objects. Formatting the plot beyond the default values requires using these handles. The following code illustrates how to use the command and apply custom formatting to the plot it produces.

```
%% plot function y(t) and vy(t)
% given vectors t, y, vy
[hax, hy, hvy]=plotyy(t/tau, y, t/tau, vy);
legend(hax(1), 'Position y', 'Velocity v_y')

% properties of time label on horizontal axis
xlabel(hax(1), 't/$\tau$',...
       'Interpreter', 'latex', 'FontSize', 14);

% properties of y  line, ticks, and label
set(hy, 'LineWidth', 1.5); % make line thick
set(hy, 'Color', 'k');     % make line black
set(hax(1), 'YTick', [-1:0.25:1], 'Ycolor', 'k');
ylabel(hax(1), 'y (m)', 'Color', 'k',...
       'FontSize', 14, ...
       'FontName', 'Times New Roman')

% properties of vy line, ticks, and label
```

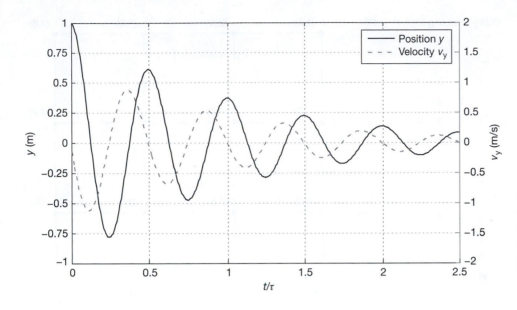

FIGURE 13.3 Two physically different quantities, with different units, can be plotted together with the `plotyy` command.

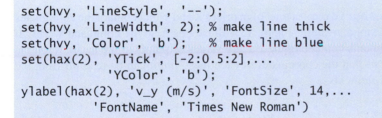

```
set(hvy, 'LineStyle', '--');
set(hvy, 'LineWidth', 2); % make line thick
set(hvy, 'Color', 'b');   % make line blue
set(hax(2), 'YTick', [-2:0.5:2],...
            'YColor', 'b');
ylabel(hax(2), 'v_y (m/s)', 'FontSize', 14,...
            'FontName', 'Times New Roman')
```

The plot that results is shown in Figure 13.3. Notice that the plot makes it easy to see, for example, that the peaks in velocity occur close to the zeroes in position and vice versa.

This example illustrates how to customize a plot by changing the properties of the lineseries objects that represent the curves. These properties include LineStyle, LineWidth, and Color. The normal `plot` command will also return a vector of lineseries handles to all the curves it produces when invoked with the syntax `hvec=plot(...)`.

The previous example also shows how to take control of the positions of tics on the axis by setting the YTick (or XTick) property to a vector containing the tic positions. The labels are formatted using the `ylabel` command with the first argument being the handle to the relevant axes.

13.3 Plotting surfaces

The `surf` command can be used to visualize a function of two variables $z = f(x, y)$. The function $f(x, y)$ can be thought of as assigning a value to each point in the xy–plane. Of course, numerically, only a finite rectangular grid of points is considered. Such a regular mesh can be considered as an array of points $\vec{r}_{j,k}$ in the plane. Each point is specified by a pair of indices (j, k) indicating the point in the jth row and kth column.

[X, Y] = meshgrid([1:4], [5:8])

X =

1	2	3	4
1	2	3	4
1	2	3	4
1	2	3	4

Y =

5	5	5	5
6	6	6	6
7	7	7	7
8	8	8	8

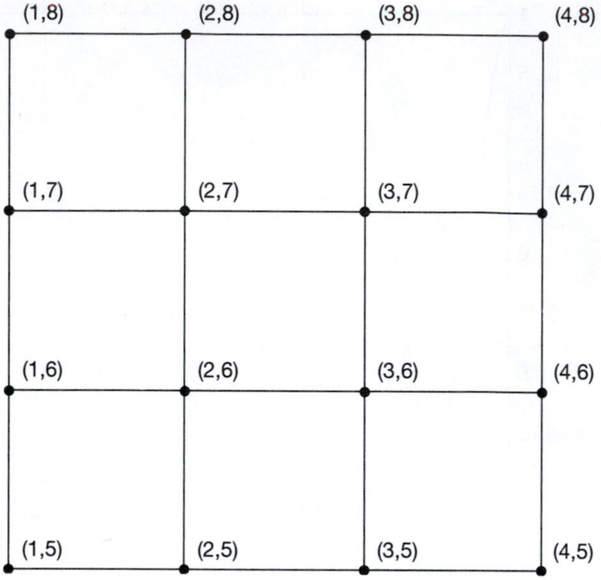

FIGURE 13.4
Illustration of the relationship between the two arrays produced by the `meshgrid` command (X and Y) and a two-dimensional coordinate grid, used for subsequent plotting.

The utility function `meshgrid` creates a set of matrices X and Y that contain the coordinates of each point in a rectangular mesh. Figure 13.4 illustrates how the command works. It takes two vector arguments containing the x and y values of points in the mesh. It returns two matrices defined so that the coordinates of each mesh point can be read off from the corresponding matrix elements.

$$\vec{r}_{j,k} = (X(j,k), Y(j,k)) \tag{13.1}$$

That is, the X matrix stores all the x-components of the mesh points' positions, and the Y matrix stores all the y-components.

$$[\vec{r}_{j,k}]_x = X(j,k) \tag{13.2}$$
$$[\vec{r}_{j,k}]_y = Y(j,k) \tag{13.3}$$

For example, to create a 50×50 rectangular mesh of points in the range $x \in [-1, 1]$, $y \in [-1, 1]$, create the vectors first using `linspace` and then invoke `meshgrid`.

```
N=50;
x=linspace(-1, 1, N);
y=linspace(-1, 1, N);
[X, Y]=meshgrid(x, y);
```

The matrices X and Y then hold the x-coordinate and y-coordinate of each point in the mesh. To compute a function of x and y, any combination of element-by-element operations on these matrices can be used to create another matrix Z, which holds the z-values corresponding to each x and y. The matrix Z must be the same size as X and Y. A few examples are shown here:

Math

$z = x^2 + y^2$

$z = \cos(x)\sin(y)e^{-x/a}$

$z = \cos(x^2 + y^2)e^{-(x^2+y^2)/a^2}$

MATLAB

$\Rightarrow$ `Z=X.^2+Y.^2;`

$\Rightarrow$ `Z=cos(X).*sin(Y).*exp(-X/a);`

$\Rightarrow$ `Z=cos(X.*X+Y.*Y).*exp(-(X.*X+Y.*Y)/(a*a));`

The following program plots the function:

$$z = f(x, y) = x^2 e^{-(x^2+y^2)}$$

in the range $x \in [-2, 2]$, $y \in [-2, 2]$

```
% demoSurf
%       Author:  Yuen D. Hertlocher

%% set parameters
Nx=50;
xmin=-2;
xmax=+2

%% make grid
x=linspace(xmin, xmax, Nx);
y=linspace(xmin, xmax, Nx);
[X, Y]=meshgrid(x, y);

%% calculate function z=f(x, y)
Z = X.^2 .* exp(-X.^2 - Y.^2);

%% plot surface
surf(X, Y, Z)
xlabel('x')
ylabel('y')
zlabel('z')
```

To rotate the image with the mouse, press the Rotate 3D icon 🔃 on the toolbar above the Figure panel. Click over the figure and drag the mouse cursor to rotate the view of the plot. To turn this on or off in a program use one of the following commands:

```
rotate3d                        % toggles rotation for current axes
rotate3d on                     % mouse-rotation on
rotate3d off                    % mouse-rotation off
rotate3d(handleOfAxes,'on');  % mouse-rotation on for axes object
rotate3d(handleOfAxes,'off'); % mouse-rotation off for axes object
```

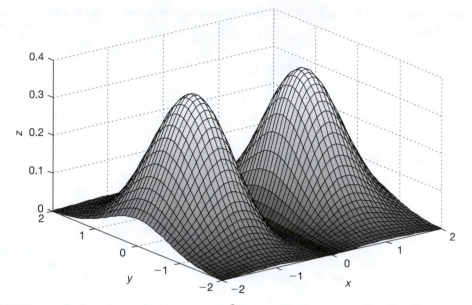

FIGURE 13.5 Surface plot produced by the surf command in the program demoSurf.

The default behavior for surf is to show the gridlines on the plot and have a constant color for each tile, as in Figure 13.5. A smoother look can be obtained with the shading command.

```
shading interp
```

This removes the gridlines and interpolates color across each facet. More control over the coloring can achieved by changing the colormap, which is covered in the documentation.

The surf command can be used to map a rectangular grid onto other shapes as well. The following program uses spherical coordinates to create a grid of azimuthal and polar angles (like longitude and latitude) and then maps this onto Cartesian coordinates through the usual transformation. The result is shown in Figure 13.6. More elaborate surfaces can be similarly created.

```
% partialSpherePlot
%    Author: Barbara Seville
%% set parameters
Nth=20;
Nph=20;
R=1;
%% make grid
phi=linspace(-pi, pi, Nph);        % azimuthal angle
theta=linspace(pi/6, pi, Nth);    % angle from z axis
[Phi, Theta]=meshgrid(phi, theta);
```

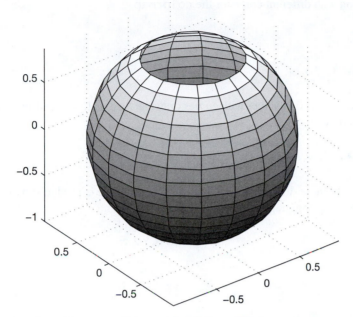

FIGURE 13.6 A surface object created by `partialSpherePlot`.

```
%% calculate rectangular coordinates
X=R*sin(Theta).*cos(Phi);
Y=R*sin(Theta).*sin(Phi);
Z=R*cos(Theta);

%% plot surface
surf(X, Y, Z)
axis equal
```

By default `surf` colors the surface by mapping the height onto different colors. A fourth argument to the `surf` command specifies the color of the surface.

```
surf(X,Y,Z,C)
```

Here C is a matrix of the same size as X, Y, and Z. The values of C, scaled from their minimum to maximum value, are mapped onto the current `colormap` to determine the colors on the tile faces of the surface. See the documentation for more on choosing or altering the `colormap`.

Surface plots with just the gridlines are provided by `mesh`, `meshc`, or `meshz`. Plots with more complicated lighting can be made with `surfl`; one needs to create light sources with the `light` command (not covered here).

The pcolor (pseudocolor) command represent a function $f(x, y)$ by associating the values of the function with different colors of the colormap.

```
pcolor(C)
   or
pcolor(X, Y, C)
```

A contour map of function values with curves drawn at Nc equally-spaced levels is produced by the contour command.

```
contour(X, Y, Z, Nc)
```

A comparison of these different visualizations of the surface is produced by the following program—the resulting graphics are shown in Figure 13.7.

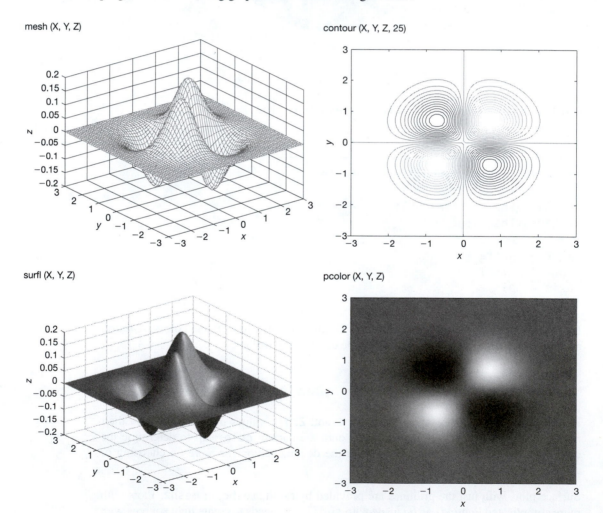

FIGURE 13.7 Four ways to visualize a function of two variables $z = f(x, y)$.

```
% demoSurfaces
%      Author:  Khan Noonien Singh

%% set parameters
Nx=60;
xmin=-3;
xmax=+3;

%% make grid
x=linspace(xmin, xmax, Nx);
y=linspace(xmin, xmax, Nx);
[X, Y]=meshgrid(x, y);

%% calculate function z=f(x, y)
Z=(X.*Y).*exp(-(X.*X+Y.*Y));

%% plot surface
figure(1)
mesh(X, Y, Z, ones(Nx))
xlabel('x')
ylabel('y')
zlabel('z')

figure(2)
surfl(X, Y, Z)
colormap gray;
shading interp
xlabel('x')
ylabel('y')

figure(3)
contour(X, Y, Z, 25)
xlabel('x')
ylabel('y')

figure(4)
pcolor(X, Y, Z)
colormap gray;
shading interp
xlabel('x')
ylabel('y')
```

13.4 Plotting vector fields

A vector field in two dimensions defines both a direction and a magnitude at each point in the plane. The vector field $\vec{v}(x, y)$ can be defined by its two Cartesian components, $v_x(x, y)$

and $v_y(x, y)$. To visualize the vector field, one typically constructs a rectangular mesh with `meshgrid`, and then computes each component of the vector field. The `quiver` command creates an array of arrows, one at each mesh point, which indicate the direction and relative magnitude of the vector field. The syntax is:

```
quiver(X, Y, Vx, Vy)
```

Vx and Vy are arrays of the same size as X and Y containing the horizontal and vertical components of the vector at each mesh point.

As an example, for each point in the plane define the vector $\vec{r}$ from the origin to the point, it's magnitude r, and the unit vector $\hat{r}$.

$$\vec{r} = (x, y) = r\hat{r}$$

where

$$r = |\vec{r}| = \sqrt{x^2 + y^2} \quad \text{and} \quad \hat{r} = \vec{r}/|r|$$

The unit vector $\hat{\theta}$ is at each point perpendicular to $\vec{r}$ in the counterclockwise direction.

$$\hat{\theta} = (-y, x)/r$$

We define a velocity vector at each point that points in the $\hat{\theta}$ direction and whose magnitude is a function of distance from the origin.

$$v_m = \sin(2\pi r/\lambda) r e^{-r/a}$$

$$\vec{v}(x, y) = v_m \hat{\theta}$$

The following program computes this vector field and plots the results with `quiver`, as shown in Figure 13.8.

```
% DemoQuiver.m
%    Author: Heino Vanderjuice
%% set parameters
Nx=30;
a=1.5;
lambda=5;

%% define grid
x=linspace(-4, 4, Nx);
[X, Y]=meshgrid(x, x);

%% compute vector field
Rmag=sqrt(X.*X+Y.*Y);
ThetaHatx=-Y./Rmag;
ThetaHaty=X./Rmag;
```

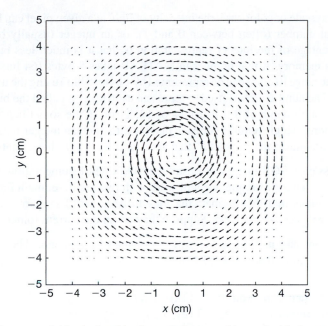

FIGURE 13.8 The vector field calculated by `DemoQuiver` and imaged with the `quiver` command.

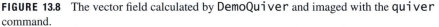

```
Vmag=sin(2*pi*Rmag/lambda).*Rmag.*exp(-Rmag/a);
Vx=Vmag.*ThetaHatx;
Vy=Vmag.*ThetaHaty;
```

```
%% plot vector field
quiver(X, Y, Vx, Vy, 'k');
axis square
xlabel('x(cm)')
ylabel('y(cm)')
```

13.5 Working with images

Importing and manipulating bit-mapped images

Bit-mapped images represent a two-dimensional image by an array of numbers indicting the color or intensity of light in each pixel. A rectangular array of pixels form an approximate representation of the spatial variation in intensity and/or color over the plane of the image. A simple grayscale image represents only the light intensity, so a 150×300 image is represented by a matrix of numbers with 150 rows and 300 columns. So-called RGB color images use an $N \times M \times 3$ array, with each of the three $N \times M$ planes representing a different color: red, green, and blue.

In either the grayscale or color case, the intensity of light at a given pixel can be represented by either a real number (often between 0 and 1), or an integer (usually between 0 and 255). The advantage of the integer representation is that it is much less burdensome for the computer's memory. A real number in MATLAB takes 8 bytes (64 bits) to represent. An integer in the range [0, 255] can be represented by 1 byte (8 bits) using the uint (unsigned integer) class. The number of bits used to represent each pixel is called the bit-depth—here we will assume a bit depth of 8. Bit-depths of 12, 14 or 16 are sometimes used. Indexed color images store a single number for each pixel, again often an integer for space reasons, and include in the image file a "palette" that associates a color with each integer.

Here we discuss only RGB images. (Consult the MATLAB documentation for many other options.) As an extended example, we will work with two public-domain images available from WikiCommons in JPEG format: the files Peace_dollar_obverse.jpg and Peace_dollar_reverse.jpg. Suppose they are in the current folder.

An image can be read in from a file with the imread command. The command will automatically recognize that it is a JPEG file.

```
dollarFront=imread('Peace_dollar_obverse.jpg');
dollarBack=imread('Peace_dollar_reverse.jpg');
dollarMask=imread('Peace_dollar_obverseMask.jpg');
```

The file Peace_dollar_obverseMask.jpg contains a mask for the coins that will be described after looking at the image.

Let's look first at the image of the front of the coin. The image can be displayed in a figure using the image command in its simple form.

```
image(dollarFront);
```

The image is stretched out (see Figure 13.9), but can be made to have the proportions of the original image by setting the axis to image mode.

```
axis image
```

Images from all three files are shown in Figure 13.10.

We can get the size of the three-dimensional array dollarFront using the size command.

```
[nrows,ncol,ncolors]=size(dollarFront)
nrows =
    217
ncol =
    220
ncolors =
      3
```

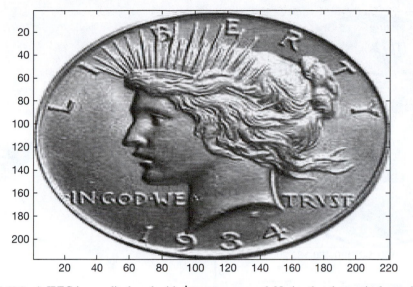

FIGURE 13.9 A JPEG image displayed with `image` command. Notice that the vertical coordinate increases in the downward axis direction.

The image is stored as a $217 \times 220 \times 3$ array of class `uint8` (eight-bit unsigned integer) with the last index determining the color sheet. So, for example, the strength of the green signal in the image is in the array `dollarFront(:, :, 2)`. Each element is an integer between 0 and 255. The (1,1) pixel in this image is white, which we can probe by displaying the three RGB values:

```
disp(['(R,G,B)=(' , num2str(dollarFront(1, 1, 1)),...
            ', ', num2str(dollarFront(1, 1, 2)),...
            ', ', num2str(dollarFront(1, 1, 3)), ')']);
```

displays:

```
(R,G,B)=(255, 255, 255)
```

A black pixel would have the values (0, 0, 0); a bright red pixel (255, 0, 0); a bright green pixel (0, 255, 0); a bright blue pixel (0, 0, 255).

Notice that the images in Figures 13.9 and 13.10 are displayed in a somewhat unusual way. The origin of the coordinate system is in the upper left corner and the vertical axis index grows larger as one moves down the image. This is the conventional way to describe a bit-mapped image: row and column indices start from the upper left and increase downward and to the right. It is different than the usual Cartesian coordinates for which the vertical dimension usually increases in the upward direction. We'd like to manipulate images within a Cartesian coordinate space, so it's necessary to flip each array, color by color, using the MATLAB `flipud` (flip up-down) command.

FIGURE 13.10 Images read from JPEG files are displayed with the `image` command and `axis image` to set the proportion of the images correctly. Each image here is 217 pixels by 220 pixels.

```
for k=1:3
    dollarFront(:, :, k)=flipud(dollarFront(:, :, k));
    dollarBack(:, :, k)=flipud(dollarBack(:, :, k));
    dollarMask(:, :, k)=flipud(dollarMask(:, :, k));
end
```

These arrays are now oriented so that we can place them in an *x-y* plane axis. We choose to set up an axis with $x \in [0, 6]$ and $y \in [0, 4]$.

```
clf
axis([0, 6, 0, 4]);
axis equal
```

We would like to place the images of the front and back of the coin separately on this axis. In manipulating images it's important to maintain the aspect ratio of the original image, so it's a good idea to first calculate this ratio. We set the width of the image to be 2.5 (the units are those of the axis just created), and we'll set the height so that the aspect ratio (here the same for both images) is maintained.

```
[ny nx n]=size(dollarFront);
coinAspectRatio=ny/nx;
coinWidth=2.5;  % picked just for demo purposes
coinHeight=coinWidth*coinAspectRatio;
```

Now the `image` command is used in its fundamental form—it creates an image object and returns a handle to the object. We will need to set several properties of the image objects.

CData: We set value of this property to the pixel data, `dollarBack` or `dollarFront`. This determines the pixels displayed on the image object.

XData and YData: The value of XData is a 1×2 vector holding the x-coordinates of the lower left and upper right corners of the image (in the axis units). The value of YData is a 1×2 vector holding the y-coordinates of the lower left and upper right corners of the image. We normally want to choose these to maintain the aspect ratio of the image, rather than stretching it out.

Parent: The value of the Parent property should be set to the handle of the axes on which the image is displayed. Here we will get the handle by using the `gca` command; in a GUI one would likely use a field in the `handles` structure (e.g., `handles.photoAxes`).

AlphaData: The value of of the AlphaData property can optionally be set to an array, of the same size as CData, which specifies the transparency of the image at each pixel. A value of 1 represents an opaque pixel (normal); a value of 0 makes that pixel invisible, an intermediate value makes the pixel correspondingly partially translucent.

We now choose the x-coordinate and y-coordinate for the lower left-hand corner of each of the two coin images. The upper right values will be calculated from the values of `coin-Height` and `coinWidth` we've calculated. The `image` command is then used to create each image object, associate it with a pixel array, and set the position within the axis.

```
xf=0.25;   yf=0;  % front of coin
xb=3.25;   yb=0;  % back of coin

hcoinFront=image('CData', dollarFront,...
                 'Parent', gca,...
                 'XData', [xf, xf+coinWidth],...
```

FIGURE 13.11 The front and back coin image objects are positioned on a Cartesian axis by setting their XData and YData properties.

```
                    'YData', [yf, yf+coinHeight]);

hcoinBack=image('CData', dollarBack,...
              'Parent', gca,...
              'XData', [xb, xb+coinWidth],...
              'YData', [yb, yb+coinWidth]);
```

The full extended areas of the image are made clearer by turning the axis off.

```
axis off
```

Figure 13.12 shows the problem that there are white corner areas of the image that we'd rather not display; they might also overlap other images. The mask image can be used to effectively remove those areas.

The file `Peace_dollar_obverseMask.jpg` was created by editing the original image file, `Peace_dollar_obverse.jpg`, in an image-processing software package (I used Photoshop®) using a combination of thresholding and painting operations. The goal in this case is to get an array of zeros and ones that can be used to make the white corners of the images invisible. Most of the values of the $217 \times 220 \times 3$ `dollarMask` `uint8` array at this point are 0 or 255 (black or white). We transform it into a 217×220 array of zeros and ones of class `double` using a logical array operation so that the mask can be used as AlphaData.

FIGURE 13.12 The two coin images are displayed with the coordinate axes turned off. This shows the problem the corners of the image might present.

FIGURE 13.13 The same image as in Figure 13.12, but now with an AlphaData mask applied to make the corners of the image transparent.

```
dollarMask=double(dollarMask(:, :, 1)>100);  %  make 0's and 1's.
set(hcoinBack, 'AlphaData', dollarMask);
set(hcoinFront, 'AlphaData', dollarMask);
```

The result is shown in Figure 13.13.

One coin can be moved smoothly over to partially overlap the other by updating the values of XData and YData in a loop. This serves also to show how the masking is effective at removing the corners so that one coin can be seen right next to the other. Note that an image object is manipulated by its handle—the pixel array is simply the value of the CData property of the object.

```
Nx=50;
xshift=linspace(0, 2.0, Nx);
yshift=0.2*xshift;
for ix=1:Nx
   set(hcoinFront, 'XData',...
                   [xf+xshift(ix), xf+xshift(ix)+coinWidth])
```

FIGURE 13.14 The left coin has moved to overlap the right coin, showing that the AlphaData mask allows one image to show through another.

FIGURE 13.15 The same image as Figure 13.14, but with additional masking to create a hole through the top coin.

```
    set(hcoinFront, 'XData',...
                    [xf+xshift(ix), xf+xshift(ix)+coinWidth])
    drawnow
end
```

Figure 13.14 shows the images after the motion is completed.

The following code constructs a more complicated mask, using the bitwise AND operator &, to create an additional hole in the top coin as shown in Figure 13.15.

```
[X, Y]=meshgrid(linspace(0, ny, ny),linspace(0, nx, nx));
R=sqrt((X-ny/2).^2+(Y-nx/2).^2);
holeMask=double( (R>nx/7) & (dollarMask>0.5) );
set(hcoinFront, 'AlphaData', holeMask);
```

Which image is on top of the other is determined by the value of the Children property of the axis. The value of this property is a column vector containing the handles of each child object, here just the two coin image objects. The order can be flipped, moving the other coin image to the top, by the following command:

```
set(gca, 'children', flipud(get(gca, 'children')) );
```

Image objects, like patch objects, can be made sensitive to user mouse-clicks and become draggable, as described in Section 12.8.

Placing images on surface objects

The surf command, introduced on page 239, can be used to create a surface object on which bit-mapped images can be displayed. The FaceColor property should be set to "texturemap" and the CData property set to the $N \times M \times 3$ bitmap array representing the image. The size of the bitmap array need not correspond to the mesh in x and y. It's usually also preferable to set the EdgeColor property to "none". The following example program places the coin image on a wavy surface.

```
% coinWavePlot
%    place image on surface
%    Author: Trillium Fortnight

%% set parameters
N=100;
lambda=1;
%% make grid
y=linspace(0, 1, N);
z=linspace(0, 1, N);
[X, Z]=meshgrid(y, z);
Y=0.2*sin(2*pi*X/lambda);
axis([0, 1, -1,  1, 0, 1]);

%% get image
dollarFront=imread('Peace_dollar_obverse.jpg' );
for k=1:3
    dollarFront(:,:,k)=flipud(dollarFront(:,:,k));
end

%% plot surface
surf(X, Y, Z,...
     'FaceColor', 'texturemap', 'CData', dollarFront,...
     'EdgeColor', 'none');
axis equal
```

Two views of the resulting image are shown in Figure 13.16.

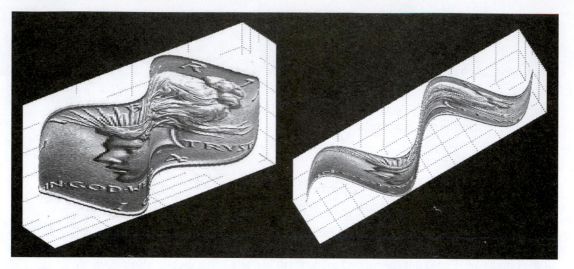

FIGURE 13.16   A bit-mapped image can be placed on a surface object by setting the CData property, as in this example produced by `coinWavePlot`.

Another example is the EdgeColor property set to an RGB value that yields light gray lines:

```
%% DrawEinstein
%  place image of Einstein on sphere surface.
%      Author: Bernhard Riemann

%% read  in image
ein=imread('einstein2.jpg');
for k=1:3
   ein(:, :, k)=flipud(ein(:, :, k));
end

%% create sphere with image on it
[X, Y, Z]=sphere(30);
surf(X, Y, Z, 'FaceColor', 'texturemap',...
          'CData', ein, 'EdgeColor', [0.6, 0.6, 0.6]);
axis equal
axis off
rotate3d('on')
```

13.6   Rotating composite objects in three dimensions

It is possible to aggregate several graphics objects together so they can be treated as one composite object, which can then be translated and rotated in space. The composite object is called an `hgtransform` object. It can have any number of graphical child objects. Child objects can be any graphical object that could be the child of an axes object with the exception of light objects.

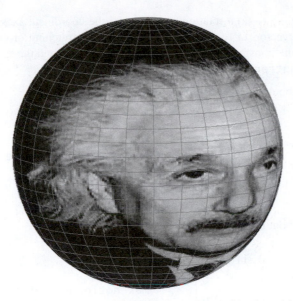

FIGURE 13.17   An image from bit-mapped file placed on a spherical surface object using the surf command.

Creating the hgtransform composite object takes only a few steps. First, create each object that you would like to aggregate (e.g., surface objects, text objects, line objects). Suppose, for this example, the handles to three such objects are hthing1, hthing2, and hthing3. Next create the, initially empty, hgtransform object.

```
hComposite=hgtransform;
```

The parent axes object can optionally be specified.

```
hComposite=hgtransform('Parent', handles.myAxes);
```

The graphical objects can now be made children of the hgtransform object by setting the value of each object's Parent property to be the handle of the hgtransform object.

```
set(hthing1, 'Parent', hComposite);
set(hthing2, 'Parent', hComposite);
set(hthing3, 'Parent', hComposite);
```

The Children property of the composite hgtransform object will automatically be set to be a column vector containing the handles of the child objects.

The hgtransform object can be manipulated geometrically by setting its Matrix property to an appropriate value representing the desired geometric transformation. The value of the Matrix property should be a 4 × 4 matrix. The function makehgtform will return the matrix corresponding to (a) a rotation about one of the coordinate axes, (b) a translation along a specified vector, or (c) a scaling of the object (stretching or compressing). The following shows the transformation matrix for each operation and the syntax for obtaining it from the `makehgtform` function.

Rotation about the x-axis by θ_x:

$$M = \begin{bmatrix} 1 & 0 & 0 & 0 \\ 0 & \cos(\theta_x) & -\sin(\theta_x) & 0 \\ 0 & \sin(\theta_x) & \cos(\theta_x) & 0 \\ 0 & 0 & 0 & 1 \end{bmatrix}$$

`M=makehgtform('xrotate',thetax);`

Rotation about the y-axis by θ_y:

$$M = \begin{bmatrix} \cos(\theta_y) & 0 & \sin(\theta_y) & 0 \\ 0 & 1 & 0 & 0 \\ -\sin(\theta_y) & 0 & \cos(\theta_y) & 0 \\ 0 & 0 & 0 & 1 \end{bmatrix}$$

`M=makehgtform('yrotate',thetay);`

Rotation about the z-axis by θ_z:

$$M = \begin{bmatrix} \cos(\theta_z) & -\sin(\theta_z) & 0 & 0 \\ \sin(\theta_z) & \cos(\theta_z) & 0 & 0 \\ 0 & 0 & 1 & 0 \\ 0 & 0 & 0 & 1 \end{bmatrix}$$

`M=makehgtform('zrotate',thetaz);`

Translation by $(\Delta x, \Delta y, \Delta z)$:

$$M = \begin{bmatrix} 1 & 0 & 0 & \Delta x \\ 0 & 1 & 0 & \Delta y \\ 0 & 0 & 1 & \Delta z \\ 0 & 0 & 0 & 1 \end{bmatrix}$$

```
M=makehgtform('translate',...
              [deltax, deltay, deltaz]));
```

Scale by scaling factors (s_x, s_y, s_z):

$$M = \begin{bmatrix} s_x & 0 & 0 & 0 \\ 0 & s_y & 0 & 0 \\ 0 & 0 & s_z & 0 \\ 0 & 0 & 0 & 1 \end{bmatrix}$$

`M=makehgtform('scale',[sx, sy, sz]));`

The transformations can be combined by matrix multiplication. For example, consider the following sequence: (a) translate by -1 along the z-axis, (b) rotate by $\pi/2$ about the *x*-axis, and then (c) translate back along the *z*-axis by +1. This can be accomplished by the following:

```
Mmz=makehgtform('translate', [0, 0, -1]));
Mrx=makehgtform('xrotate', pi/2));
Mpz=makehgtform('translate',[ 0, 0, +1]));
set(hComposite, 'Matrix', Mpz*Mrx*Mmz);
```

The operations are performed in sequence from right to left. Performing additional transformations can be accomplished by getting the current Matrix value, multiplying it by a new transformation, and setting the result to be the new Matrix value. The 4×4 identity matrix, returned by eye(4), represents the identity transformation. Setting the Matrix property to the identity undoes any previous transformations.

The following program illustrates the process of creating a composite object, and rotating it. The center of rotation is not the origin, so the transformation is made by combining the operations of translation to the origin, rotation about the *x*-axis, and translation back to the original position. Snapshots of the resulting animation are shown in Figure 13.18. The MATLAB sphere(N) function returns the coordinates of a discretized sphere with $N \times N$ faces.

```
% rotateDumbbell.m
%    Make hgtransform object and rotate it
%    around object center, which is displaced
%    from the origin.
%    Author: Marty McFly

%% create two spheres connected by a line
[X, Y, Z]=sphere(12);
hs1=surf(X, Y, Z, 'FaceColor', [0.8, 0.8, 0.8]);
hold on
    hs2=surf(X+3, Y, Z, 'FaceColor', [0.4, 0.4, 0.4]);
hold off
axis equal

hL=line([1, 2], [0, 0], [0, 0], 'LineWidth', 7);
axis([-2, 4, -2, 4, -2, 3]);
xlabel('x'); ylabel('y'); zlabel('z')

%% aggregate into Dumbbell object
hDumbbell=hgtransform('Parent', gca);
set(hs1, 'Parent', hDumbbell);
set(hs2, 'Parent', hDumbbell);
set(hL,  'Parent', hDumbbell);
drawnow
```

```
%% rotate around center of dumbbell
%      at r=(1.5, 0, 0)
Delta=[1.5, 0, 0];
Nth=60;
theta=linspace(0, 2*pi, Nth);
for ith=1:Nth
    Mt1=makehgtform('translate', -Delta);
    M=makehgtform('yrotate', theta(ith));
    Mt2=makehgtform('translate', Delta);
    set(hDumbbell, 'Matrix', Mt2*M*Mt1);
    drawnow
end
```

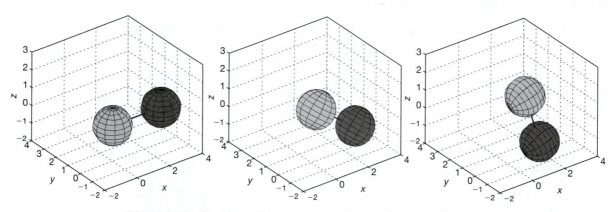

FIGURE 13.18 Snapshots of the rotating dumbbell, an `hgtransform` composite object, produced by the `rotateDumbbell.m` program.

Placing graphics in GUI Tools

In this chapter we have included individual scripts that illustrate the graphics commands. To employ them in a GUI tool, these commands would be incorporated into an appropriate function that would itself be invoked from a GUI callback function. The `handles` structure would then be available so that the handle for each axes object could be obtained. For high level plotting commands, the handle to the axes object on which you want the plot to appear can be inserted as the first argument of the command. Examples are shown here (these are separate examples not a program):

```
plot(handles.EnergyAxes, t, E1, t, E2);
xlabel(handles.EnergyAxes, 'Time (s)');
ylabel(handles.EnergyAxes, 'Energy (eV)');

semilogy(handles.PowerAxes, v, P);
grid(handles.PowerAxes, 'on')
```

```
loglog(handles.GrowthAxes, t, G);

surf(handles.SurfAxes, X, Y, Z);
rotate3d(handles.SurfAxes, 'on');
shading(handles.SurfAxes, 'interp');

pcolor(handles.FirstAxes, X, Y, Z);
contour(handles.SecondAxes, X, Y, Z);
quiver(handles.vectorAxes, X, Y, Vx, Vy);
```

For lower level commands, the target axes object must be made the parent of the graphical object by explicitly setting the Parent property of the graphical object to the handle of the axes. (The plotyy command is somewhat unusual in this respect.) Examples are shown here:

```
hline=line(x, y);
set(hline, 'Parent', handles.PlotAxes, 'Color', 'blue');

hLine2=line(x, y2, 'Parent', handles.PlotAxes);

htext=text(xp, yp, 'This is a label.');
set(htext, 'Parent', handles.PlotAxes);

dollarFront=imread('Peace_dollar_obverse.jpg');
him=image(dollarFront);
set(him, 'Parent', handles.MainImageAxes);

[X, Y, Z]= sphere(30);
surf(X, Y, Z, 'Parent', handles.FigAxes);

[hax, hE, hP]= plotyy(t, E, t, P);
set(hax, 'Parent', handles.MainAxes);
```

More Mathematics

We've already seen how a physical model, like ballistic motion (page 106) or simple harmonic motion (page 109), can be transformed into a mathematical model, such as coupled differential equations, that can in turn be expressed as a computational model, and become the basis for a GUI tool. The purpose of the tool is to gain insight into the behavior of the model and, finally, of the actual physical system. In this chapter we point to several mathematical techniques that may prove useful in constructing computational models of various systems.

This chapter has the character of a reference section to which one can turn for pointers on MATLAB capabilities. It is not meant to be comprehensive; as always, more detail is available in the online documentation. The following topics are covered:

Derivatives Given a mathematical function realized as a MATLAB function, or a tabulated set of function values, approximate derivatives of the function can be calculated. The key MATLAB command, `gradient`, is described in Section 14.1.

Integration Given a mathematical function realized as a MATLAB function, or a tabulated set of function values, approximations for the definite integral of the function over a specified range can be calculated. Key MATLAB commands, `trapz` and `quadl`, are described in Section 14.2.

Root finding Given a mathematical function of one variable $f(x)$, which is realized as a MATLAB function, the zeros of the function in a specified range can be found with the MATLAB command `fzero` (Section 14.3).

Function minimization Given a mathematical function of one variable $f(x)$, which is realized as a MATLAB function, a minimum of the function in a specified range can be found with the MATLAB command `fminbnd`. For a function of several variables, use `fminsearch`. This minimization process for several variables is useful for fitting data with a multi-parameter function. It can also be used to solve a system of simultaneous nonlinear equations. These are described in Section 14.4.

Solving systems of ordinary differential equations (ODEs) A set of coupled first-order differential equations can be solved using one of a family of MATLAB ODE solvers. The workhorse solver is `ode45`, explained in Section 14.5. The use of the `quiver` command to plot slope fields for ODEs is also described.

Eigenvalues and eigenvectors In linear algebra, one often needs to find the eigenvalues and eigenvectors of a square matrix. The key MATLAB command that accomplishes this is `eig`, described in Section 14.6.

14.1 Derivatives

Derivatives of mathematical functions expressed as MATLAB functions

The derivative represents the instantaneous rate of change of a mathematical function.

$$\frac{df}{dx} \equiv \lim_{\Delta x \to 0} \frac{f(x + \Delta x) - f(x)}{\Delta x} \tag{14.1}$$

If we have the mathematical function realized as a MATLAB function, we can calculate a numerical approximation to the derivative by taking a very small, but finite, increment Δx.

$$\frac{df}{dx} \approx \frac{f(x + \Delta x) - f(x)}{\Delta x} \tag{14.2}$$

Similarly, the second derivative can be calculated as a ratio of finite differences of the first derivative.

$$\frac{d^2 f}{dx^2} \equiv \lim_{\Delta x \to 0} \frac{\left.\frac{df}{dx}\right|_{x+\Delta x} - \left.\frac{df}{dx}\right|_x}{\Delta x} \tag{14.3}$$

$$\approx \frac{\frac{f(x+2\Delta x)-f(x+\Delta x)}{\Delta x} - \frac{f(x+\Delta x)-f(x)}{\Delta x}}{\Delta x} \tag{14.4}$$

$$\frac{d^2 f}{dx^2} \approx \frac{f(x + 2\Delta x) - 2f(x + \Delta x) + f(x)}{\Delta x^2} \tag{14.5}$$

The following program computes and plots values and derivatives of the *sinc* function:

$$\mathrm{sinc}(x) = \frac{\sin(\pi x)}{\pi x} \tag{14.6}$$

Here `sinc` is defined as an anonymous MATLAB function. The MATLAB function `eps` returns the smallest real number that MATLAB can represent; it's used here to avoid division-by-zero errors. The first and second derivatives are computed using the finite difference equations (14.2) and (14.5) directly (shown in bold in the program).

```
% findDerivs.m
%    demo finding derivative for function y(x)=sinc(x)
%           Author: Norma Leigh Lucid

%% define sinc function
%            eps in denominator avoids division by zero
sinc = @(z)  sin(pi*z)./(pi*z+eps);

%% set grid for evaluating function and derivatives
Nx=300;
xmin=-5; xmax=+5;
x=linspace(xmin, xmax, Nx);

%% tabulate y, first derivative y', and second derivative, y''
y=sinc(x);
dx=1e-6;
yp=(sinc(x+dx)-sinc(x))/dx;
 % from Eq(14.2)
ypp=(sinc(x+2*dx)-2*sinc(x+dx)+sinc(x))/(dx^2);
 % from Eq(14.5)

%% plot function and derivatives
subplot(3, 1, 1)
plot(x, y)
grid on
xlabel('x')
ylabel('$$y(x)$$' ,'Interpreter', 'latex', 'FontSize', 16)

subplot(3, 1, 2)
plot(x, yp);
grid on
xlabel('x')
ylabel('$$\frac{dy}{dx}$$' ,'Interpreter', 'latex', 'FontSize', 16)

subplot(3, 1, 3)
plot(x, ypp)
grid on
xlabel('x')
ylabel('$$\frac{d^2y}{dx^2}$$', 'Interpreter', 'latex',
 'FontSize' ,16)
```

Notice that the program sets the quantity dx to a value of 1×10^{-6}. One must choose a value that is small compared to the scale over which the function changes significantly. In this case, this value works very well because, as one can see from the graph, the function changes very slightly over such a range. If, by contrast, the function had oscillations with a very small period, one would need a smaller dx. Making it too small, however, will introduce numerical noise.

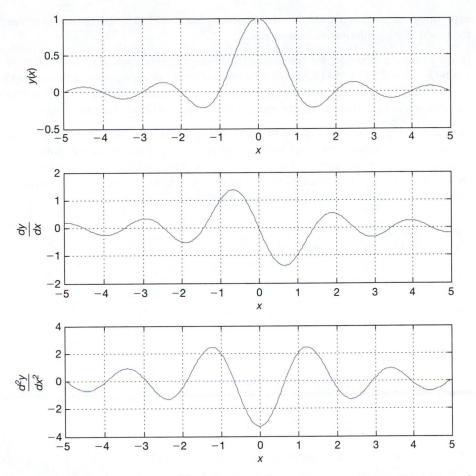

FIGURE 14.1 Graphical output from findDerivs.m illustrating the calculation of derivatives of MATLAB functions by taking finite differences.

The subplot command used here constructs a rectangular array of axes objects. The command subplot(3, 1, 2) generates a 3×1 array of axes (3 rows and 1 column), and directs subsequent plotting commands to the second axes object (i.e., it becomes the *current axes*). The third argument specifies which axis is made the current axis. The axes in the subplot array are numbered left to right along the rows and from top to bottom. For example, subplot(3, 2, 4) would create, if it doesn't already exist, an array of axes objects with 3 rows and 2 columns, and make the fourth axes object—the one in the second row and second column—the current axes, to which plotting commands will be directed.

Notice, also, the mathematical labels on the *y* axes of the plots, made by setting the Interpreter property to 'latex'. See Appendix B for a brief summary of LaTeX commands.

Derivatives of tabulated functions

Often, one wants to calculate the derivative of a function that is already tabulated. It may have taken some effort to calculate the values of the function, or perhaps they came from an experiment, or perhaps it's simply inconvenient to create a MATLAB function to represent the function whose derivative is to be calculated.

In the following example, we consider a fourth-order polynomial, $y(x)$, that has roots at $x = [-3, -2, 1, 2]$. The MATLAB function `poly` takes as an argument a vector containing the roots and returns a vector of the polynomial's coefficients. It is then a simple matter to tabulate values of the function, here represented by the MATLAB vectors x and y.

To find the numerical derivative of the tabulated function, use the MATLAB `gradient` function. This assumes a uniform spacing of the tabulated points, and also requires the size of the spacing as an argument. Iterated calls can be used to find higher-order derivatives as shown. The `gradient` command can also be used to find the vector gradient of two- and three-dimensional scalar fields (see the online documentation).

```matlab
% plotPolyDerivs.m
%     plot a polynomial and its derivatives
%     to illustrate the gradient command
%             Author: Ima Levingood

%% construct quartic polynomial with roots at xr
nx=300;
xmin=-3;  xmax=3;
ymin=-50; ymax=50;
x=linspace(-3, 3, nx);
xr=[-3, -2, 1, 2];       % position of roots
c=poly(xr);              % coefficients of polynomial
y=c(1)*x.^4+c(2)*x.^3+c(3)*x.^2+c(4)*x+c(5);

%% calculate first, second, and third derivatives, y', y'', y'''
dx=x(2)-x(1);
yp=gradient(y, dx);
ypp=gradient(yp, dx);
yppp=gradient(ypp, dx);

%% plot function, roots, and derivatives
plot(x, y, 'k-',...
     x, yp, '--', ...
     x, ypp, 'k-.',...
     x, yppp, 'k:',...
     [xmin, xmax], [0, 0], 'k',...      % draw x axis
     [0, 0], [ymi, ymax], 'k',...       % draw y axis
     xr, zeros(1, length(xr)), 'ro'); % put circles on roots
axis([xmin, xmax, ymin, ymax]);
hleg=legend('$f(x)$','$$\frac{df}{dx}$$',...
            '$$\frac{d^2f}{dx^2}$$',...
            '$$\frac{d^3f}{dx^3}$$');
set(hleg, 'Interpreter', 'latex')
set(hleg, 'Location', 'Southeast')
xlabel('x')
```

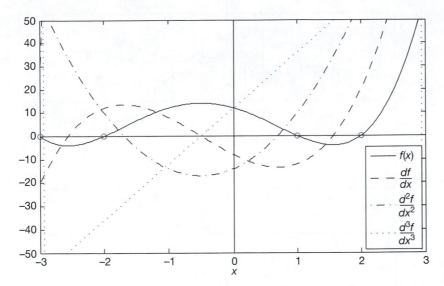

FIGURE 14.2 Graphical output from `plotPolyDerivs.m` illustrating use of `gradient` to find numerical derivatives of tabulated functions.

The program also illustrates the use of LaTeX formatting commands for the legend, and positioning the legend by adjusting its Location property.

14.2 Integration

Integrating tabulated functions

For a mathematical function $f(x)$ defined on at least the interval $[a, b]$, the definite integral of the function from a to b is the area between the graph of the function $f(x)$ and the x-axis. Suppose we have a tabulation of the function consisting of a regularly spaced set of N x-points, $\{x_1, x_2, x_3, \ldots, x_N\}$, and the corresponding function values, $\{f_1, f_2, f_3, \ldots, f_N\}$, where $f_k = f(x_k)$. We define the *grid spacing* $\Delta x = x_{k+1} - x_k$ (the same for any k). Δx becomes smaller if N is increased.

We can approximate the area under the curve by the sum of the area of all the rectangles of width Δx and height $f(k)$ as shown in Figure 14.3.

$$\int_a^b f(x)dx \approx \sum_{k=1}^{N} f(x_k)\Delta x \tag{14.7}$$

In the limit that the number of tabulated points, $N \to \infty$, Δx approaches 0, and this sum becomes exactly the definition of the integral.

$$\int_a^b f(x)dx \equiv \lim_{N \to \infty} \sum_{k=1}^{N} f(x_k)\Delta x \tag{14.8}$$

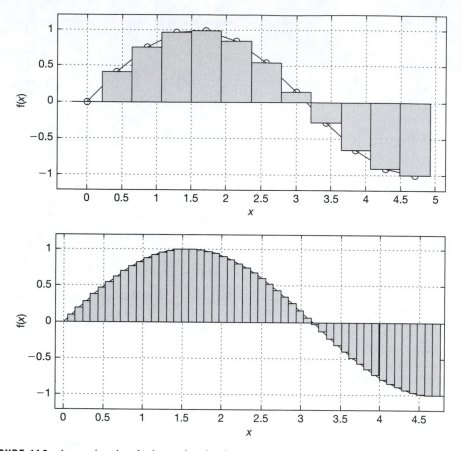

FIGURE 14.3 Approximating the integral under the curve by summing the area of rectangles. The top figure shows $N = 12$ rectangles; the bottom shows $N = 50$.

Since we always have only a finite number N of tabulated points, equation (14.7) can serve as a numerical approximation for the integral; the approximation will improve as N increases.

In MATLAB, if the finite tabulation is stored in vectors `x=[x(1), x(2), x(3),...,x(N)]`, and `f=[f(1), f(2), f(3),...,f(N)]`, then the integral can be calculated using equation (14.7) and the `sum` function, which sums the of the elements of a vector.

```
deltax=x(2)-x(1);  % regular spacing
Integ=sum(f)*deltax;
```

For example, find an approximation to integral of three-quarters of a sine wave,

$$\int_0^{3\pi/2} \sin(x)dx$$

whose exact value is 1.

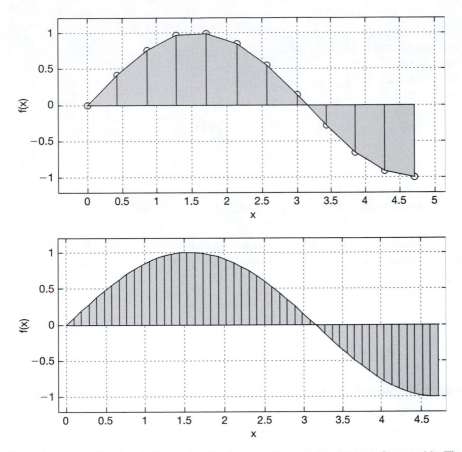

FIGURE 14.4 Approximating the integral under the curve by summing the area of trapezoids. The top figure shows $N = 12$ trapezoids; the bottom shows $N = 50$.

```
N=300;
x=linspace(0, 3*pi/2 ,N);
f=sin(x);
deltax=x(2)-x(1);
Integ=sum(f)*deltax;
disp(['Approximate integral (rectangles) = ', num2str(Integ)]);
```

```
>> Approximate integral (rectangles) = 0.9921
```

A significantly better approximation to the integral is obtained by summing the trapezoids formed by each pair of function values and the corresponding points on the x-axis, as shown in Figure 14.4. The area of each trapezoid is just the average value of the function values times the width of the trapezoid, Δx.

```
N=300;
x=linspace(0, 3*pi/2, N);
f=sin(x);
deltax=x(2)-x(1);
Integ=0;
for k=2:N
    Integ=Integ+0.5*(f(k)+f(k-1))*deltax;
end
disp(['Approximate integral (trapezoids) = ', num2str(Integ)]);
```

```
>> Approximate integral (trapezoids) = 0.99998
```

This technique is so useful that MATLAB provides a built-in function for it: `trapz`. Suppose one has a tabulation of a function $y(x)$ represented by the vectors x and y, where both have the same length N and the values of x are equally spaced. If a =x(1) and b =x(N), then the integral

$$I = \int_a^b f(x)dx$$

can be calculated by the MATLAB command

```
dx=x(2)-x(1);
I=trapz(y)*dx;
```

More generally, even if the x values are not equally spaced, one can use `trapz` with the x array as an additional argument.

```
I=trapz(x, y);
```

An example of using `trapz` is shown in the following program. The normalized sinc function is defined by

$$sinc(x) = \frac{\sin(\pi x)}{\pi x}$$

The program uses an anonymous MATLAB function (see page 128) to represent this function. One grid of x-values is used to tabulate the function for plotting on the range $x = [-4, 4]$. To calculate the integral from $x = -1$ to $x = +1$, a finer tabulation is made using xs and ys.

```
% findIntegTrapz.m
%  finding integral of function y(x)=sinc(x)
%     from x=-1 to x=+1 using TRAPZ
%                   Author: Rudy Blatnoyd
%% define sinc function
%           eps in denominator avoids division by zero
sinc = @(z)  sin(pi*z)./(pi*z+eps);
```

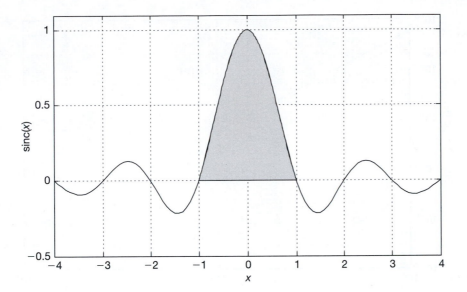

FIGURE 14.5 Plot of sinc function and the area under the curve from $x = -1$ to $x = +1$, to be found by integration using `trapz`.

```
%% plot the function
x=linspace(-4, 4, 300);
y=sinc(x);
plot(x, y);
xlabel('x');
ylabel('sinc(x)')
axis([-4, 4, -0.5, 1.1])
%    shade the region from -1 to 1
N=500;
xs=linspace(-1, 1, N);
ys=sinc(xs);
   hold on
fill(xs, ys, 'b')
hold off
grid on
```

```
%% integrate the area under the curve
I=trapz(xs, ys);
disp(['N=', num2str(N),...
        ' Area under sinc [-1, 1] (trapz)= ', num2str(I,6)]);
```

```
>> N=500 Area under sinc [-1, 1] (trapz)= 1.17898
```

Figure 14.5 shows the graphical output and the area under the curve being calculated.

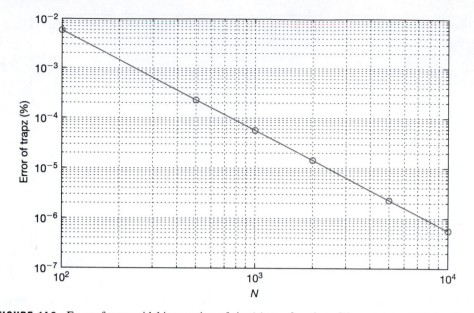

FIGURE 14.6 Error of trapezoidal integration of sinc(x) as a function of the number of tabulated points.

As the number of tabulated values increases, so does the accuracy of the numerical approximation. Figure 14.6 shows the numerical error for the previous sinc function integration. The error for uniformly spaced trapezoidal integration decreases as the square of the number of tabulated points.

Integrating mathematical functions expressed as MATLAB functions

Calculating a numerical approximation to the definite integral of a mathematical function is particularly simple and straightforward if the mathematical function is realized as a MATLAB function. The integral from a to b can be calculated using the `quadl` command. The syntax is:

```
IntegValue=quadl(<function handle>, a, b, tolerance);
```

As an example, consider the integral

$$I = \int_0^{20} \frac{1}{1 + e^{x-1}} - \frac{1}{1 + e^{x+1}} dx \tag{14.9}$$

The integrand is represented by a MATLAB function `myfunc`, which is stored in the file `myfunc.m`.

```
% myfunc.m
function z=myfunc(x)
z=1./(1+exp(x-1)) - 1./(1+exp(x+1));
```

To find the integral, invoke `quadl` and pass a handle to the function to be integrated as follows:

```
>> Integ=quadl(@myfunc, 0, 20, 1e-7)
Integ =
      1.999999985094934
```

The function passed to `quadl` must take a single argument, which can be a vector, and it must return a single scalar. The result returned has an absolute error in `Integ` of less than or equal to 1×10^{-7}; it is shown here with `format long` so that the level of convergence is visible.

The `quadl` command uses a sophisticated numerical method (adaptive Lobatto quadrature) to evaluate the function to the desired accuracy with as few function evaluations as possible, thereby making it faster than tabulation and trapezoidal integration in almost all cases.

Using function handles

The first argument of `quadl` is a function handle, a standard MATLAB data class. A function handle holds the encoded memory address of the function and can be treated much like any other MATLAB data. It can be copied:

```
bestFcn=@myfunc;
```

This stores a handle to the function `myfunc` in a variable named 'bestFcn'. The function `myfunc` must be accessible (for example, `myfunc.m` may be in the current folder or in a folder listed in the MATLAB path). One can invoke the action of the function referenced by the function handle by using its name, just as one would a usual function.

```
>> z=bestFcn(0)
z =
      0.4621
```

For anonymous functions, the function handle is already stored in a variable so the @ attached to the function name is not necessary in a call to `quadl`.

```
sinc = @(z)  sin(pi*z)./(pi*z+eps);
I=quadl(sinc, -1, 1, 1e-7)
disp(['Area under sinc [-1, 1] (quadl)= ',num2str(I,6)]);
```

```
Area under sinc [-1 ,1] (quadl)= 1.17898
```

Integrating functions with multiple arguments

A complication in using quadl can arise because one often encounters an integrand that has one or more parameters associated with it. For example, a normalized Gaussian function of width a centered at x_0 is defined by:

$$G_{a,x_0}(x) = \frac{1}{a\sqrt{2\pi}}\, e^{\frac{-(x-x_0)^2}{2a^2}} \tag{14.10}$$

The integrand can be computed by the following MATLAB function, stored in gauss.m. Here one is treating x as the independent variable, with x0 and a considered as parameters— but to the MATLAB function they're all on the same footing.

```
function y=gauss(x,x0,a)
%   returns value at x of Gaussian function centered
%   on x0, with width a
y=(1/(a*sqrt(2*pi)))* exp( -(x-x0).^2/(2*a^2));
```

Suppose one wants to check the normalization of this function by finding the integral,

$$I_{a,x_0} = \int_{-\infty}^{\infty} G_{a,x_0}(x)dx \approx \int_{-10a}^{+10a} G_{a,x_0}(x)dx \tag{14.11}$$

and verify that it is 1, as it should be. (Integrating from $-10a$ to $+10a$ is nearly the same as integrating from $-\infty$ to $+\infty$ because the function decays so rapidly.) This presents a problem because quadl must be passed a function that takes a single argument, and gauss takes three. The solution is to embed the function with several arguments, in this case gauss, in a function that takes only one, and that therefore can be passed to quadl. The embedding can be done with either a nested function or an anonymous function. Here is a solution with a nested function.

```
function checkNormalization1
%    check that the integral under the
%    gaussian function in gauss.m
%    is indeed 1 for various values of the width
%    Use a nested function.
%                      Author: S. Robert Squarepants
widths=[0.1, 0.25, 0.5, 1, 2, 10];
for iw=1:length(widths)
    a=widths(iw);
    x0=0;
    I=quadl(@gaussf, -10*a, 10*a, 1e-6);
    disp(['I=', num2str(I,12), ' for a=', num2str(a,4)]);
end
    function y=gaussf(x)
        y=gauss(x, x0, a);
    end
end
```

This results in the following output:

```
I=0.999999999991 for a=0.1
I=0.999999999991 for a=0.25
I=0.999999999991 for a=0.5
I=0.999999999991 for a=1
I=0.999999999991 for a=2
I=0.999999999991 for a=10
```

The key is that because the function gaussf is a nested function, rather than being a subfunction or an external function, variables defined in the calling function, such as a and x0, are available to it. To use the nested function approach, it is necessary to have the main computation reside in a function, here checkNormalization1, rather than a script.

The same result can be achieved using an anonymous function. The anonymous function approach has some advantages—it's more compact and it can be employed within a script. The following script file checkNormalization2 does the same calculation as checkNormalization1, but uses an anonymous function gaussf to wrap the function gauss so it has only one argument.

```
% checkNormalization2.m
% check that the integral under the
% gaussian function in gauss.m
%    is indeed 1 for various values of the width
%    Use an anonymous function.  Author: Genghis Cohen
widths=[0.1, 0.25, 0.5, 1, 2, 10];
for iw=1:length(widths)
    a=widths(iw);
    x0=0;
    gaussf = @(x) gauss(x,x0,a);
    I=quadl(gaussf, -10*a, 10*a, 1e-6);
    disp(['I=', num2str(I,12), ' for a=', num2str(a)]);
end
```

It's important to recall that the values of the parameters used by the anonymous function, here a and x0, are associated with the anonymous function only when the anonymous function is created; they are are not automatically updated when the values of a and x0 change. As a result, one must be careful to create the anonymous function anew each time the parameters are changed. In the previous program, this necessitates putting the anonymous function assignment statement inside the loop.

14.3 Zeros of a function of one variable

Any equation in one variable, linear or nonlinear, can be put in the form $f(x) = 0$. The task of finding a solution of the equation is then equivalent to the task of finding the zeros of a function. No general technique exists for finding all the zeros of an arbitrary function. For polynomial functions, see documentation for the roots command.

Consider a very simple algorithm for finding the zero of an arbitrary function $f(x)$. We start with an initial guess, x_1, and evaluate the function there, $f(x_1)$. Suppose this is positive, i.e., above the x-axis. We are seeking the value of x for which $f(x)$ crosses zero—that is, the graph of $f(x)$ intersects the x-axis. If we pick a small quantity Δx and evaluate $f(x_2 = x_1 + \Delta x)$, we can tell if the function is increasing or decreasing as we move to the right. If it is decreasing to the right, we choose another point farther to the right, say $x_3 = x_2 + \Delta x$, and evaluate the function there (if not, we look to the left of x_1). This process continues until a zero-crossing occurs between two successive points, that is, $f(x_k) > 0$ and $f(x_{k+1}) < 0$. The sign change signals that the function crossed the x-axis. Now we know the zero is between x_k and x_{k+1}. We can start at the left-hand side and repeat the above process with a smaller Δx. In this way we can zoom in on the zero-crossing to within a desired accuracy.

This algorithm is unsophisticated, but reveals the essential idea that a numerical search for a zero can start with an initial guess, and then iteratively (and more cleverly than the previous process) search for a nearby zero-crossing, characterized by the function changing sign. The MATLAB command that does all this automatically is `fzero`. It takes as arguments a handle to the function and the initial guess.

```
x0=fzero(@fun, xguess);
```

Alternatively, if it is already known that the function changes sign in a particular segment $[x_{left}, x_{right}]$, then `fzero` can be invoked to find the zero in that segment.

```
x0=fzero(@fun, [xleft, xright]);
```

Suppose, for example, we want to find a solution of the transcendental equation (which arises in the theory of quantum wells):

$$\tan(x) = \sqrt{x^2 + 1} \tag{14.12}$$

We can recast the problem to that of finding a zero of the function:

$$f(x) = \tan(x) - \sqrt{x^2 + 1} \tag{14.13}$$

To illustrate, the following program `findZeros` plots the left-hand and right-hand sides of equation (14.12), and the function $f(z)$ defined by equation (14.13). It then finds the zero of $f(z)$, realized in the MATLAB function `fqwell`, using `fzero`, and plots it.

```
function findZeros
%   find zeros of function
%      f(x)=tan(x)-sqrt(x^2 +1)
% Author: Anita Job

%% plot function
xmax=0.5*pi;
x=linspace(0, xmax, 400);
```

```
y=fqwell(x);    % see function below
RHS=sqrt(x.^2+1);  % right-hand side of Eq.(14.12)
LHS=tan(x);        % left-hand side of Eq.(14.12)
plot(x, RHS, 'k--', x,LHS, 'k-.', x, y, '-k');
hleg=legend('$$\sqrt{x^2+1}$$',  '$$\tan(x)$$',...
            '$$f(x)=\tan(x)-\sqrt{x^2+1}$$');
set(hleg, 'Interpreter', 'latex', 'Location', 'northwest');
axis([0, xmax, -1, 5])
xlabel('x');
grid on
```

```
%% find zero
xguess=0.4;
x0=fzero(@fqwell, xguess);
disp(['zero at x=', num2str(x0)]);
%% plot zero on plot
hold on
    plot(x0, 0, 'ro');
hold off
```

```
function f=fqwell(z)
f=tan(z)-sqrt(z.^2 +1);
```

When the function `findZeros` is run, it produces:

```
zero at x=0.94146
```

and the graphical output shown in Figure 14.7. The zero of the function is, of course, where the left-hand and right-hand sides of equation (14.12) are equal.

One can gain some knowledge about the function and its zeros by plotting the function. Another strategy is to loop through a regular array of initial guesses and collect all the zeroes (many will be duplicates). There is no guarantee that one has found *all* the zeros of an arbitrary unknown function—the function could always have quickly sneaked across the x-axis and back between the x-values one has examined. For realistic, fairly smooth functions, this is not a problem.

Note that, since `fzero` searches for a place where the function changes sign, it cannot locate the zero of a function like $f(x) = (x-1)^2$, which just touches the x-axis at $x = 1$.

14.4 Function minimization

Finding a minimum of a function of one variable

In some cases, one desires not to find the zero of a function, but rather to locate a local minimum. MATLAB provides the function `fminbnd`, which returns a local minimum of a function in the region between `xmin` and `xmax`.

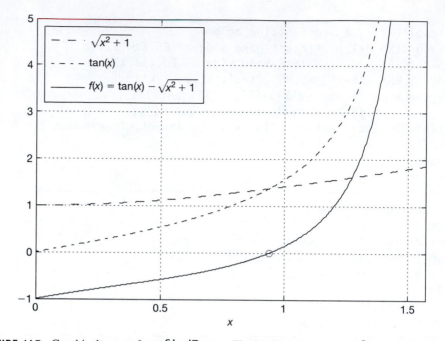

FIGURE 14.7 Graphical output from `findZeros`. The MATLAB command `fzero`, called with an initial guess $x_{guess} = 0.4$, finds the value $x_0 = 0.94146$, for which the function is zero.

```
xc=fminbnd(@fun, xmin, xmax);
```

The following example shows its use:

```
function findMinimum;
%    demonstrate using fminbnd to find local minimum
%    between 2 and 5 of sin(x)^2 + sqrt(|x|)
%                         Author: Iona Ford

%% plot function
xmin=2;   xmax=5;
Nx=100;
x=linspace(xmin, xmax, Nx);
y=myfun(x);
plot(x, y)
grid on
xlabel('x');
ylabel('y');

%% find minimum in this range
xc=fminbnd(@myfun, xmin, xmax);
disp(['x at local min is ', num2str(xc)]);
```

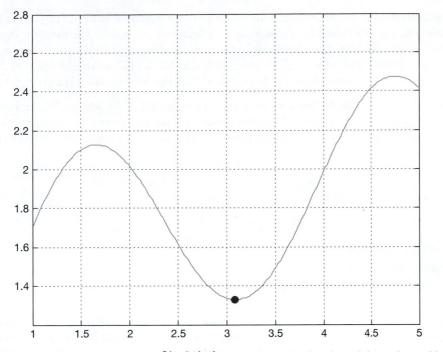

FIGURE 14.8   Graphical output from `findMinimum`, showing the function minimum located by `fminbnd`.

```
%%  plot the position of the minimum
hold on
    plot(xc, myfun(xc), 'ro', 'MarkerFaceColor', 'r')
hold off
```
```
function y=myfun(x)
y=sin(x).^2 + sqrt(abs(x));
```

The graphical output of `findMinimum` is shown in Figure 14.8.

Be aware that `fminbnd` yields *one* local minimum, but there may be others in the range specified. If there are, there is no guarantee that the one found by `fminbnd` yields the smallest value of the function. So it's most useful when you already know something about the function's behavior.

Multidimensional minimization

MATLAB provides a general-purpose function `fminsearch` that locates a local minimum for a real scalar function `fun` of N variables. An initial guess, a vector of length N, is required.

```
xmin=fminsearch(@fun, xguess);
```

The command `fminsearch` returns the vector `xmin` for which the value of `fun(x)` is a local minimum. The independent variable `x` can be a vector of any size N. The function `fun(x)` must assign a single real number to any point in the N-dimensional space of vectors `x`. For example, if the length of `x` is 13, `fminsearch` searches a 13-dimensional space to find a local minimum for `fun(x)`. If N is large, this can take some time, but it is a powerful tool.

It is often the case that the function one wants to minimize (i.e., for which a local minimum is sought) has other parameters. A common idiom is to use an anonymous function to set the parameters, and then pass the function handle of the anonymous function to `fminsearch`.

```
% set parameters
a=3.2;
b=12;
minfunc = @(x) myfun(x, a, b);

% find minimum
xguess=[1.2, 3.3, 0.01];
xmin=fminsearch(minfunc, xguess);
```

In this example, the function `myfun` must return a scalar function of the three-dimensional vector `x`, with parameters `a` and `b`. Note that again, since the variable `minfunc` is already a function handle, it is not necessary to add an `@` to its name when calling `fminsearch`.

The following sections give examples of using this multidimensional minimization technique for two specific classes of problems: curve-fitting and solving simultaneous nonlinear equations.

Fitting to an arbitrary function by multidimensional minimization

Suppose we have data in the form of N_d measurements of (x, y) pairs

$$(x_1, y_1), (x_2, y_2), \ldots, (x_k, y_k), \ldots, (x_{N_d}, y_{N_d})$$

as plotted in Figure 14.9. The data has noise in both x and y. We suspect that it can be described by a sum of two Gaussian lineshapes, each with height y_{max}, center x_0, and width a.

$$y = G(x) = y_{max}^{(1)} e^{-(x-x_0^{(1)})^2/2a_1^2} + y_{max}^{(2)} e^{-(x-x_0^{(2)})^2/2a_2^2} \tag{14.14}$$

We would like to know the values of these six parameters that optimally match the data. The problem can be formulated as a minimization problem. Consider the six parameters as forming a vector in a six-dimensional space.

$$\vec{g} \equiv [y_{max}^{(1)}, y_{max}^{(2)}, x_0^{(1)}, x_0^{(2)}, a_1, a_2] \tag{14.15}$$

Each different choice of these six parameters specifies a different vector $\vec{g}$, and for each such vector there is a corresponding lineshape given by equation (14.14), which we can now write:

$$y = G_{\vec{g}}(x) = g_1 e^{-(x-g_3)^2/2g_5^2} + g_2 e^{-(x-g_4)^2/2g_6^2} \tag{14.16}$$

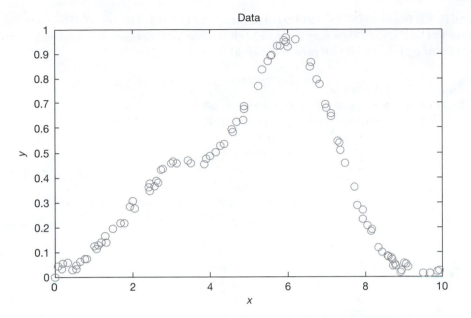

FIGURE 14.9 Data in the form of (x, y) pairs to be fit with a double-Gaussian lineshape.

Some choices of parameters $\vec{g}$ result in a lineshape that doesn't fit the data very well at all, while other choices provide better fits. We'd like to find the optimal choice. To make that notion precise, we need to define a function that quantifies how well a particular choice fits the data. A good way to do this is to find the root-mean-square (RMS) deviation of the data from a particular lineshape. For each data point value x_k, we calculate the value of y_k^g predicted by the lineshape function equation (14.16).

$$y_k^g = G_{\vec{g}}(x_k) \qquad \text{for} \quad k = [1, 2, \ldots, N_d] \qquad (14.17)$$

The superscript g indicates that this function depends on the values of the parameters currently in $\vec{g}$. The square root of the sum of the squares of the difference between the y_k data values and the values y_k^g predicted by equation (14.16) is then calculated.

$$\Delta_{RMS} = (1/N_d)\sqrt{(y_1 - y_1^g)^2 + (y_2 - y_2^g)^2 + (y_3 - y_3^g)^2 + \ldots}$$

$$= \frac{1}{N_d}\sqrt{\sum_k^{N_d} (y_k - y_k^g)^2} \qquad (14.18)$$

This RMS goodness-of-fit measure assigns a single real number to each $\vec{g}$, given the set of N_d pairs of (x, y) data, and we'd like to find the $\vec{g}$ for which this number is the smallest.

The following program fitGaussians loads in the (x, y) data and constructs an initial guess, gguess, for the six Gaussian parameters that determine the vector $\vec{g}$. The MATLAB function twoGaussian(x,g) calculates the lineshape using equation (14.16). The RMS error for a particular choice of g is calculated using equations (14.17) and (14.18) by the

MATLAB function RMSdeltaTwoGaussianError(xdata,ydata,g). The main function fitGaussians then uses fminsearch to search the six-dimensional space for the vector of optimum Gaussian parameters gopt.

```matlab
function fitGaussians
%  fit data to sum of two Gaussians
%  use multidimensional minimization
%   to find optimal parameters
%          Author: Lindsey Noseworth

%% load data
load('SignalData');  % loads vectors xdata and ydata
xmin=min(xdata);
xmax=max(xdata);

%%  find best fit of Gaussian parameters
%  initial guess [ymax1, ymax2, x01, x02, width1, width2]
guess=[0.4, 0.9, 3, 6, 2, 1];
minfunc=@(gs) RMSdeltaTwoGaussianError(xdata, ydata, gs);
gopt=fminsearch(minfunc, guess);

%% plot data and fit
x=linspace(xmin, xmax, 300);
[yopt, y1, y2]=twoGaussian(x, gopt);

figure(1)
plot(xdata, ydata, 'o');
axis([0, 10, 0, 1]);
xlabel('x');
ylabel('y');
title('Data')

figure(2)
hp=plot(xdata, ydata, 'ko',...
        x, yopt, 'k',   x, y1, 'k--',   x, y2, 'k--');
set(hp(2), 'LineWidth', 1.5) % make fit line thicker
axis([0, 10, 0, 1]);
xlabel('x');
ylabel('y');
title('Data and fit')

%% report parameters
clc;
prec=3;
disp('Optimum parameters:')
disp(['  height of Gaussian 1: ', num2str(gopt(1), prec) ]);
disp(['  height of Gaussian 2: ', num2str(gopt(2), prec) ]);
```

```
disp(['    zero of Gaussian 1: ', num2str(gopt(3), prec) ]);
disp(['    zero of Gaussian 2: ', num2str(gopt(4), prec) ]);
disp(['   width of Gaussian 1: ', num2str(gopt(5), prec) ]);
disp(['   width of Gaussian 2: ', num2str(gopt(6), prec) ]);
```

```
function rmserror=RMSdeltaTwoGaussianError(xdata,ydata,g);
%   root-mean-square error between
%   data and sum of two Gaussians with
%  gaussian parameters g=[ymax1, ymax2, x01, x02, width1, width2]
deltay=ydata-twoGaussian(xdata,g);
rmserror=(1/length(xdata))*sqrt(sum(deltay.^2));
```

```
function [y, y1, y2]=twoGaussian(x, g);
% returns sum of two Gaussians and components
% Gaussian parameters
% g= [ymax1, ymax2, x01, x02, width1, width2]

y1=g(1)*exp( -(x-g(3)).^/(2*g(5)^2));
y2=g(2)*exp( -(x-g(4)).^/(2*g(6)^2));
y=y1+y2;
```

```
Optimum parameters:
   height of Gaussian 1: 0.422
   height of Gaussian 2: 0.927
     zero of Gaussian 1: 3.12
     zero of Gaussian 2: 6.12
    width of Gaussian 1: 1.27
    width of Gaussian 2: 1.13
```

The graphical output of `fitGaussians` is shown in Figure 14.10. The graph shows the initial data and the optimal fit and the two individual Gaussian components that comprise it.

Solving simultaneous nonlinear equations by multidimensional minimization

Another use for the multidimensional minimization capabilities of the `fminsearch` command is finding the solutions of systems of nonlinear algebraic equations. For ease of visualization, we will use a two-dimensional example. Suppose we seek a solution to the following pair of nonlinear equations.

$$x \cos(y) = y \sin(x) + 2$$
$$x \sin(y) = y \cos(x) + 4 \tag{14.19}$$

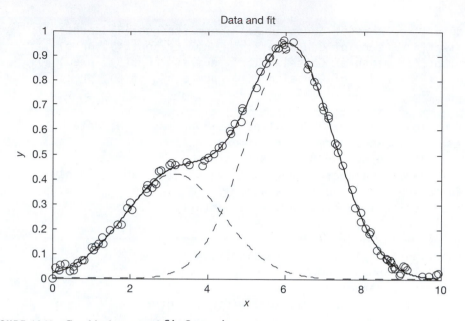

FIGURE 14.10 Graphical output of `fitGaussians` showing the optimized fit of the data in Figure 14.9 to the double-Gaussian lineshape of equation (14.14).

We first recast the task of finding a solution to equations (14.19) as the problem of finding a zero of two functions simultaneously.

$$f_1(x, y) = x\cos(y) - y\sin(x) - 2 = 0$$
$$f_2(x, y) = x\sin(y) - y\cos(x) - 4 = 0 \tag{14.20}$$

The problem of finding a simultaneous solution to equations (14.20) can, in turn, be transformed into a minimization problem by defining another function.

$$f_{min}(x, y) = \sqrt{[f_1(x, y)]^2 + [f_2(x, y)]^2} \tag{14.21}$$

Note that the function f_{min} is always positive, so that if there is a point (x, y) where $f_1(x, y)$ and $f_2(x, y)$ are both zero, that point will be a local minimum of f_{min}. Therefore, if we find values x_0 and y_0 for which

(a) $f_{min}(x_0, y_0)$ is a local minimum, and

(b) the value $f_{min}(x_0, y_0)$ is numerically very close to zero,

then we have very likely found a solution to equations (14.20) and therefore to equations (14.19). Of course, numerically the value of the function at the minimum will never be *exactly* zero; we have to content ourselves with a very small value.

The following function `solveSimulNonlinear` illustrates using `fminsearch` in this way. The command `optimset` is used to set the tolerance for the function value. It returns an object of class `struct` that holds various options for the search.

```
function [x,y,z,xy0]=solveSimulNonlinear;
%   demonstrate using fminsearch to solve
%   two simultaneous nonlinear equations
%       Author: Nell Fenwick
%
% Solve these two equations simultaneously:
%       x.*cos(y) - y.*sin(x)-2 = 0  Equation 1
%       x.*sin(y) - y.*cos(x)-4 = 0  Equation 2
```

```
%% plot the function for visualization
xx=linspace(0, 6, 50);
[x, y]=meshgrid(xx);
z=myFun(x, y);
contour(x, y, z, 30);
xlabel('x');
ylabel('y');
```

```
%% find minimum
xyguess=[3, 1];
options=optimset('TolFun',1e-9);
myMinFun = @(r) myFun(r(1),r(2));
xy0=fminsearch(myMinFun, xyguess, options);
```

```
%% plot result and report
hold on
    plot3(xy0(1), xy0(2), 0, 'rp')
hold off
clc
disp(['minimum at x0= ', num2str(xy0(1)) ]);
disp(['           y0= ', num2str(xy0(2)) ]);
disp(['         fmin= ', num2str(myFun(xy0(1), xy0(2))) ]);
```

```
function z=myFun(x, y)
f1=x.*cos(y) - y.*sin(x)-2; % =0  Equation 1
f2=x.*sin(y) - y.*cos(x)-4; % =0  Equation 2
z=sqrt(f1.^2+f2.^2);
```

```
minimum at x0= 3.4363
           y0= 1.0555
         fmin= 1.7119e-009
```

Figure 14.11 shows a contour plot of the function $f_{min}(x, y)$ with the located zero. The function f_{min} over this range, $x = [0, 6]$ and $y = [0, 6]$, is of order 1; examination shows the

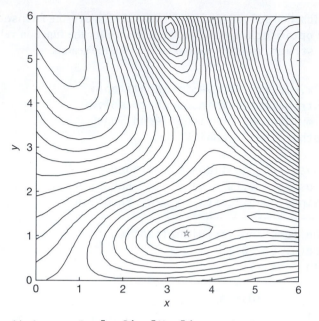

FIGURE 14.11 Graphical output of `solveSimulNonlinear` showing a contour plot of the function $f_{min}(x, y)$ defined by equations (14.20) and (14.21). The star indicates the zero located by `fminsearch`. The zero corresponds to a solution of the simultaneous nonlinear algebraic equations (14.19).

maximum value is more than 14. So finding the value at the computed minimum to be more than 9 orders of magnitude smaller convinces us that this is truly a zero. But other solutions exist—the plot suggests that there is another zero near $(x, y) = (3, 5.5)$. The point near $(5.5, 1.4)$, by contrast, is a local minimum that is not a zero; f_{min} at that point is about 0.42.

In a large-dimensional space, corresponding to more simultaneous equations, it's not possible to plot the contours of the function; one is to some extent always in the dark about the functional landscape. A reasonable strategy is to make a sparse grid of initial guesses, loop through each and do a minimum search, and then examine the resulting minima to find the true zeros. It's never possible to be completely sure that a zero hasn't gone undetected.

14.5 Solving ordinary differential equations

Modeling physical phenomena frequently results in differential equations, equations that involve variables and derivatives of variables. A differential equation that include no partial derivatives is called an "ordinary differential equation" (ODE). One example, Newton's second law, was solved using the velocity Verlet method in Chapter 6.

MATLAB offers a more general approach, using the built-in function `ode45`, one of a suite of ODE solvers that also includes `ode23`, `ode113`, `ode15s`, `ode23s`, `ode23t`, and `ode23tb`. For a given problem, one of the other solvers may be more efficient, but it's usually best to start with `ode45`; they all use the same syntax.

Consider the second-order differential equation describing a damped driven harmonic oscillator.

$$\frac{d^2x}{dt^2} = -\omega^2 x - g\frac{dx}{dt} + c\, s(t) \tag{14.22}$$

In this equation, $x(t)$ is the time-dependent position of a particle, ω is the angular resonant frequency of the oscillator (the period $T = 2\pi/\omega$), g is a frictional damping coefficient, and the last term represents the effect of a time-varying external force, which is here taken to be a square-wave. (The fact that the last term is not a function of x or its derivatives means that this ODE is classified as nonhomogeneous.)

A second-order (or higher) ODE can always be written as a set of simultaneous first-order ODEs. In this case we can write:

$$\frac{dv}{dt} = -\omega^2 x - gv + c\, s(t)$$

$$\frac{dx}{dt} = v \tag{14.23}$$

These equations can be expressed as a first-order vector differential equation:

$$\frac{d\vec{y}}{dt} = \vec{f}(t, \vec{y}) \tag{14.24}$$

where the vector of the unknown functions of time is:

$$\vec{y}(t) = \begin{pmatrix} y_1(t) \\ y_2(t) \end{pmatrix} = \begin{pmatrix} v(t) \\ x(t) \end{pmatrix} \tag{14.25}$$

and the derivative vector is:

$$\frac{d\vec{y}}{dt} = \begin{bmatrix} \frac{dy_1}{dt} \\ \frac{dy_2}{dt} \end{bmatrix} = \vec{f}(t, \vec{y}) = \begin{bmatrix} f_1(t, \vec{y}) \\ f_2(t, \vec{y}) \end{bmatrix} = \begin{bmatrix} -\omega^2 y_2 - g y_1 + c\, s(t) \\ y_1 \end{bmatrix} \tag{14.26}$$

To solve such a system with ode45, invoke it with the following syntax:

```
[t,y]=ode45(@odefun, [Tinit, Tfinal], y0);
```

The ODE function odefun(t,y) must have exactly two arguments: t is a scalar and y is a vector of length N (in this example, N$=2$). Its job is to return, for that t and $\vec{y}$, a column vector containing the derivatives of each component of $\vec{y}$, as in equation (14.26). Because odefun can have only the two arguments, t and y, it is common to make it a nested function so that other necessary parameters can be accessed from the outer calling function. The second argument is a vector of initial and final times defining the time span to be solved for. The third argument y0 is a column vector representing the initial state of $\vec{y}$. The function ode45 returns a vector t of length Nt (determined by the solver), and an Nt $\times$ N matrix y. Together they represent the solution $\vec{y}(t)$.

The function demoODE solves this problem using ode45.

```
function demoODE
%   solve 2nd order inhomogeneous ODE
%       x''= -w^2 x -g x' + c s(t)
%           where s(t) is square wave with period Ts
%           s(0)=0 and s(t) steps between 0 and 1
%   transform to
%       v'= -w^2 x -g v + c s(t)
%       x'= v
%                Author: Eaton Wright

%% set parameters
w=1;            % angular frequency
g=0.2;          % damping coefficient
y0=[0; 0];      % initial condition v=0,x=0
T=2*pi/w;       % period of oscillation
Ts=20*T;        % square wave period
c=5;            % amplitude of square wave
Tfin=1.5*Ts;

squarewave = @(t) (1-sign(cos(2*pi*t/Ts)))/2;

%% solve ODE
[t, y]=ode45(@dampedODE, [0, Tfin], y0);
    function dydt= dampedODE(t, y)
    % ode  function returns column vector of derivatives
    % y(1) is v     dydt(1) is v'
    % y(2) is x     dydt(2) is x'=v
    %     w, g, c defined in outer function
        dydt=zeros(2, 1);
        dydt(1)= -w^2*y(2) - g*y(1) + c* squarewave(t);
        dydt(2)= y(1);
    end
x=y(:, 2);
v=y(:, 1);

%% plot results
figure(1)           % x(t)
plot(t/Ts, x);
xlabel('t/Ts', 'FontSize', 16);
ylabel('x', 'FontSize', 16);
figure(2)           % phase plot x vs. v
plot(x,v);
xlabel('x(t)', 'FontSize', 16);
ylabel('v(t)', 'FontSize', 16);
xlims=get(gca, 'XLim'); % save scaling
```

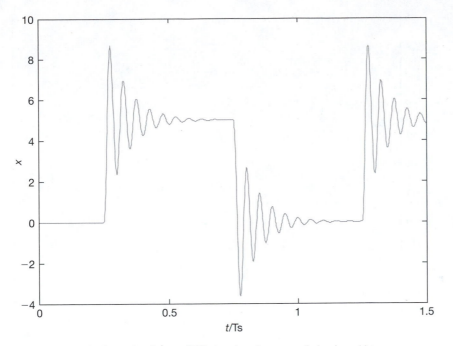

FIGURE 14.12   Graphical output of demoODE showing the system behavior $x(t)$.

```
ylims=get(gca, 'YLim')
end
```

Figure 14.12 shows the calculated behavior for $x(t)$. Figure 14.13 shows a so-called *phase space* plot of $v(t)$ and $x(t)$, showing how the square-wave forcing function switches the stable state (known as an *attractor*) between two points. A three-dimensional plot of $v(t)$ and $x(t)$ can be made using the plot3 command with the following additional code; the result is shown in Figure 14.14.

```
%% make 3d plot
figure(3)
plot3(t/Ts, x, v, 'k');
xlabel('t/Ts', 'FontSize', 16);
ylabel('x(t)', 'FontSize', 16);
zlabel('v(t)', 'FontSize', 16);
grid on
rotate3d('on')
```

Plotting a slope field

The slope field is the vector field $d\bar{y}/dt$, as in equation (14.26), plotted in the phase space of the problem. In the previous problem, the slope field changes in time when the square-wave driver turns on and off. Consider the system response for just the part of the motion when the

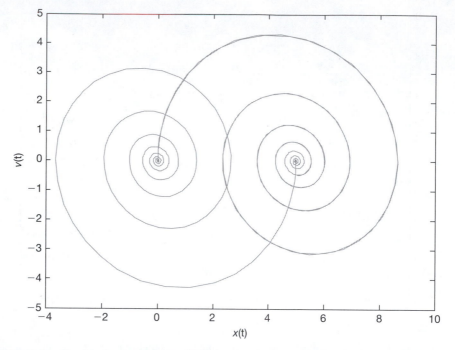

FIGURE 14.13 Graphical output of demoODE showing the system behavior as calculated by ode45 in phase space, a parametric plot of $v(t)$ and $x(t)$.

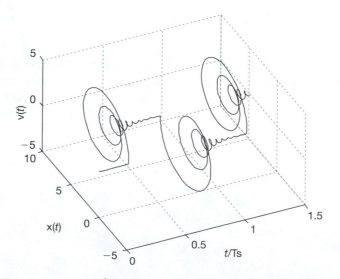

FIGURE 14.14 Graphical output of demoODE showing the system behavior as calculated by ode45 in three-dimensional space plotting $v(t)$ and $x(t)$.

square-wave turns off and the system relaxes to $x = 0$. We can plot that slope field with the MATLAB quiver command, which plots a vector field. The additional code that is added to the function demoODE to calculate the slope field and plot it is shown as follows, along with its graphical output.

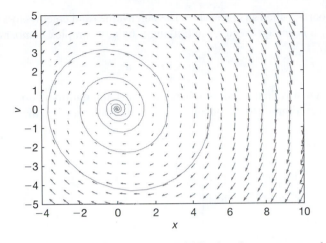

FIGURE 14.15 Slope field for the ODE in equation (14.26) when the square-wave driver is off $(s(t) = 0)$ and the system is relaxing to $x = 0$, $v = 0$. The vector field is created by the MATLAB `quiver` command.

```
%% append this to function demoODE to make slope field plot
x0=c/w^2; % x-coordinate of stationary point with driver on
c=0;      % turn off driver
[t, y]=ode45(@dampedODE, [0, Tfin], [0;x0]);

Ns=20;
xs=linspace(xlims(1), xlims(2), Ns);
vs=linspace(ylims(1), ylims(2), Ns);
[X, V]=meshgrid(xs, vs);

Uv=-w^2*X-g*V;
Ux=V;
figure(4)
plot(y(:,2) ,y(:,1));
hold on
    quiver(X, V, Ux, Uv);
hold off
axis([xlims, ylims])
xlabel('x', 'FontSize', 16)
ylabel('v', 'FontSize', 16)
```

14.6 Eigenvalues and eigenvectors

Consider an $N \times N$ matrix $\mathbf{A}$. A column vector $\mathbf{u}$ is said to be an eigenvector of $\mathbf{A}$ if, and only if, it satisfies the equation:

$$\mathbf{A}\mathbf{u} = \lambda\mathbf{u} \qquad\qquad (14.27)$$

for some number λ, called an eigenvalue. The eigenvalues and eigenvectors can, in general, be complex. If $\mathbf{u}$ is an eigenvector, multiplying $\mathbf{u}$ by any complex number c also yields an eigenvector.

$$\mathbf{A}(c\mathbf{u}) = \lambda(c\mathbf{u}) \tag{14.28}$$

Two eigenvectors of $\mathbf{A}$ that are not simply related by scalar multiplication are called distinct eigenvectors. It is common to consider normalized eigenvectors, i.e., those with a unit norm.

$$\| \mathbf{u} \|^2 \equiv \mathbf{u}^\dagger \mathbf{u} = [u_1^*, u_2^*, u_3^*, \ldots, u_N^*] \begin{bmatrix} u_1 \\ u_2 \\ u_3 \\ \vdots \\ u_N \end{bmatrix} = |u_1|^2 + |u_2|^2 + |u_3|^2 + \ldots + |u_N|^2 = 1 \tag{14.29}$$

Here, $*$ indicates complex conjugation and $\dagger$ indicates the complex conjugate of the transpose.

An $N \times N$ real matrix has up to N distinct eigenvectors. If the matrix is nonsingular (i.e., has a nonzero determinant), then there will be exactly N distinct eigenvectors, and N eigenvalues. The eigenvalues need not be unique; some may be repeated. The eigenvalues of a real matrix will either be real, or will occur in complex conjugate pairs. A matrix for which $\mathbf{A}^\dagger = \mathbf{A}$ is said to be Hermitian; a matrix for which $\mathbf{A}^T = \mathbf{A}$ is said to be symmetric. Both Hermitian matrices and real symmetric matrices have only real eigenvalues.

The MATLAB function `eig` finds the eigenvectors and eigenvalues of an $N \times N$ matrix A.

```
[V,D]=eig(A);
```

The function `eig` returns two matrices. The columns of V are normalized eigenvectors of A, satisfying both the eigenvalue equation (14.27) and normalization condition (14.29). The matrix D is a diagonal matrix (all off-diagonal elements are 0) whose diagonal entries are the eigenvalues of A. A vector of eigenvalues can be extracted from D using the `diag` command:

```
lambdas=diag(D);
```

The kth eigenvalue, `lambdas(k)`, corresponds to the kth eigenvector `V(:,k)`. If the eigenvalues are all real, they are returned sorted from smallest to largest.

```
% findEigs.m
%    find lowesttwo eigenvalues and
%    associated eigenvectors of
%    energy (Hamiltonian) matrix
%       Author: Zane Toadflax
g=-0.1;
```

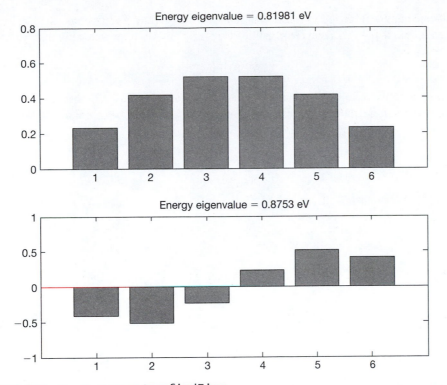

FIGURE 14.16 Graphical output from findEigs.

```
H= [ 1    g   0    0   0   0;
      g   1   g    0   0   0;
      0   g   1    g   0   0;
      0   0   g    1   g   0;
      0   0   0    g   1   g;
      0   0   0    0   g   1];

%% find eigenvalues and eigenvectors
[V, D]=eig(H);
es=diag(D);  % eigenvalues
psi1=V(:, 1); % lowest eigenvector
psi2=V(:, 2); % next eigenvector

%% plot results
subplot(2, 1, 1);
bar(psi1)
title(['Energy eigenvalue = ', num2str(es(1)), ' eV']);
subplot(2, 1, 2);
bar(psi2)
title(['Energy eigenvalue= ', num2str(es(2)), ' eV']);
```

Hierarchy of Handle Graphics Objects

In the MATLAB graphical object hierarchy, all figures are children of the root object. Each figure can have children that are axes objects or user-interface objects. User-interface objects (buttons, sliders, checkboxes, etc.) allow the user to control program execution through Callback functions. Axes objects can display graphical plots, and can also have children that are one of several types of graphical objects. Graphical objects can both display information and respond to user mouse-driven input. The table below shows an overview of the hierarchy of these objects. Each of these objects has a long list of properties whose values determine the appearance and behavior of a particular instance of the the object. Consult the online documentation for a complete listing. For example, search for "lineseries properties," "image properties," or "annotation arrow properties."

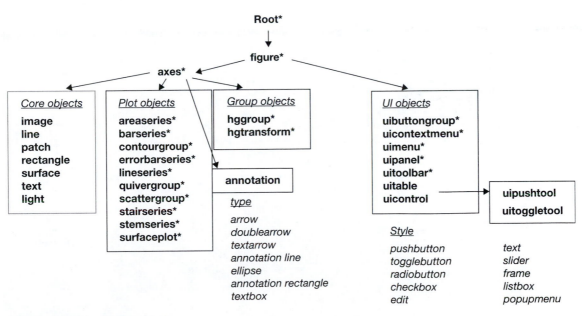

*Can be parent to children objects

Using LaTeX Commands

TEX is a technical typesetting language, created by Donald Knuth, which is widely used for formatting mathematical expressions. LaTeX is a set of macros created by Leslie Lamport, which expand the power of TEX and made it easier to use. By default, several MATLAB text-related commands, including `xlabel`, `ylabel`, `title`, and `text`, automatically interpret a subset of TEX commands. For example, basic subscripts can be created using the underscore symbol "_", and superscripts by the caret symbol "^". Curly brackets group symbols together. For example, the following text codes in the `title` or `xlabel` string will be displayed as shown:

$$x\text{\textasciicircum}2 \quad \rightarrow \quad x^2$$

$$y\text{\textasciicircum}\{2n\text{-}1\} \quad \rightarrow \quad y^{2n-1}$$

$$g\_0\text{\textasciicircum}2(x) \quad \rightarrow \quad g_0^2(x)$$

$$e\text{\textasciicircum}\{\text{-}ax\text{\textasciicircum}2\} \quad \rightarrow \quad e^{-ax^2}$$

The Interpreter property of a text object can be set to 'tex' (the default), 'latex', or 'none'. To use the more advanced LaTeX formatting, set the value of Interpreter to 'latex' and embed the formatting command between single or double dollar signs. Many special LaTeX symbols begin with a backslash character—the the square-root symbol, for example, is written \sqrt. Thus, the command

```
title('Characteristic $\sqrt{1-|\chi(x)|^2}$',...
'Interpreter', 'latex')
```

results in the plot title:

$$\text{Characteristic} \quad \sqrt{1-|\chi(x)|^2}$$

Fractions are encoded using the `frac` command.

$$\text{(a+x)/(a-x)} \quad \rightarrow \quad (a+x)/(a-x)$$

$$\backslash\text{frac}\{1\text{+}x\}\{1\text{-}x\} \quad \rightarrow \quad \frac{1+x}{1-x}$$

$$\backslash\text{frac}\{dy\}\{dx\} \quad \rightarrow \quad \frac{dy}{dx}$$

$$\backslash\text{frac}\{d\text{\textasciicircum}2y\}\{dx\text{\textasciicircum}2\} \quad \rightarrow \quad \frac{d^2y}{dx^2}$$

$$\backslash\text{frac}\{\text{-}b\backslash pm\backslash sqrt\{b\text{\textasciicircum}2\text{-}4ac\}\}\{2a\} \quad \rightarrow \quad \frac{-b \pm \sqrt{b^2-4ac}}{2a}$$

Larger math symbols like sums and integrals are handled as shown:

$$\texttt{\char92 int\_0\char94 \char92 infty f(x) dx} \quad \rightarrow \quad \int_0^\infty f(x)dx$$

$$\texttt{\char92 sum\_\{k=0\}\char94 N \char92 frac\{1\}\{k\char94 n\}} \quad \rightarrow \quad \sum_{k=0}^{N} \frac{1}{k^n}$$

$$\texttt{\char92 left(\char92 frac\{1\}\{a\} \char92 right)\char94 \{2k+1\}} \quad \rightarrow \quad \left(\frac{1}{a}\right)^{2k+1}$$

$$\texttt{\char92 lim\_\{x\char92 to\char92 infty\} \char92 frac\{x\}\{x+a\} = 1} \quad \rightarrow \quad \lim_{x\to\infty} \frac{x}{x+a} = 1$$

The following program gives several examples of embedding LᴬTᴇX formatting in text objects. Double dollar signs generally yields a larger equation. [Recall that `text(x, y, 'String')` places a text string at position (x, y) on the current axis.]

```
% testingLatex
clf
axis([0 1 0 1]);
title('Testing Latex Math: $\sqrt{1-|\chi(x)|^2}$',...
      'Interpreter','latex')
text(0.2,0.25,'$$ \int_0^\infty f(x) dx $$',...
            'Interpreter','latex','FontSize',14);
text(0.2,0.45,'$$ \sum_{k=0}^N \frac{1}{k^n}  $$',...
            'Interpreter','latex','FontSize',14);
text(0.2,0.65,'$$ \left(\frac{1}{a} \right)^{2k+1}    $$',...
            'Interpreter','latex','FontSize',14);

text(0.2,0.80,'$ \sum_{k=0}^N \frac{1}{k^n}  $',...
            'Interpreter','latex','FontSize',14);
text(0.6,0.80,'$ \frac{d^2y}{dx^2}    $',...
            'Interpreter','latex','FontSize',14);
text(0.6,0.65,'$$ \frac{d^2y}{dx^2}    $$',...
            'Interpreter','latex','FontSize',14);
text(0.6,0.45,'$$ \frac{-b\pm\sqrt{b^2-4ac}}{2a}  $$',...
            'Interpreter','latex','FontSize',14);
text(0.6,0.25,'$$ \frac{1-\beta}{1+\alpha} $$',...
            'Interpreter','latex','FontSize',14);
text(0.4,0.9,'$$  $$',...
            'Interpreter','latex','FontSize',14);
xlabel('\alpha_1^2')
ylabel('$$\frac{1-x}{1+x}$$','Interpreter','latex')
%  results are shown in Figure B.1
```

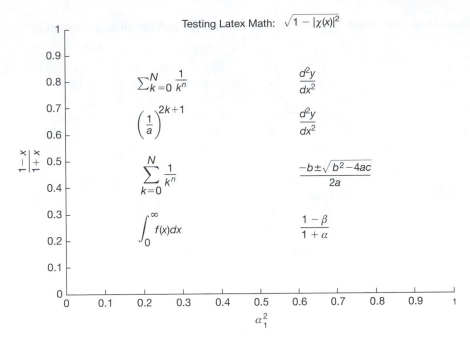

FIGURE B.1 Demonstration of program `testingLatex` to illustrate the use of the LATEX interpreter.

Codes for lowercase Greek letters are given in Table B.1. The lowercase Greek letter omicron is represented by a Latin "o" so it needs no special symbol.

\alpha	α	\beta	β	\gamma	γ	\delta	δ
\epsilon	ϵ	\varepsilon	ε	\zeta	ζ	\eta	η
\theta	θ	\vartheta	ϑ	\iota	ι	\kappa	κ
\lambda	λ	\mu	μ	\nu	ν	\xi	ξ
\pi	π	\varpi	ϖ	\rho	ρ	\varrho	ϱ
\sigma	σ	\varsigma	ς	\tau	τ	\upsilon	υ
\phi	ϕ	\varphi	φ	\chi	χ	\psi	ψ
\omega	ω						

TABLE B.1 Lowercase Greek letters.

Several uppercase Greek letters are identical with the normal Latin alphabet: A, B, E, H(Eta), I, K, M, N, O, P(Rho), T, X(Chi), Z. Those requiring special codes are given in Table B.2.

\Gamma	Γ	\Delta	Δ	\Theta	Θ	\Lambda	Λ
\Xi	Ξ	\Pi	Π	\Sigma	Σ	\Upsilon	Υ
\Phi	Φ	\Psi	Ψ	\Omega	Ω		

TABLE B.2 Upper case Greek letters.

Some other useful LaTeX symbols (not a comprehensive list) are given in Table B.3.

\pm	$\pm$	\cap	$\cap$	\mp	$\mp$	\oplus	$\oplus$
\cup	$\cup$	\times	$\times$	\otimes	$\otimes$	\div	$\div$
\oslash	$\oslash$	\ast	$\ast$	\odot	$\odot$	\star	$\star$
\vee	$\vee$	\bigcirc	$\bigcirc$	\circ	$\circ$	\wedge	$\wedge$
\dagger	$\dagger$	\bullet	$\bullet$	\setminus	$\setminus$	\ddagger	$\ddagger$
\cdot	$\cdot$	\leq	$\leq$	\geq	$\geq$	\equiv	$\equiv$
\sim	$\sim$	\perp	$\perp$	\simeq	$\simeq$	\mid	$\mid$
\ll	$\ll$	\gg	$\gg$	\parallel	$\parallel$	\subset	$\subset$
\supset	$\supset$	\approx	$\approx$	\subseteq	$\subseteq$	\supseteq	$\supseteq$
\cong	$\cong$	\neq	$\neq$	\doteq	$\doteq$	\in	$\in$
\ni	$\ni$	\propto	$\propto$				

TABLE B.3 Binary operations.

\hat{x}	$\hat{x}$	\dot{x}	$\dot{x}$	\ddot{x}	$\ddot{x}$	\acute{x}	$\acute{x}$	\vec{x}	$\vec{x}$
\bar{x}	$\bar{x}$	\tilde{x}	$\tilde{x}$						

TABLE B.4 Accents.

\leftarrow	$\leftarrow$	\longleftarrow	$\longleftarrow$	\uparrow	$\uparrow$
\Leftarrow	$\Leftarrow$	\Longleftarrow	$\Longleftarrow$	\Uparrow	$\Uparrow$
\rightarrow	$\rightarrow$	\longrightarrow	$\longrightarrow$	\downarrow	$\downarrow$
\Rightarrow	$\Rightarrow$	\Longrightarrow	$\Longrightarrow$	\Downarrow	$\Downarrow$
\leftrightarrow	$\leftrightarrow$	\longleftrightarrow	$\longleftrightarrow$	\updownarrow	$\updownarrow$
\Leftrightarrow	$\Leftrightarrow$	\Longleftrightarrow	$\Longleftrightarrow$	\Updownarrow	$\Updownarrow$
\mapsto	$\mapsto$	\longmapsto	$\longmapsto$	\nearrow	$\nearrow$
\hookleftarrow	$\hookleftarrow$	\hookrightarrow	$\hookrightarrow$	\searrow	$\searrow$
\leftharpoonup	$\leftharpoonup$	\rightharpoonup	$\rightharpoonup$	\swarrow	$\swarrow$
\leftharpoondown	$\leftharpoondown$	\rightharpoondown	$\rightharpoondown$	\nwarrow	$\nwarrow$
\rightleftharpoons	$\rightleftharpoons$	\leadsto	$\leadsto$		

TABLE B.5 Arrows.

\ldots	$\ldots$	\cdots	$\cdots$	\vdots	$\vdots$	\ddots	$\ddots$
\aleph	$\aleph$	\prime	$\prime$	\forall	$\forall$	\infty	∞
\hbar	$\hbar$	\emptyset	$\emptyset$	\exists	$\exists$	\Box	$\Box$
\imath	$\imath$	\nabla	∇	\neg	$\neg$	\Diamond	$\Diamond$
\jmath	$\jmath$	\surd	$\surd$	\flat	$\flat$	\triangle	$\triangle$
\ell	ℓ	\top	$\top$	\natural	$\natural$	\clubsuit	$\clubsuit$
\wp	$\wp$	\bot	$\bot$	\sharp	$\sharp$	\diamondsuit	$\diamondsuit$
\Re	$\Re$	|	$\|$	\backslash	$\backslash$	\heartsuit	$\heartsuit$
\Im	$\Im$	\angle	$\angle$	\partial	∂	\spadesuit	$\spadesuit$
\mho	$\mho$						

TABLE B.6 Other symbols.

LATEXcommands can also be used within MATLAB comments, which are interpreted when the code is "published" using the the 'File | Publish' command (not covered in this book).

This book was composed by the author using LATEX and the PCTEX program (`http://www.pctex.com`). For more information on LATEX the following resources are recommended:

```
http://www.latex-project.org/
```

```
http://www.ctan.org/
```

```
http://en.wikibooks.org/wiki/LaTeX
```

The TEXbook, Donald E. Knuth (Addison-Wesley, Reading, MA, 1984).

LATEX: A Document Preparation System: User's Guide and Reference Manual, Leslie Lamport (Addison-Wesley, Reading, MA, 1994).

The LATEXCompanion (Tools and Techniques for Computer Typesetting); Second Edition, Frank Mittelbach, Michel Goossens, Johannes Braams, David Carlisle, and Chris Rowley (Addison-Wesley, Reading, MA, 2004).

Index